JARDINE
MATHESON

JARDINE MATHESON

*Traders of the
Far East*

ROBERT BLAKE

Weidenfeld & Nicolson
LONDON

First published in Great Britain in 1999
by Weidenfeld & Nicolson

© 1999 Robert Blake

The moral right of Robert Blake to be identified as the
author of this work has been asserted in accordance
with the Copyright, Designs and Patents Act of 1988

A CIP catalogue record for this book
is available from the British Library.

ISBN 0 297 82501 1

Typeset by Selwood Systems, Midsomer Norton

Set in Minion

Printed in Great Britain by
Butler & Tanner Ltd, Frome and London

Weidenfeld & Nicolson

The Orion Publishing Group Ltd
Orion House
5 Upper Saint Martin's Lane
London, WC2H 9EA

Contents

Illustrations

All photographs are courtesy of Matheson & Co.

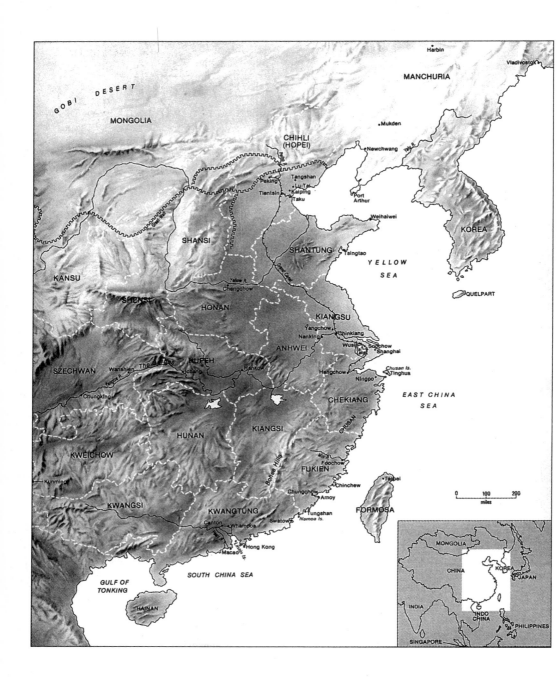

Introduction

At the request of Mr Henry Keswick, Chairman of Matheson & Co., I undertook in 1980 to write a history of the most remarkable firm of traders to be involved in the opening up of China. Jardine Matheson (Jardines, JM or the Firm, as it is varyingly called) played a key and often highly controversial role in this process from the 1830s onwards. Although my first interest has been the political history and biography of nineteenth- and twentieth-century Britain, I have always been fascinated by the impact of British economic power on distant and alien lands. I explored one aspect of this in my history of Rhodesia (Zimbabwe). Although the situations were very different and nothing existed in southern Africa to compare with China, the last great non-European empire, some of the same issues were *mutatis mutandis* involved. There was a similar vast technological gap, a similar mutual incomprehension, a similar Western arrogance and greed, and a similar indigenous delusion of invulnerability. So I was intrigued by the subject and readily accepted Henry Keswick's offer.

It has been a fascinating task exploring this previously unknown world (to me at least). I have tried to avoid the minutiae of financial transactions while showing in broad outline how Jardine Matheson fared both in absolute terms and in comparison with its rivals. I have kept in mind the wider historical context in which Jardine Matheson operated and given some analysis of Sino-British relations in which the Firm played at times an important part. There is therefore more general history than is perhaps usual in a company history.

1

We agreed at the outset to end in 1949, the year when Jardine Matheson was, as it seemed then, finally expelled from mainland China by the Communist revolution. The Firm continued its activities in Hong Kong which had been its headquarters. There it has indeed flourished with great success. But interesting though the last 50 years have been, there are reasons to protect commercial confidence and the position of personalities and their families still living. We agreed that it was better to finish at the end of a definite period in the Firm's history and leave its post-1949 revival to a future chronicler.

I would like to acknowledge the help I have had in Hong Kong and London from conversations with members of Jardine Matheson – in particular, the late Sir John Keswick and his brother Sir William; also Henry Keswick and Jeremy Brown. I would also like to acknowledge the help I had from the late Alan Reid who supervised the Firm's archives and wrote a number of useful monographs on various aspects of its history. An invaluable source of information has been *The Thistle and the Jade*, a beautifully illustrated book of essays privately published by the Firm to mark its 150th anniversary in 1982. Finally I would like to express my great gratitude to the late Major-General Douglas-Withers RA who analysed with immense perseverance the highly complicated early trading accounts of the company. I could not have written a very important part of the book without his help.

Robert Blake

ONE

The China Trade

Jardine Matheson & Co. was founded in Canton on 1 July 1832, the lineal descendant of a confusing series of partnerships which in Alan Reid's words, 'start to look like the intricate toing and froing of some Scottish reel'.[1] The earliest of these partnerships dates back to 1787. Dr William Jardine, however, first saw Canton in 1802 at the age of eighteen as a ship's surgeon in the employment of the East India Company. In 1825 he became a partner in Magniac & Co., the immediate predecessor of Jardine Matheson, and he was joined three years later by James Matheson. The Firm has had a longer continuous existence than any other British, European or American business connected with the China trade. It is the only one surviving from 'pre-Treaty' days – the time before the Treaty of Nanking in 1842 opened China to foreign commerce on a major scale, and it played a very important part in that process. Based originally in Canton, the only city where foreigners were allowed to conduct business before 1842, it soon moved to the newly ceded colony of Hong Kong. Its name has always been associated with the island. 'Jardines *is* Hong Kong' someone (not a member of the firm) once asserted to the author – an exaggeration of course but pardonable. With branches all over China until 1949, it has been, for most of the nineteenth and twentieth centuries, the most important and prestigious commercial enterprise in the colony. Hong Kong reverted to Chinese sovereignty in 1997 but, providing the 1984 agreement is upheld, Jardine Matheson is likely to remain a major feature of the place and may well pay a renewed role in mainland China far into the twenty-first century.

The history of the Firm reflects the way the newly industrialized western world impacted upon a much older civilization – one which was self-sufficient, self-satisfied, profoundly xenophobic and convinced of its superiority to all other cultures. Any account of the story of Jardine Matheson must begin with some description, however cursory, of the world which the West was seeking to 'open up'. It is important to emphasize that the last thing which the Chinese Imperial authorities wanted was for their country to be 'opened up' at all: the merchants and sailors of the seaboard may have had a different outlook but they cut no ice in Peking: the Chinese governing class which controlled the empire upon which eighteenth-century Europeans impinged was proud, suspicious and rigidly conservative.

China had first become a recognizable national entity as long ago as 221 BC when the Ch'in dynasty from which the country derives its name unified what were called 'the Warring States' into a single vast empire. There were to be many periods of division and disintegration afterwards, such as the Sixteen Kingdoms between AD 304 and 449 and the Ten Kingdoms in 907–79. The latest was the rule of the War Lords between 1916 and 1928 – an experience which had traumatic effects and goes far to explain the acceptance of the Maoist regime. For behind all the vicissitudes of Imperial and post-Imperial China, there are two closely connected concepts. One is that a vast country so diverse ethnically, culturally, geographically and climatically can only be held together by an authoritarian centralized regime. The other is the feeling of nationalism which insists that all people of Chinese ancestry, wherever they live, belong to 'Mother China'. It explains why China's leaders are obsessed with Taiwan and why the sovereignty of Hong Kong was never negotiable. These two deeply felt sentiments account for that strong desire for unity to which the Chinese people have constantly returned, despite interludes of rebellion, anarchy, foreign conquest and civil strife.

There is no need here to trace the rise and fall of successive dynasties. One may note that many of them were foreign, but the English, who have not been ruled by a family of English origin since 1066, need not find anything odd about that. Nor should they be surprised that Chinese culture and civilization, like those of England or of Greece in the days of Imperial Rome, had a great capacity for assimilating foreign invaders. The 'Barbarians' from the north and west soon became almost more Chinese than the Chinese. The Mongol conqueror Kublai Khan, who was the grandson of Chinghis (Ghengis) Khan, could never speak Chinese properly, but his descendants were completely Sinicized. A similar process occurred between George I and George III in England.

The civilization which Western traders encountered in the closing years of the eighteenth century was very old, far older than any European counterpart. Egypt alone had a longer history. Not only was Chinese civilization extremely old, it was also very remote. Separated by a vast and arid landmass it was almost completely cut off from the influence of European culture. The Chinese, naturally enough, looked at the situation the other way round. To them it was Europe that was cut off from the only true civilization. China was the 'Middle Kingdom', and 'middle' meant the centre of the world. All outside it were 'Barbarians'. The Middle Kingdom was ruled by an emperor who owed his authority to 'the Mandate of Heaven'. When dynasties were overturned, a convenient fiction reconciled this apparent contradiction. The Mandate was only conferred by Heaven on those fit to govern. An emperor who fell to a rival claimant or a conqueror was by definition not fit to govern – an inversion of the doctrine enunciated in Sir John Harrington's famous couplet:

> Treason doth never prosper; what's the reason?
> For if it prosper none dare call it treason.

China had developed over the centuries an idiosyncratic social order to which there has been no parallel elsewhere. The key to the continuity of the state was the civil service, the mandarinate. It was recruited by competitive examination of the most rigorous nature in the principles and writings of Confucius – a sage born in the middle of the sixth century BC whose doctrine as reported to posterity emphasized tradition, obedience, duty, hierarchy and good order. The official class was an élite within an élite. In theory open to all, it was in practice recruited from what European historians misleadingly call the 'gentry'. This expression has to be distinguished from its English connotations.

The 'gentry' were those who had passed certain examinations in traditional classical scholarship. They had special privileges and special immunities. They might or might not be landowners. They could be teachers, assistants or secretaries to the mandarins or hold other positions such as magistrates or tax collectors. They were sharply differentiated from the peasantry, the vast majority of the population, some 85 per cent, who lived off the land. The gentry are estimated to have been two per cent of the population – in 1800 perhaps 8 million out of 400 million. The official class was probably not more than two per cent of that figure – around 40,000.

The mandarinate dated back continuously to the T'ang dynasty (AD 618–907) although its origins were even earlier. This remarkable administrative body, with which the British Civil Service has often but erroneously been compared, preserved the basic unity of China despite all the changes of regime. Although recruited from the gentry, the Confucian scholar-officials felt no special obligation towards the class from which they had been drawn. They were not like the public servants of eighteenth-century England or of Japan under the Shogunate. They had moved into a different and higher world. They were the Emperor's servants, and their moral prestige, material privileges and social status put them only below the Imperial family itself. To avoid undue favouritism, they were not allowed to hold office in the provinces whence they came or to hold land in the provinces to which they were sent. They could not have relatives in the same administrative branch. Of course none of these provisions in practice precluded corruption and 'squeeze', which were notorious by the time of the European impact and were an integral part of the system, for state salaries were pittances; extortion, bribes and 'presents' alone assured a proper style of life. Believing, perhaps rightly from their own viewpoint, that all concessions to dissent from within or pressure from without would be disastrous to the regime, the Confucian officials were hostile to innovation and devoted to tradition. In the whole of history there has probably never been a more conservative and more long-lasting governing class.

Another important unifying factor in China was the written language. It has retained to this day its pictographic form whereas almost all others have adopted a phonetic alphabet. In China such a change would affect the vital unity of north and south which is hard enough to preserve anyway. The two principal languages, Mandarin in the north and Cantonese in the south, are when spoken so different as to be mutually incomprehensible, but the written language is the same. The result of preserving this ancient form of writing is the need to learn some 4000 different characters – which is bad luck on Chinese children although it may be the necessary price of cohesion.

The population of China at any historical time has always been immense in comparison with other countries, and it has always constituted one of China's greatest problems. It is reckoned to have been 80 million in AD 1400, twice as much in 1600, and something like 430 million by 1850. The pressure of numbers on food resources in a country in which four-fifths of the total population were peasants, cultivating small plots and living on subsistence agriculture, has been a constant feature of Chinese history. It was from time to time 'relieved', if one can use the word, by fearful floods and famines or by horrific wars, whether of rebellion or invasion. The Mongol conquest, completed by the end of the thirteenth century, may have cost 30 million lives – more than a quarter of the entire population. The Manchu invasion in the seventeenth century probably resulted in some 25 million deaths. In the Taiping rebellion, which was only suppressed in 1864 after fourteen years of ferocious strife, more people perished than in all the countries involved in the First World War. To those figures must be added the casualties of natural disasters. Yet all these catastrophes were only shortlived checks to a seemingly inexorable process of growth.

At the time when this history commences – the beginning of the nineteenth century – the population problem was one that also worried observers in Europe. Hence the gloomy predictions of Malthus, and the famous passage in Disraeli's *Sybil* (1845) in which one of the characters is made to say:

I speak of the annual arrival of more than three hundred thousand strangers in this island. How will you feed them? How will you house them? They have given up butcher's meat. Must they give up bread? ... See the fall of the great Roman Empire – what was that? ... What are your invasions of the barbarous nations, your Goths and Visigoths, your Lombards and Huns to our Population Returns?

In fact the pessimistic prophecies of Malthus were not fulfilled in the West. The situation was transformed by the agricultural and industrial revolutions which originated in Britain in the mid-eighteenth century and gradually spread first over western then eastern Europe, although in the latter case more slowly and never completely. New techniques enormously increased the productivity of land, and industrialization made it possible to exchange manufactured goods for food and other commodities from all over the world. Supplies in Europe more than kept up with population. Nineteenth-century Europe and its vast extensions in America and Australasia experienced an unexampled rise in the standard of living.

No comparable revolution occurred in China. It was not that the Chinese had ignored science and technology. They had made many discoveries long before Europe: paper, printing, gunpowder, glass, the magnetic compass and the casting of bronze and iron; the Great Wall, a barrier against the nomadic northern invaders extending for 1400 miles (2240km), was a remarkable feat of military engineering. It survives still, one of the wonders of the world. Yet for some reason there was never in China the breakthrough, the 'take off' which occurred in Europe. At a very early stage the Chinese had invented a wheelbarrow superior to all others, but there was no follow-up. They discovered new techniques but did not exploit them. Population perpetually pressed upon a narrowing margin of subsistence. The Malthusian thesis may have proved inapplicable to Europe and North America, but it was highly relevant to contemporary China and is to modern Africa.

The differences between civilizations are seldom susceptible to simple explanation. It may seem surprising that Chinese culture, for all its contributions to the heritage of the world – ceramics, porcelain, silk paintings, bronzes, statues, calligraphy, literature – remained so curiously fossilized. There existed great cities, larger than most in Europe, but they were never characterized by the civic liberties which contributed so much to European intellectual vigour and to their challenge to established orthodoxies. They never became the focus of radicalism or revolution. There was a rich and grand aristocratic world of much splendour, but one cannot imagine a Chinese equivalent of the 'Canal Duke' of Bridgwater, Coke of Norfolk or 'Turnip Townsend'. All countries are governed by an élite, and always have been whether the regime is monarchical, oligarchical, democratic, capitalist, communist or something else. The English élite was exceptionally libertarian; it presided over a pluralistic and 'open' society in which innovatory practices and new ideas flourished. Such conditions did not guarantee a 'take off', but they made it possible. Indeed without them it would not have occurred. The contrast with the hierarchical bureaucracy of China could scarcely be more striking. No doubt Coke of Norfolk was pretty remote from the average agricultural labourer, but the Chinese élite was still more remote from the peasant masses whose numbers they counted and whose taxes they collected; it was more exclusive, more rigid, more hostile to change than any comparable class elsewhere. It may be that its very success in achieving the prime objectives of unity and continuity, and in absorbing the 'Barbarians' into Chinese culture, contributed to this all-pervasive conservatism. Whatever the reason, Chinese technology lagged far behind that of Europe. The mandarinate was the route to power, wealth and above all to status. The Confucian scholars who constituted the official class despised merchants, engineers, technicians and – even more dangerously – soldiers. In any armed conflict with a European power the Chinese Empire was almost certain to be defeated.

When William Jardine, the founder of the Firm, first saw Canton in 1802, China was governed by what turned out to be the last of her many dynasties. The Ch'ing were Manchus, a northern people who had invaded and conquered Peking in 1650, overthrowing the Ming emperor. The first great Ch'ing ruler was K'ang Hsi who reigned for 60 years from 1662 to 1722. He has been compared for magnificence with his near contemporary on the other side of the world, Louis XIV. Like many of the invading northerners of the past, he was a great admirer of the culture he had conquered. He rebuilt Peking, which had been devastated by his armies, in the traditional Chinese manner. To quote Dr J.M. Roberts, 'It was as if Versailles had been put up in the Gothic style or London rebuilt in the Perpendicular after the Great Fire.'[2] He took over the civil service which carried on much as it had before. It was now open to Manchus, and the odd custom of wearing pigtails was introduced – a Manchu usage which always surprised European visitors. But the indigenous Chinese retained their positions and there was no attempt at replacement *en masse*. Despite this tolerance Manchu rule was never fully accepted, particularly in the south, and when things were beginning to go wrong, as they palpably were in the early nineteenth century, the dynasty, still regarded as foreign, soon came in for blame.

Europe's first impact on China coincided with, although did not in itself cause, the onset of a slow long-term deterioration in the social and economic conditions of the Empire. The reason was traditional and was internal, not external – the rocketing growth of population pressing upon the means of subsistence; the expanding peasantry was forced to live off the produce of plots of land which could at best be only marginally enlarged. The symptoms were also traditional – increasing misery among the 80 per cent of the nation who cultivated the soil, famine, rebellions in the 1770s and 1780s, the growth of secret societies like the 'Triads' and the appearance of millenarian sects. This deterioration was to have important consequences later for European traders, but naturally enough they did not notice it at the time, for they had no contact at all with the rural population which constituted the overwhelming majority of this 'last of the great universal empires of antiquity', as Professor John Fairbank describes it in a brilliant essay.[3] And even if they had, they probably would have been no more aware of the causes than the dynasty itself, which remained confident and complacent in the knowledge that it had the Mandate of Heaven and pretended that all other countries paid tribute to it.

In 1795 when Lord Macartney went on his famous abortive mission to Peking, the envoy of Britain was firmly rebuffed. He asked for equality of diplomatic representation in both countries and freedom of trade. The Emperor saw no reason to grant either. In that xenophobic capital all other nations were regarded as so unimportant that no equivalent of the Foreign Office even existed. In trade China was virtually self-sufficient. Lord Macartney had to return, with a flea in his ear, to what the Emperor, in his message of reply, called 'the lonely remoteness of your island cut off by the intervening wastes of sea.' It is true that George III was politely congratulated on his 'submissive loyalty in sending this tribute mission' but that was hardly the answer which either the Monarch or his First Minister expected to receive. A similar mission by Lord Amherst in 1816 was given similarly disdainful treatment.

There was, however, a weak point in the apparently monolithic attitude of Manchu China. Professor Fairbank has pointed out that 'the major tradition of China's agrarian-bureaucratic empire was accompanied by a minor tradition of what we can call Maritime China. On the sea coast south of Shanghai there were merchants who lived by coastal foreign trade and pirates who lived off the merchants.'[4] This minority Chinese world is of key importance in any assessment of the role of Jardine Matheson. The coastal trade was very large. There were said to be some 10,000 junks employed in it by the end of the eighteenth century. To quote Professor Fairbank again:

> The junk trade, as Westerners called it, was a flourishing business of Maritime China throughout the seventeenth and eighteenth centuries. One wing of it traded at Nagasaki where Japan in seclusion allowed only the Chinese and the Dutch. Another wing traded at Manila under the Spaniards who needed Chinese silks to laden their Manila galleon in order to go and get the silver of Spanish Mexico. Another wing of the Chinese junk trade supplied Chinese goods to the ports of Malaya and the East Indies and brought the rice surplus of Bangkok to Canton to feed South China.[5]

There had always been a very substantial waterborne trade on the lakes, rivers and canals of mainland China, but it was subject to the red tape and extortion of the mandarins. The coastal and foreign shipping was in theory equally under the rule of the officials. In practice, seaborne trade was much less restricted, although it was far from being wholly free, as events in Canton were soon to show.

Maritime China was the area with which European traders interacted. Of the peasant masses they knew nothing and could not have known anything even if they had been interested, since foreign travel within China was forbidden. Of the mandarinate, what little they saw

inspired ridicule and contempt. In Canton they were regarded as pro-
claimers of absurd restrictive decrees couched in condescending
language emanating from a far northern court wholly out of touch
with the modern world. But Chinese merchants and sea captains made
sense. Their objects and needs were like those of the Europeans –
pilots, warehouses (or 'godowns' as they were termed), credit facilities, low taxes and commercial good faith. This was a part of China
whose outlook the European merchant could understand even if the
language remained incomprehensible. It was one of the problems of
Canton in the 1830s that only two Europeans in the place could speak
Cantonese.

The earliest long-distance traders with China were the Arabs. They
were followed by the Parsees. Described sometimes as the 'Jews of
India', they were descended from Persians adhering to the Zoroastrian
faith, who migrated after the Muslim conquest of their country in the
mid-eighth century AD. Centred on Bombay they had the stamina,
determination and commercial shrewdness which has often characterized displaced minorities. One of them was to be much involved in the
affairs of Jardine Matheson. From 1600 onwards, however, most of the
foreign trade with China was conducted by the European chartered
companies of which the British East India Company was by far the most
important – 'The Honourable East India Company' as it was called.
When William Jardine entered its employment, it still had a monopoly
of all British trade east of the Cape of Good Hope, and it governed
India, subject in the last resort to ministerial and parliamentary control. But that mysterious and indefinable phenomenon, 'the spirit
of the time' or 'the climate of opinion' was against monopolies,
in Britain anyway, the country that mattered, and especially in
its northern kingdom whence so many eastern traders originated
along with their arch-ideologue, the great Adam Smith. Monopolies
authorized by the state were not to be revived until the Labour
administration of 1945–51 and they now seem to be on their way out
yet again.

The East India Company was under constant attack from the last
quarter of the eighteenth century onwards. The question of the renewal
of its charter came up in 1813. The company was given another 20 years,

but its monopoly of the India trade was abolished, and it retained only that of China. On 28 August 1833 this, too, was abrogated by Act of Parliament with effect from 21 April 1834. The company continued to govern India until it was replaced by direct rule from Whitehall after the Mutiny in 1856, but its commercial monopoly was everywhere at an end.

The circumstances under which trade was conducted with China were anything but easy; they will be described in detail in the next chapter. It is enough to say that trade was confined to a single city, Canton, as far away from Peking as possible and was subjected to a multitude of elaborate restrictions carefully calculated to cause the maximum of inconvenience and produce the maximum of extortion compatible with not driving the 'Barbarians' out altogether – the Chinese government wanted their money but not them. Why did Europeans bother at all about commerce with such an unfriendly and intransigent country? What could be got from China, which could not be got elsewhere? There were two commodities that Europe sought. Silks had been from time immemorial one of them. There had been a demand for many centuries dating back to the Roman Empire and the period of the Han dynasty.

The other commodity, much more recently in demand, was tea. Pronounced 'tay' it had become fashionable in early eighteenth-century England, coffee having been hitherto *de rigueur*. Alexander Pope referred to Queen Anne as:

> … Great Anna whom three realms obey
> Who sometimes counsel takes and sometimes tea.

China was the only country which grew tea until India competed with a different variety in the second half of the nineteenth century. In 1783 Britain imported 6 million pounds of tea, when the duty was 100 per cent; the following year it was reduced to twelve and a half per cent and imports rose to 15 million pounds. But this remission was reversed by drastic tax increases during and after the Napoleonic Wars. In the early 1830s, however, despite these imports, Britain and Ireland consumed some 30 million pounds. The price in the previous decade had averaged between five and six shillings a pound. The 'deleterious produce of China', as it was described by Sir F. Eden in his enquiry, *The State of the Poor* (1797), could not have done the average labourer on nine to eighteen shillings a week much harm, even 30 years later. It was a luxury import and remained as such for a long time to come. But the same could be said of silks. The political consequences of commerce in luxuries can be just as significant as that in necessities, if indeed one can draw any definable boundary between the two. Moreover, tea was an important element in the British budget. Its duty regularly contributed some £3 million to the Exchequer, enough to pay half the cost of the British Navy. The Chancellor could no more have done without it than his modern successor could dispense with taxes on tobacco or alcohol.

All foreign trade depends on a balance, however indirect and complicated, in the exchange between countries of commodities, manufactures and services. The Chinese Empire had poor communications, a very low *per capita* income, virtual economic self-sufficiency and an anti-commercial governing class. The problem for the West and for Britain in particular, was to find something that the Chinese would accept in exchange for silks and tea. The discovery took a long time. Wool and cotton goods, Britain's major exports, did not serve this purpose. Woollen textiles were of little use to a country where the rich in the bitter northern cold wore furs or silk and the peasants padded cotton which was produced locally. There was a market for raw cotton from India, but its value fluctuated with the success of China's own immense cotton crop and it could not be relied upon to fill the gap. There was also a market for jewelled watches, toys and musical boxes which amused the Mandarins and which were produced in James Cox's goldsmith shop off Fleet Street. They were called 'singsongs' in China. Their contribution to the balance of payments was negligible. Sir Robert Hart, the Director of Chinese customs, wrote in the 1890s: 'The Chinese have the best food in the world, rice; the best drink, tea; the best clothing, cotton, silk, fur. Possessing these staples and their innumerable native adjuncts they do not need to buy a pennyworth's elsewhere.' But there was a general feeling in the mercantile world that some solution must be found other than the export of gold and silver coins or bullion, which was regarded as injurious to the national economy. From about 1800 the answer began to appear –

Indian-grown opium, an illicit contraband for which the Chinese demand seemed almost insatiable and which founded the fortunes of the great European and American commercial houses engaged in the eastern trade, not to mention those of an even more numerous category of Chinese merchants. It should never be forgotten that a section of the indigenous traders did just as well out of opium as the foreigners.

TWO

The Canton System

The conditions under which foreign merchants traded in China were unique. The so-called Canton system dated from 1760. Earlier the great Emperor K'ang Hsi had been so confident that in 1685 he threw all his ports open to foreigners, subject to certain restrictions. His motive was not an enlightened anticipation of the principles of Adam Smith but a desire to augment the Imperial revenues by taxes, duties, levies and extortion. He soon decided that he had gone too far and that the risks of indiscriminate liberalism outweighed the advantages. Trade was confined to three ports: Amoy, where the Spaniards were allowed to do business, although by 1800 they had almost ceased to send ships there;[1] Macao, where a Portuguese settlement had existed since 1557; and, by far the most important, Canton, which, under the famous 'Eight Regulations' laid down in 1760 and amended 20 years later, was the only entrepôt of any significance. Life in Canton was by no means agreeable. The foreigners were confined to an enclave in a suburb of the city on the north bank of the river. The regulations were numerous and irksome, disease was rife and the climate for much of the year stiflingly hot and humid; but the fortunes that could be made by astute dealing were immense.

Throughout the eighteenth century, and for several years into the nineteenth, the dominant institution in the China trade was the East India Company. By 1715 it was well established in Canton. It possessed, as we saw, a monopoly in all trade undertaken by British subjects, between the Cape of Good Hope and the Magellan Straits. Its charter gave it immense powers, and its social and economic ramifications in Britain were so extensive that Burke could declare: 'to say the Company was in a state of distress was neither more nor less than saying that the Country was in a state of distress'. The Company relaxed its monopoly in certain respects. Its employees on its 'East Indiamen' were allowed to carry a certain amount of 'privileged' cargo on their own account and trade with it personally according to their best ability. Dr William Jardine started his business career by taking advantage of this concession when he became surgeon on the East Indiaman, *Brunswick*. He did so well on a series of voyages that in 1817 he left the Company's employ to become a private merchant.

The existence of private merchants was another and much more important modification of the Company's monopoly. Since 1787 it had suited the Court of Directors in London to allow what were called 'Houses of Agency' to operate in India. By 1790 fifteen of these private partnerships were based in Calcutta and concerned with what came to be called, for reasons that remain obscure, 'the Country Trade', referring to trade within India and eastwards. The Agency Houses acted for British manufacturers and foreign investors, were bankers and insurers, and financed indigo cultivation – an important part of the 'remittances' which contributed to the complicated balance of payments of the East India Company. The private merchants operating in Canton were closely connected with these Agency Houses, and themselves often constituted similar partnerships. The Company had an ambivalent attitude towards them. On the one hand, the Court of Directors was anxious to avoid having any private competition in Canton itself. On the other hand, the Country Trade was becoming more and more important, particularly in respect of opium which the Company dared not handle, because of the official disapproval of the Chinese authorities who might make trouble over its tea monopoly. Ideally the Company would have liked 'Country' ships to convey their cargoes to China and then return as soon as possible, with whatever they could buy apart from tea; but in practice the Select Committee of Supercargoes,[2] which regulated matters in Canton, often winked at individual merchants staying in Canton or Macao on one pretext or another. By 1770 there was a substantial group of them in Canton, but in 1780 there was a clampdown by the Company, which legally had the right to expel British subjects. By 1783 there was only one British Country Merchant left – John Henry Cox.

He was there on a different basis from the others who had been expelled. His father James had sold 'singsongs' to the Chinese merchants of the Co-hong,[3] who were alone allowed to trade with the East India Company. Along with Francis Magniac of Clerkenwell he was one of the principal suppliers. On James Cox's death, John Henry was allowed to come out in order to collect the debts owing to his father's estate. Since many of the Hong merchants were bankrupt, he often had to take payment in goods, and it was a short step to trading on his own account. In 1787 he entered into partnership with Daniel Beale who had evaded the Company's veto by becoming Prussian Consul in Canton and thus gaining diplomatic immunity. Cox and Beale were the lineal progenitors, after numerous intermediate changes in partners, of Jardine Matheson. The Company managed to eject Cox but they dared not touch Beale, who then went into partnership with one John Reid, who had also adopted the diplomatic ruse and had come out to Canton in 1780 as Austrian Consul. Cox returned with a commission in the Swedish Navy in 1791. The Select Committee tried to refuse him permission to land but he promptly hoisted Prussian colours. He died that year and Thomas Beale, Daniel's brother, came out to succeed him, describing himself as the Prussian Consul's Secretary.

The assumption of consular roles was widely adopted. James Matheson took out Danish papers. Thomas Dent, originator of the firm which became the great rival of Jardine Matheson, was Sardinian Consul. His partner, W.S. Davidson, went one better, maintaining that he was a Portuguese subject when in China, but British anywhere else. There were merchants operating under Swedish, Sicilian, Genoese, Hanoverian and even Polish protection, although the Polish Kingdom was almost extinct. The Company gave up. Its own attempt to act as a House of Agency was a complete flop and was abandoned shortly before 1800. It could not do without the 'private English', as they were called, although most of them were Scottish, nor without the Parsees, who became an increasingly important element in the Country Trade.

The degree of dependence can be shown by the figures analysed for

1828 by Michael Greenberg.[4] Rounded to the nearest $100,000, British imports into China were $20.3 million [5] of which $4.5 million was on the Company's account and $15.8 million on private accounts. The Company's imports were almost exactly half Western products and half Eastern, woollens constituting the bulk of the former and raw Indian cotton nearly all of the latter. The private imports amounted to $11.2 million of opium and $2.5 million of raw cotton, the rest being made up of other Eastern products plus a small amount from Europe. British imports from China totalled $18.1 million of which just over half was on private account. The Company's share of $8.5 million was virtually all tea. Of the $9.6 million imported on private account $6.1 million was sent in silver. The next largest item, amounting to $1.1 million, was raw silk. The silver went for the most part to the Company's treasury at Canton exchanged by the private merchants for Bills drawn on the Company either in India or London. The crucial importance of the illicit opium trade which will be analysed in more detail below can thus be easily seen.[6]

Figures are one thing, people another. What was it like to be involved in the Canton system? It was all based on India. Indeed British political control over the subcontinent, which had been increasingly consolidated since the days of Clive and then Warren Hastings, was a major factor shaping the China trade. The Company's appropriation of revenues in kind – diwani – its monopolies first in the cultivation of the opium poppy and later in the manufacture of the finished product, its effective control over the weaving of cotton cloth, its monopoly of salt-petre, all contributed to the export trade upon which the import of tea to Britain depended. Moreover, the private firms in India which engaged in the China trade were nearly all offshoots of the old and well-established East India houses which the Company had allowed to operate despite its monopoly. The young adventurer seeking his fortune in China would sail to Bombay or Calcutta first.[7] Thence he would proceed, whether on an Indiaman or a Country vessel, via Singapore to the Gulf of Canton, taking advantage of the summer south-west monsoon and arriving in September. His ship would probably put in at the Taypa, the anchorage close to Macao, to take on board a pilot for the Pearl River. Before 1815, if his ship was carrying any opium, he would certainly be delayed for some days, while it was trans-shipped to one of the receiving ships stationed there. Until 1815 Macao was the principal opium mart.

Macao, situated on a narrow isthmus on the western edge of the Gulf some 40 miles from Hong Kong on the eastern side, had by all accounts, then as now, an air of seedy yet romantic decay. It had been a Portuguese settlement since 1557 but the Portuguese were there as tenants at the will of the Emperor. Chinese law prevailed and local Mandarins supervised their administration with varying degrees of assiduity. It was not until 1849 that Lisbon effectively claimed sovereignty. Macao was commercially on the decline, the once great Portuguese sea-borne empire was falling into decrepitude, and whatever prosperity Macao possessed was to be killed by the cession of Hong Kong to Britain in 1842. Nevertheless it remained and still remains a most attractive place. Described as the Naples of the Orient Macao is situated on a wide curving bay. The broad esplanade of the Praya Grande with its elegant baroque houses painted in pink, blue and white looks on to the outer harbour. There are splendid churches and buildings, and a wonderful view from the Monte Fort looking towards the blue enigmatic hills of China from which one feels under perpetual silent and suspicious observation. The English Church and its graveyard are moving reminders of the time when the Canton merchants would repair there for rest, relaxation and cool breezes when the trading season (September to March) came to an end. Today and for many years past it has been little more than a large fishing village financially sustained by gambling. The Hong Kong Chinese pour into it on weekends and spend up to 48 hours on endless games of chance conducted in hideous multi-storey casinos surveyed by hidden cameras to detect cheating. To an outside observer the spectacle of these fanatical gamblers seems almost as depressing as the descriptions one reads of an opium den. Yet Macao is still worth a visit. Its narrow streets and its strange merchandise are probably the last vestiges of an 'old China' now obliterated by the modernizing dogma of Beijing and the sky-scraping philistinism of Hong Kong.

Our traveller would then sail to the Canton River through the Bocca Tigris or 'Bogue', as it was generally called. It was guarded by forts with fixed guns incapable of being swivelled and thus totally useless. His ship would anchor at Whampoa, some thirteen miles from Canton, and the nearest anchorage permitted for foreign ships. There he might see a remarkable and picturesque spectacle – a multitude of vividly painted junks and launches and cutters from the big ships, some manned by English sailors in blue jackets and straw hats, some by Indian lascars in white robes and coloured turbans, some by Malays in scarlet cloth. In the trading season there might be a line of merchant ships three miles long with 3000 sailors on board. The men were allowed on shore only in small parties to visit the brothels and drink-shops of what was called Bamboo Town. In the latter they regaled themselves into insensibility on a compound of hard liquor, arsenic, tobacco and sugar. The senior commander of the East India Company's fleet was in charge of all British ships at Whampoa. Each of them had a cutter for conveyance to Canton. At sunrise and sunset the band on one of the ships would play for an hour. An attempt to put on a similar performance at Canton was a failure. The Chinese could not listen with pleasure to European music.

The next stage was the short journey to Canton itself. The foreign merchants were confined to a narrow overcrowded compound on the north bank of the river in one of the suburbs of the city. The area was about 300 yards by 200. There were thirteen 'factories' – long narrow buildings with frontages some 50 to 200 yards from the river. The word 'factory' has nothing to do with its modern sense. It stems from the Portuguese word 'feiter', meaning an agent, and was simply the description of a trading house. From the river they looked like single buildings, but they were in reality a collection of separate houses arranged in depth and opening on to inner courts. They stretched back as much as 200 yards. On the ground floors there would be godowns (warehouses), offices and safe-rooms or treasuries; on the first floors were spacious dining- and reception-rooms as well as bedrooms if these were not situated on the second floors which some factories possessed.

Between the frontages and river lay an open and unpaved area called Respondentia Walk,[8] which swarmed with pedlars, beggars and impor-tuners of every description. The frontage itself was divided by three narrow alleys going northwards to Thirteen Factories Street which ran east–west dividing it from the factories. The most notorious of these was the most eastern, Hog Lane, which ran alongside and west of the English Factory. It was packed with disreputable drink shops where British sailors on the spree from Whampoa (limited in theory to two visits only) were wont to drink the same poisonous brew available in Bamboo Town. Although many of the factories in 1800 still bore the names of the European Companies which had originally settled there, the names of only four corresponded to current reality: the English, the American, the Dutch and the French. The New English, which was double the size of the others and by far the grandest, was occupied by the East India Company. It paid £20,000 per annum for the lease from the Co-hong, the so-called Hong[9] merchants, sometimes termed Hongists or Mandarin Merchants who had purchased the monopoly of business with the Barbarians. In the 1830s Jardine Matheson occupied the Creek, the most eastern of these establishments, separated by the Dutch from the New English Factory. Its name derived from a small malodorous stream which ran into the Canton River and marked the eastern boundary of the factory area.

Some of the Chinese Hong merchants made huge fortunes, others went bankrupt or teetered on the verge. It was an office which many of them were glad to get rid of. All were subject to the extortion of the Mandarins. No city in China was more corrupt. The principal civil officials were the Hsun or Governor of Canton and the T'sung Fu or Viceroy of the provinces of Kuangsi and Kuangtung, in the latter of which the city was situated. As far as Canton was concerned, the two acted jointly. The military administration was in the hands of the Chiang Chün, normally translated as Tartar General. Unlike his two civil colleagues, who were Chinese, he was always a Manchu, usually a relative of the Emperor. More important than any of these for the foreign traders was the superintendent of marine customs at Canton, known as the Hoppo.[10] He too was a Manchu and generally a member of the Imperial clan. His task was to milk both the foreign and Chinese merchants on behalf of the Emperor – and also, of course, himself – and he made a great deal of money. The Hong merchants were held responsible for the good behaviour and obedience to law of the foreign devils. All communication between the factories and the officials had to be made through them in the form of petitions. This rule emphasized the inferior status of the foreigners and avoided the embarrassment of any direct official dealings with them.

The merchants in the factories were in theory allowed to stay there only for the trading season from September to March, which was delimited by the monsoon winds. The south-west monsoon in the summer carried the East Indiamen and other ships up the South China Sea laden with goods and bullion; in the spring the north-east monsoon would take them on the reverse voyage laden with tea. As soon as the season ended, the foreigners were supposed to depart to Macao. The regulation was not difficult to evade for those who wanted to do so, but most preferred the summer climate of Macao which was cooler and healthier than the humid heat of Canton.

Macao had another important asset – sex. One of the more irksome restrictions in Canton was that foreigners were forbidden to bring women – wives, daughters, mistresses or whatever – and this was a rule strictly enforced and not possible to evade.[11] This apart, most creature comforts were available. Food and drink were lavish. There are vivid descriptions of the East India Company's hospitality – dinner parties of 30, each guest with his own Chinese servant standing behind him, a band playing, a multi-course repast washed down with sherry, Madeira, claret, champagne and port. The Company had a library of 4000 books. But, although wine and song were present, women were not. The famous flower boats, floating brothels, were forbidden to foreigners, and those who took the risk often lived, and sometimes died, to regret it. But the import of girls from these boats into the factories was not unknown, although condemned severely by the authorities. 'If any dare … to employ young boys as servants for foreigners, who will lead them secretly to drink and pass the night with courtesans, or under cover of darkness will take native prostitutes to the factories, let the patrols, the watchmen and the constables seize them.'[12] In Macao there was no problem. European merchants who brought out their wives and families could settle them there and return after the Canton trading season had ended. The far larger number who went unaccompanied to the Far East could take Portuguese or sometimes Chinese mistresses, the process being facilitated by the remarkable surplus among the Portuguese of women over men, more than two and a half times as many.[13] It was one of the benevolent functions of Jardine Matheson, as it had been of their predecessor firms, to act as discreet trustees or executors for the 'pensioners', as they were politely described, of deceased employees and for their illicit offspring.

In Canton conditions were far less agreeable. The city, surrounded by walls 30 feet high, was forbidden territory. It was, in theory, permissible to go into the hinterland, but one could only do so through a noisome, crowded suburb, and few felt inclined to try. Foreigners could visit the public gardens on Honan Island, opposite the factories, three times a month, but had to be back before dark, avoid getting drunk and refrain from conversing with the public. They were not allowed to learn Chinese. The number of servants employed was limited, and licences had to be obtained for them as well as for boatmen, pilots, agents, etc. Business was supposed to be conducted through 'linguists' who knew little English and were often even ignorant of their own language. No vessels of war were allowed in the Canton river. A host of complicated regulations affected the smaller boats which plied between Whampoa and Canton. There were tedious rules about customs and excise duties. Most frustrating of all were the endless delays while minor officials haggled about this and that petty detail.

The merchants of the Co-hong were the only people legally allowed to trade with foreigners. There were never more than thirteen of them, and on occasion as few as four. They formed a loose association, trading not as a combine but individually. Although some made vast fortunes like the redoubtable Howqua, who reckoned his wealth in 1824 to be $26 million, they tended to be under-capitalized, and there were frequent bankruptcies. These, however, were met by a fund called the Consoo Fund, fed by a levy of three per cent on foreign trade. So foreign merchants in Canton were in the unique position of being able to rely on reimbursement against default, an asset available nowhere else. In a period of immense trading risks, this was a notable advantage. One can contrast the great crash in Calcutta, where there was no such safety net, in 1830–3; the principal houses went bankrupt to the tune of

$15 million, bringing down many London houses with them.[14] The Chinese government regarded the Co-hong as responsible for the good behaviour of the foreign merchants with whom they dealt. They were supposed to 'secure' ships and merchants. The reality was different. The East India Company did indeed abide by the rules and trade only with the 'Hongists', but there was also a multitude of traders outside the Co-hong known as 'shopmen', and the 'private English' dealt regularly with them despite the Co-hong's legal monopoly. Among other commodities traded there was the ever-rising volume of opium imports. The actual cargoes were kept away from Canton, and the smuggling trade was physically conducted elsewhere, but the finance and broking were done in Canton and the prices were regularly published in the English language *Canton Register* started in 1827, which also printed the latest gossip and information.

The British traders in Canton were sharply divided in outlook. 'The Select' were for peace at any price and their tea monopoly was their sole concern. They were 'doves' while the 'private English' were 'hawks'. The 'private English' came to believe more and more strongly that China should be opened to British trade. They saw great opportunities which, as events turned out, they overestimated, and they believed that it was vital to obtain proper diplomatic relations with Peking. They were infuriated by the attitude of the Chinese officials.

To a Westerner it was undoubtedly very irritating. Foreign trade was treated as a benevolent condescension on the part of the Celestial Emperor. The Barbarians were there on sufferance, and very lucky to be allowed to engage in their activities at all through the kindness of the Emperor. If they disliked the conditions, they could go away. But the Barbarians were fully aware that both the Emperor's privy purse and the Imperial equivalent of the Inland Revenue obtained a vast income from Canton – one-third of all the duties on Chinese trade. The Hoppo was particularly responsible for remits to the privy purse, and during his three-year term of office he had to satisfy the Emperor and the Government's Exchequer, and make his own fortune. On the other hand he could not go too far in extortion. He would be held accountable if the Canton trade declined or disappeared, for this would be a disaster for the Emperor's private income and the Government's official revenue. It was difficult to steer the line between maximizing taxation and driving the Barbarians out altogether. Guile and diplomacy were needed as well as authority.

The importance of opium in the China trade can be demonstrated by one simple statistic. Between 1800 and 1810 China gained something like $26 million in her world balance of payments. Between 1828 and 1836 she lost about $38 million.[15] It was the import of opium which produced this startling reversal. In effect the British tea exports from China, which had been financed by the import of Indian raw cotton and other goods plus bullion to make up the deficit, were now financed by these plus opium, which not merely eroded the surplus but produced a deficit for which China, in her turn, now had to pay in bullion. The sale and smoking of opium had been prohibited as long ago as 1799 by the Ch'ing Government, but, like many other edicts of the Middle Kingdom, this was regarded more as the expression of a moral precept than as a law to be effectively enforced. A parallel perhaps would be the prohibition of alcohol in America between the World Wars. It would be wrong to think that the opium trade was as easy and straightforward as trade in other commodities, or that the law was completely ignored. Traders often complained of the measures sporadically taken by the Mandarin, but, however irritating, these were no effective barrier to a startling rise in opium imports from 1800 onwards.

The figures of what were essentially contraband sales cannot be wholly reliable, but they are more likely to be an underestimate than an exaggeration. From 1800 to 1821 the opium traffic averaged a little over 4500 cases (140lb [63.5kg] to a case), but from 1821–2 it began to increase rapidly. In the next decade the average number of cases was 10,000. Then, for reasons connected with Indian production, it escalated to 19,000 in 1831–2, 40,000 in 1838–9, just before the clampdown, which led to the First Opium War. The principal source of 'the drug', as it was called, was India – the opium poppy grown in Bengal. The two favoured varieties were called 'Patna' and 'Benares'. The East India Company had a monopoly in both the sale and manufacture, as far as its own domains were concerned, and organized them very efficiently, but it had no control over an allegedly inferior brand called Malwa and grown in the Native States which were not ruled by the Company. Eventually, Malwa was to become a flood and destroy the Company's cautious policy of restricting the production of Bengal in order to keep up prices.

It took about eighteen months to two years for opium to appear on the market after the poppies had been sown in October. For example, opium sown in the autumn of 1826 would be harvested from February to April 1827, made up in the factory into six-inch cakes from May to September, sent by river to Calcutta in a series of successive fleets from the beginning of November. The earliest auctions were held shortly after Christmas and could continue until as late as July 1828. There was, therefore, at any single moment a great deal 'in the pipeline', if one can use that metaphor.

The opium monopoly was extremely profitable. By the 1830s it was producing something like one-seventh of the entire income of the Company. If one remembers that the export of opium from India to China was the key to the import of tea from China to Britain, and that tea duties amounted to nearly one-tenth of the revenue of the British budget, it is easy to see what immense vested interests were involved in both countries, extending right down to the *ryots*, the Bengal peasants who sowed and harvested the crop. Nor was there any substitute for opium if the system was to continue at all. Cotton was the only other article which the Chinese wished to import, but since 1819 the cotton market had been in a state of depression. In 1823, the value of opium imports into China for the first time exceeded the value of cotton imports, and this remained the pattern thenceforth.[16]

That opium addiction could be dangerous and deleterious was well known in Britain, but certain points can be made in extenuation of the trade. In the first place, the purchase and use of opium in Britain itself was entirely legal. One could buy what was openly on offer. In 1830, 22,000lbs (9980kg) were imported – the equivalent of about 150 cases. This was, of course, far less than the Chinese figures quoted above, but the population of China was twenty-five times that of the UK; if one applied that factor, the British imports would be the equivalent of 3750 cases – obviously a great deal less than the average of 10,000 which actually prevailed in China at that time, but not massively lower. In

1860, Britain was reckoned to be importing 88,000lbs (39,920kg) – 600 cases.[17] Comparison with China has to be modified in the light of social structure, income per capita, lack of transport, and many other considerations. Nevertheless an Englishman or Scotsman engaged in the trade would not necessarily feel especially guilty, in view of what was happening in Britain.

In Britain, opium was taken partly as a medicament to soothe babies and children in such products as Godfrey's Cordial, Batley's Sedative Solution and Mother Bailey's Quieting Syrup and partly to relieve pain among adults suffering from various complaints – indigestion, toothache, hangovers, alcoholism and gout. The use of it was very old. The opium poppy was first grown in Egypt and Asia Minor, and there are many allusions to it in the literature of Antiquity. There are various ways in which it can be administered. In the early nineteenth century the most common form in Europe was liquid – laudanum, which was opium dissolved in alcohol, often known as a 'tincture'.[18] This was a relatively weak mixture, and far less damaging than opium smoked in a pipe, which was the Oriental usage and almost universal in China. Smoking has a much more direct and harmful effect than laudanum, but in contemporary Britain the practice was almost unknown, certainly very rare.

It was, after all, possible for people, not perhaps very many, to live for many years on moderate daily doses of laudanum. William Wilberforce, the great Evangelical crusader against slavery, was a case in point. He died at 74, having taken laudanum every day for the last 45 years of his life. The general attitude before De Quincey's celebrated work, and long afterwards, was that opium resembled alcohol. A person so inclined could destroy himself by too much of either, but this was no reason for banning them.[19] In fact, we now know that alcohol is far less dangerous than opium. It is eliminated from the body much more quickly than even the softest of soft drugs, and its effects, although certainly damaging when it is taken in excess, are slower and less destructive. These facts were not known in the early nineteenth century, nor could many people in Britain have appreciated the difference between smoking opium and drinking laudanum.

The extent of opium addiction in China at this time has never been calculated with any accuracy. In 1836 there was a European estimate of about 12.5 million smokers. Jonathan Spence reckons that in the late 1880s the figure may have been some 15 million.[20] Of greater significance was the impression which the big urban centres gave of widespread addiction. Moreover it was the upper class in which the practice was prevalent, for it required both money and leisure. The Chinese peasant was in no position to afford it. The habit, therefore, was damaging the very class upon which Imperial rule depended. It was alleged that one-fifth of the officials of the central government were smokers, and four-fifths of the *yamen* clerks. It was also very prevalent in the army – a factor among many others in the crushing defeats inflicted upon China in the two Opium Wars. The Imperial Court had every cause for alarm at the spread of a vice which was corrupting the élite of the nation, physically, morally and financially. The danger was appreciated but, though repeated edicts declared the traffic to be illegal, evasion was not difficult, and the opium traders took care to operate away from Canton itself, first at Macao, then at Whampoa and finally at Lintin Island, outside the Bogue, until the outbreak of the Opium War.

By the time Jardine Matheson was formed in 1832, the opium trade was making vast fortunes for Scottish, English, American, and Parsee merchants. It produced large revenues directly for India and indirectly for the British Exchequer. Peasants in Bengal and the Princely States depended upon it, and the value of land was reckoned in certain areas to be four times as high as it would have been but for the opium poppy. In China itself, opium brokers, merchants and smugglers profited immensely. The consequential bribery lined the pockets of the mandarins. Even the Emperor's court was rumoured to be involved. The Emperor himself was a beneficiary, probably unconsciously; if there had been no illicit trade in opium outside Canton, the remittances of the Hoppo from legal trade within the city would have been much less, for the volume depended on opium imports. Yet the fact remained that it was a contraband trade and therefore fundamentally precarious. The more it grew, the more precarious it became.

THREE

William Jardine
and James Matheson

William Jardine was born at Broadholm, a farm near Lochmaben in Dumfriesshire, on 24 February 1784.[1] He was the fourth child and second son of Andrew Jardine, who died when William was only nine. He was supported by his elder brother David through his studies at the Medical School in Edinburgh. He remained throughout his life deeply grateful for this help – an example of family solidarity which he was himself to follow when prosperity came his way. Although he never married, he was most generous to his nephews and cousins. We do not know why he chose his profession, merely that he was registered as attending classes in various branches of medicine in 1800 and 1801, obtaining the full diploma of the Royal College of Surgeons in Edinburgh on 2 March 1802 at the surprisingly early age of just over eighteen. Nor do we know what prompted him to seek a career as a surgeon at sea on the Indiamen, the ships chartered by the East India Company for trade with the East. All we know is that he travelled to London as soon as he was qualified and contacted, through whatever influences, one of the most experienced managing owners, Thomas Newte, who had a vacancy for a surgeon's mate on one of his ships, the *Brunswick*, a 1200-ton vessel which had come into service for the China run in 1793. On 15 March Jardine signed a receipt for £5 for the customary two months' advance. It was not lavish but there were other opportunities. On 30 March the *Brunswick* weighed anchor and in company with two other ships set out on the long voyage to China. For the first time in some years, a naval escort was unnecessary. The Treaty of Amiens of 1801 had suspended, though not for long, the war with France. A defective rudder caused the *Brunswick* to put in for repairs at a Brazilian port. Thence she sailed until 7 August, apparently without a pause, to the Anjer Road in the Sunda Strait which divides Java and Sumatra. After four days to fill up with fresh food and water she set sail again, soon entering the China Sea. Helped by the south-west monsoon she was off Macao on 4 September and moored at Whampoa three days later.

The captains of the three ships then repaired to Canton to do business, especially over their privileged tonnage – the real source of their income. A commander had 56 tons outward and 38 tons on the return voyage. The average profit was reckoned at some £6000 (over £100,000 today). A surgeon was entitled to three tons and a surgeon's mate to only two, but quite a lot could be done with that by a shrewd operator, though we do not know what Jardine did with his portion. The surgeons would also take up temporary residence in the Factory area forming a 'mess' on their own. On his first voyage young Jardine would almost certainly have been left on board the *Brunswick* to look after the health of the crew, for Whampoa was a notoriously insalubrious place. But he would have had ample opportunity of at least paying short visits to Canton itself and meeting some of the principal figures there. One of them was a senior surgeon, Thomas Weeding. Another was Charles Magniac, recently made a partner in Reid, Beale & Co., which occupied the Creek Factory. Jardine was to have important dealings with both Weeding and Magniac in later years.

His first stay in China lasted some six weeks. By 29 November the *Brunswick* was loaded with tea and left Whampoa for Lintin. Then with her accompanying ships she sailed for Macao, dropped the pilot and headed back with the north-east monsoon across the China Sea. On 19 December they were clear of the Sunda Strait, by 1 February 1803 they were rounding the Cape of Good Hope and fourteen days later were anchored off St Helena where a capital ship, HMS *Rodney*, was to escort the convoy home. The renewal of war with France was regarded as imminent and inevitable, and risks could not be taken. There was no trouble, however, and the *Brunswick* anchored at Long Reach above Greenhithe near Gravesend on 25 April 1803. The whole voyage had lasted thirteen months and eleven days.

Jardine enjoyed a respite from the sea for the next ten months, but in the autumn he was promoted to surgeon on the *Brunswick* in succession to the previous holder, who had retired and presumably given a good report of his junior officer. The *Brunswick* was to carry the 66th Regiment of the King's Troops, later the Royal Berkshires, to Ceylon – one of three troopships and five other Indiamen proceeding in convoy under naval escort. The voyage began on 26 February 1804 and was to be the most perilous in which Jardine was involved. He had now moved upwards in the elaborate Indiaman pecking order, being 'entitled to a canvas cabin and a servant, also the right to walk on the weather side of the quarterdeck'.[2] On 17 July the troopships landed the 66th Regiment at Trincomalee and thence sailed to Madras. They loaded raw cotton, and again, under naval escort, sailed for China. They encountered a violent typhoon in the China Sea. No ships were lost, but a few days later the *Brunswick* ran aground in the Canton River on 13 October. She was floated off and no damage was suspected at the time.

Having unloaded her cargo and filled up with tea, the *Brunswick*, as part of a convoy of eight Indiamen bound for England and seven Country ships bound for India, sailed on 8 January 1805 from China, again under naval protection.

She soon began to leak. The damage in the Canton River had been greater than suspected. Instead of sailing from Penang to England she had to put in at Bombay. The tea cargo was discharged and shipped to England in another Indiaman, and the *Brunswick* prepared to return to Canton with a load of raw cotton. There she would pick up a fresh cargo of tea. One of the passengers bound for Canton was a Parsee, Jamsetjee Jejeebhoy,[3] whom Jardine came to know well and with whom he had many dealings, mostly, but not invariably, cordial. Captain James Ludovic Grant was supposed to sail under naval protection, but he departed on 1 July before the convoy had assembled, his obvious motive being to reach the Canton market before the other cargoes flooded the cotton market and brought the price down. He was intercepted off Point de Galle in Ceylon on 11 July by two French warships under the command of Admiral Linois and was obliged to surrender ship.

Jardine was now, along with the rest of the crew, a prisoner of war. Most of them were transferred to the French Admiral's flagship, the *Marengo,* but Jardine was ordered to remain on the *Brunswick* , which sailed under the guns of the *Marengo* for the Cape of Good Hope. The Treaty of Amiens had handed the Cape back to the Dutch Republic, which was now an ally of the French. The two ships reached Simon's Bay on 29 August – mid-winter in South Africa. A storm resulted in the *Brunswick* parting with her anchors and running ashore, becoming a total loss though all hands were saved. Jardine and the rest were transported to Cape Town. Admiral Linois allowed them to return to England on parole in a neutral American ship. They sailed via St Helena and there joined HMS *Howe* which was conveying home the Governor-General of India, the Marquess Wellesley, elder brother of the future Duke of Wellington. Thus less than three months after Trafalgar, William Jardine returned to Britain, arriving in the Thames in late January 1806. There was a company rule that if a ship was lost, whatever the reason, the personnel forfeited all wages due, the theory being that wages were based on freight – therefore no freight, no wages. It was not quite as harsh in practice. Advances were not reclaimed and compassionate allowances could be made. Jardine lost £40 in wages but his privileged tonnage had been sent home from Bombay by another ship and he was entitled, as surgeon, to ten shillings a head for looking after the troops on the outward journey, amounting to about £175.

There is no space to describe in detail Dr Jardine's later voyages. The interested reader should consult Captain Williamson's fascinating book. It is enough to say that he was involved in five more of these adventures, four of which were undertaken in wartime. However, after Trafalgar and the British recapture of the Cape, the French navy counted for little. One of the worst voyages was in 1809 when it became extremely hazardous to go from Lintin to Whampoa, because of a notable eruption of Chinese pirates based on some 2000 junks in the approaches to the Canton River. It was for the time being impossible for the Europeans in Macao to make their seasonal return to Canton by Chinese passenger boats, and Indiamen with armed escort had to be their refuge. There is still perhaps in some people's minds a vaguely romantic and exciting association with piracy. Any account of what actually happened in the China Sea should dispel that notion. The pirates were brutal murderers, who cut to pieces or threw to the sharks every single person on the ships they boarded. They dared not allow a witness to survive. If the pirates were ever identified and captured, death was certain. It was one of the ironies of the relations between East and West that the Chinese government was ready to execute ruthlessly the criminals who preyed upon ships conveying contraband goods to its own shores and breaking China's own criminal law, although it is fair to say that discrimination between vessels carrying legitimate and illegitimate cargoes was not easy. This was not the only 'looking-glass' aspect of the strange topsy-turvy world in which the China trade was conducted. British merchants constantly referred to the 'persecution of the mandarins', rather as if today a drug pedlar were to talk of the 'persecution of the police'.

The last of Jardine's voyages as a ship's surgeon was in 1816–17. His arrival in Canton coincided with the return of Lord Amherst from his ill-fated mission to Peking. He would certainly have met the repulsed envoy, and the episode must have confirmed him in his conviction of the futility of engaging in diplomatic negotiations with the Imperial authorities. The Indiaman *Windham*, in which Jardine made the voyage, returned as usual via St Helena which was, surprisingly, governed not by the Crown but by the East India Company, whose permission had to be sought for Napoleon's sojourn there. Everyone who landed wanted to be presented to that extraordinary personality. The captain of the *Windham* very probably was, but the surgeon may well have had to content himself with a view of the great man pacing up and down in the grounds of Longwood.

We do not know about this and so many other matters in what must have been the most interesting part of William Jardine's life. He did not keep a diary, or if he did, it has not survived. Most tantalizing of all the gaps is the financial success of his voyages. That it must have been considerable cannot be disputed, but there is now no means of knowing its extent. Whatever it was, he decided at the age of 33 in 1817, to give up the profession of surgeon at sea and take to a business career. The transition was not a great one. From the beginning he must have been as much concerned with the commercial as the medical side of his job.

This is not to impugn his ability as a doctor, of which nothing is known except that he clearly commended himself to his predecessor on the *Brunswick*. It is merely to say that a major objective for any ship's officer on an Indiaman was to make money out of privileged tonnage.

He finished his last voyage as a surgeon on 25 May 1817. He took up residence in London and entered into some sort of association with Thomas Weeding, another former ship's surgeon, whom he first met in Canton in 1802, and who had retired from medicine to the City in 1805. Jardine had, in fact, replaced him as ship's surgeon on one of his voyages. Weeding had later acted as Jardine's agent in respect of sales in London of privilege tonnage, and was well placed to advise him on the practice and opportunities of banking and commerce in the world's greatest financial centre. In August 1818, Weeding applied to the East India Company, saying that he needed an agent in India and would like permission to send William Jardine. The request was peremptorily refused. Free Merchants' Indentures needed the nomination of a director, and none was supplied. The defect was soon remedied. John Thornhill, a new director, filled the gap and Jardine was duly given the necessary indentures. In November, he and Weeding agreed on a joint venture with a Bombay Parsee, Framjee Cowasjee, in a ship, the *Sarah*, yet to be built. Jardine meanwhile went out to establish himself in Bombay, where he had been only once before, despite his many Eastern voyages. He was there in the autumn of 1819 and met up again with Jamsetjee Jejeebhoy. In the following spring he met James Matheson for the first time, although it was to be some years before they formed their famous partnership. Before he left London, William Jardine had the pleasure of helping his eldest sister's son, Andrew Johnstone, to follow in his footsteps as a surgeon at sea in one of the East India Company's few 'own ships' as opposed to those it chartered. The officers of these were regarded as a superior élite. Andrew Johnstone was to be briefly, in the mid-1830s, a partner of his uncle in Canton, but retired early, presumably with sufficient on which to live. Like his uncle he never married, but was reputed to be 'much attached to horses and women'.[4]

Jardine was generous to his nephews and cousins as long as they were respectable, sensible and industrious. He was ready to assist the son of one of them, 'who is a fine grown-up lad and ought to have a farm of his own...but the assistance must be considered for the general benefit of the family, not as an advance to Frank individually; which might make him play the fool.' He goes on in the same letter to Andrew Johnstone in Dumfries:

> You are aware I have a strong objection to extravagance and idleness, and I trust you will impress this on the minds of your young cousins. I can never consent to assist idle and dissipated [characters?] however nearly connected with me, but am prepared to go to any reasonable extent in supplying such of my relations as conduct themselves prudently and industriously.[5]

The letters of William Jardine suggest all the seriousness, probity and high business standards which characterized the early nineteenth-century work ethic. It was very marked in Scotland where relative poverty produced a heightened desire to make one's way in the world, but it was to be found all over Britain. Occasionally, he would deviate into slightly ponderous humour. To a friend in London, one F. Halliburton, he wrote in the same month, 'success to your matrimonial scheme, the commission of a handsome workbox being left unexecuted till I shall have heard of your having obtained the consent of the lady; and secured her heart and hand by means of your own insinuating manner, and a few words from the parson.' But his letters are for the most part businesslike and rather dry, although he could at times be scathing about other members of the merchant community in Canton, in particular 'the Select' with whom he seldom saw eye to eye. He could also be very sharp even with friends if he thought they had let him down in matters of business, as in a letter to Jamsetjee Jejeebhoy in Bombay, written in January 1833 from Canton:

> We have already addressed you at considerable length, respecting your account; and I revert to it here with no other view than that of expressing to you the very great annoyance your letter No 27 – addressed to the firm – has occasioned us. More particularly, when combined with your peremptory instructions respecting remittance this season, as they have left us a choice of evils only. Whatever view you may take of the subject ... we have

acted throughout with a view to your interest and advantage in preference to our own, and trusting to your liberal feelings for giving us credit for having so acted.[6]

It would be difficult, perhaps impossible, to disentangle the points in dispute, nor likely to be at all interesting. But one can well imagine that in the 'cabin'd, cribb'd, confin'd' conditions of the foreign enclave in Canton tempers could easily become frayed, even for such a solid and equable character as Dr Jardine.

To return to his partnership with Weeding and Framjee Cowasjee, little is known about his dealings in 1820–22 nor about the *Sarah*. What is clear is that in the latter year he decided to base himself in Canton, spending the non-trading season in Macao. In his first year in the Factory area he engaged in what seems to have been his earliest transactions in the opium trade, selling 649 chests of Malwa for $813,000. By 1824, he was well established, and when Charles Magniac of the leading opium firm in Canton – Charles Magniac & Co. – became ill Jardine was invited to take over the management of his affairs until Charles's brother, Hollingworth Magniac, could get back from London. Charles returned to England and died soon afterwards. Charles Magniac & Co. had been highly successful until Charles's health began to fail. Hollingworth himself was anxious to retire to England and eventually did so in 1827. But it was a natural step at this stage, in 1825, to invite William Jardine to become a partner in the firm now named Magniac & Co. It was an opportunity not to be missed. Jardine promptly accepted. He made a short visit to Bombay to clear up his affairs. On 12 August, he returned to Canton and took up his residence at the Creek Factory, his partnership in the Firm having been promulgated in July 1825. He was based there until his final retirement to Britain twelve years later. By then he was a very rich man indeed. As a new partner he had a mass of business to conduct and much midnight oil was consumed. He believed in combining courtesy with expedition. The story is that he had no chairs in his Canton office in order to discourage loquacity on the part of callers. He was a tough character. The Chinese were addicted to pejorative nicknames for foreigners and Jardine's was 'Iron-headed Old Rat'. It was bestowed after a particular incident when he was presenting a document at the Petition Gate in Canton. He was struck on the head with a bamboo pole, but never even turned round. The episode was symbolic of his whole career.

James Matheson was born at Lairg in Sutherland in 1796. He came from a cadet branch of an old and pedigree-conscious family, the Mathesons of Lochalsh and Attadale in the south-west corner of Ross and Cromarty. The Mathesons had connections with the East India Company. In the subtle social hierarchy of nineteenth-century Scotland, Matheson was a modest cut above Jardine. In the 1820s he was the only Country Merchant in Canton to be on equal terms with the members of the Select. Highlanders and Lowlanders did not always hit it off. Their worlds were, and are still to some extent, very different. Fortunately he and Jardine were to have the happiest relations throughout their joint business lives. This is not to say that they never differed, merely that the differences did not last. The fact that Matheson's background was rather more advantageous and cultivated than that of the older man – doctors did not then count high socially – caused neither condescension on the one side nor resentment on the other.

Matheson was educated at Edinburgh University, which, along with Glasgow, was one of the two best seats of learning in Britain. Oxford and Cambridge still lagged well behind. He then went to London where, after a short while, family influence procured him Free Merchants' Indentures from the East India Company in 1815 – at a far earlier age than Jardine. He joined his uncle's firm, Mackintosh & Co., in Calcutta, but was evidently not a success. He seems to have got into some sort of youthful scrape which annoyed his employers. For whatever reason, he was on the shelf in Calcutta in 1818, when in June he met Robert Taylor, a former Indiaman purser, who persuaded him to go out to Canton in an informal partnership concerned with insurance. In 1819 they involved themselves in opium dealings too complicated to record in detail; it is enough to say that Matheson was nearly ruined. Taylor, who was much older, died on 4 August 1820. His affairs were in chaos and he left a load of debts. James Matheson was faced with financial disaster, but a sudden rise in the price of opium saved him. He sold a consignment at a high profit, but was always cautious thereafter, for he never forgot the nerve-racking risk he had run. He had a 'decent house' in Macao in 1821, and began a trading relationship with Xavier Yrissari, a Spaniard, who had a connection with M. Larruleta & Co., a major firm in Calcutta. By then, Matheson, who had acquired the Danish Consulship in Canton, was beginning to make his way. As Consul he could defy the East India Company's rules, and when he became Yrissari's partner in July 1821, he was on the road to success. On 19 June he had written: 'I had the great gratification last night of welcoming Mr Yrissari to Macao, and if anything else could add to my pleasure it is the unexampled magnitude of the business with which he will enable us to commence our establishment, far exceeding the most sanguine hopes I could have formed.'[7] The Yrissari connection was a turning point in his career, and from then he never looked back.

Matheson was evidently a man who gave some thought to the problems of his modern world. He was widely read, he studied science, law and economics, and he was a keen disciple of Adam Smith. He was something of a publicist. He was to write in 1836 a pamphlet entitled *Present Position and Future Prospects of Trade in China,* which stated the Western case for trade in unequivocally doctrinal terms; they were scarcely calculated to conciliate the Chinese, whose policy he attributed to their 'marvellous degree of imbecility and avarice, conceit and obstinacy'. He started in 1827 the *Canton Register,* largely a news and gossip sheet, but useful to the merchants in shamelessly announcing the current prices of opium. No doubt there were as few Chinese people who could read English as Britons who could read Chinese. So perhaps no great harm was done. Matheson was, however, more interested than most of his colleagues in Chinese culture. He bought Morrison's *Grammar of the Chinese Language* and three numbers of his Chinese dictionary. Like Jardine, he was equally generous towards his relations, although he did not have quite so many to provide for, since the family had other commercial connections which could help.

Matheson was the earliest of the opium merchants to engage personally in the seaborne traffic up the east coast, instead of relying on Chinese intermediaries. In 1822, the first great opium boom had collapsed and Yrissari & Co., which had tried to corner the market in Patna, was faced with a major crisis. It had large stocks but no takers from its usual clientele. It was decided to see what could be done by direct personal salesmanship on the coast instead of depending on Chinese intermediaries. In June 1823, Matheson sailed east under Spanish colours in a 200-ton brig, *San Sebastian*, commanded by a cousin, John McKay. He first put in at Amoy, which was the official port reserved for Spanish trade. But an official port was hardly the place, even in China, for disposing of a cargo of contraband opium. The *San Sebastian* then proceeded further up the coast to Chinchew. There Matheson sold $80,000-worth of opium, not a startling success but enough to encourage another voyage in the autumn of the same year. This produced $132,000, but more by luck than good judgement. Stormy weather forced the *San Sebastian* to shelter in a bay 30 miles (48km) short of Chinchew. The place luckily turned out to be the principal opium centre of the district, and a roaring trade was done. But his success did not last. Other firms, notably Dent & Co., followed suit, and Matheson, on behalf of Yrissari & Co., pulled out. Some years later he and Jardine were to revive the coastal trade on a major scale, but by then the circumstances had greatly changed.

In October 1826, Yrissari died in Calcutta. In his will he left $500 to his partner 'to purchase something as a token of my regard from one who yielded to no one in the admiration of his excellent character, of which, during the period we have lived together [in Canton], no one had better opportunities of experiencing the benefit.'[8] Matheson was thus deprived of a partner for the second time. He had to go out to Calcutta to settle Yrissari's affairs. Early in March 1827, he notified his clients that the firm's day-to-day business would be carried on by two clerks, one being his nephew Alexander Matheson, and that the general conduct of the business would be in the hands of William Jardine. When he returned to Canton in September he announced that the firm would henceforth be known as Matheson & Co. This arrangement was short-lived. Just as death had removed Yrissari from Yrissari & Co., so death, retirement and unfitness[9] had removed all the Magniacs from Magniac & Co. The latter was the largest house in Canton, the runner-up being Dent & Co., with which Jardine Matheson was later to be on terms of bitter personal rivalry. It was hardly surprising that the survivors of the two partnerships who knew and trusted each other should have come together; early in 1828 Matheson joined the firm that was still called Magniac & Co. He is said to have brought with him $60,000.[10]

It took four years to wind up the affairs of the Magniac family. Until this was done Hollingworth remained a sleeping partner, and it would have been awkward for many reasons to change the name; but on 30 June 1832 Magniac & Co. finally closed its doors in order to reopen in Canton next day under the name of Jardine Matheson & Co. This is the formal date of the beginning of the famous Firm[11], but one can fairly say that, for practical purposes, it had come into being at the beginning of 1828 and has had a continuous existence ever since that year.

FOUR

The Coastal Trade

We have seen that the opium trade boomed from the late 'teens of the nineteenth century. Competition between the products of Bengal and the Native States led to a fall in prices, an increase in consumption and a greater demand than ever. 'Opium is like gold,' wrote Robert Taylor in 1819, 'I can sell it at any time.'[1] But the vast rise of opium imports into China between 1819 and 1839 was accompanied by abrupt and startling changes of price. It was a highly speculative affair, and the general progress of the trade was marked by sudden temporary crises, which could be ruinous to those concerned. In July 1819 Patna opium could be bought for $1170 a chest. Magniac & Co. started to buy all the opium they could get and cornered the market. By February 1820 it reached $2500. Then the Magniacs wisely sold out, because renewed 'persecution' by the mandarins led to an alarming slump. Patna, in March 1822, was below $2000, but in August that year it shot up again beyond $2500 and could be sold for nearly $3000. In its turn Yrissari & Co. now tried to corner the market, but the official anti-opium campaign was renewed. A slump ensued. By September 1823 Patna had fallen to $1420. Only Matheson's opium-selling voyages on the east coast saved the firm from ruin.

These violent fluctuations were caused largely by the sporadic attempts of the Chinese government to enforce its laws. Although the mandarins were corrupt to a high degree, there were always some limits to what the opium dealers could get away with. For example, in 1820, W.S. Davidson of Dent & Co. was ordered to remove his opium ship from Whampoa and 'no money could reverse the decree'.[2] That summer the Viceroy and the Hoppo issued edicts obliging the Hong merchants to search ships for opium and bear full responsibility for the ships they had 'secured', for which they had given surety. Worse followed. There was the affair of the *Topaz*, a ship discovered to be carrying opium by the officials on one of their surprise searches. In July 1821 a Macao opium dealer called Asee was imprisoned on some local charge and revenged himself on the officials by sending his account books to Peking, revealing the bribes that he had been paying to the mandarins. The authorities were stimulated into unwonted zeal, and the Hong merchants now refused to 'secure' any ships which even had a part cargo of opium. Charles Magniac declared it to be 'the hottest persecution we remember'. Matheson was concerned with three of the four ships specifically named by the Chinese authorities. He deemed it wise to leave Whampoa and anchor them outside the Bogue at Lintin Island.

Clearly, Whampoa was no longer viable. The question was where to find a safe base for the transshipment of 'the drug'. The topic was much debated. The Portuguese would have welcomed the choice of Macao. They already did a fair amount of trade in Malwa, exported from their colonial ports in India. It could not be consigned direct to Whampoa, because Portuguese ships were not allowed up the Canton River. But Macao had two disadvantages. The Portuguese were, as we saw, mere tenants-at-will of the Chinese government, and at any moment the mandarins might clamp down on the traffic. In 1822 there was a revolution in the city which was reversed a year later and the restored regime sought to make Macao the sole base for the opium trade, suggesting that a duty should be levied on every chest. It would produce some $200,000 per annum 'to bribe the Mandarins and keep them always contented'.[3]

Matheson strongly opposed the idea. He wrote:

The dependence of the settlement on the Chinese appears to us to be an insuperable bar to the plan. Hitherto the consumers have had some check on the mandarins in being able when not willing to yield to their extortions, to resort to the markets of Canton and Lintin. But, if all the opium were fast in their clutches at Macao, as the Portuguese propose and expect, it is difficult to foresee to what unheard-of pitch the avarice of the mandarins would reach.[4]

There were other problems. The supply of opium was abundant. Had it been in short supply, a monopoly market might have made it easier to combine to exact a high price, but with a surplus 'the proposed union must have a hurtful tendency, since our object should be to promote consumption by diffusing the supply through as many channels as possible.'[5] Nor was this all. The Macao administration was inordinately venal. The only judge was elected from the inhabitants and currently (1825) was a ship's doctor. 'It cannot be supposed that he knows much about the law.' To have any hope of securing justice it was essential to use influence in Lisbon, which was far away. Matheson's attorney, in a case he was bringing, was pressurized into going over to the other side and acting for the defendant – 'a crime punishable with transportation by the laws of Portugal, but countenanced at Macao by all from the Governor downwards'. The next attorney employed by Matheson was imprisoned on a trumped-up charge of contempt of court. Then it transpired that the judge was the brother-in-law of one of the defendants against whom Matheson was claiming. In the end he gave up and dropped the case. Jardine bitterly observed that the government was 'conducted on principles which precluded all confidence of safety in the property of foreigners coming under its control'. It was clearly hopeless to use Macao as a depot.

What were the alternatives? Serious consideration was given to the use of a port entirely outside Chinese jurisdiction – Singapore or Manila. Both of them not only had that advantage, but also the asset of low charges for storage, insurance and demurrage. But the distances were large and it would not be easy to maintain a fleet of ships on a shuttle service, capable of beating up the China coast against the northeast monsoon between October and March. Nor had Matheson's attempt at direct dealing with coastal opium centres been entirely successful. The decision was in favour of a Chinese depot, despite the problems raised by Chinese jurisdiction. Both Formosa (Taiwan) and Amoy were considered, but in the end the place chosen was Lintin Island – a mountain in the Pearl River estuary rising to some 2000 feet (610m). The name means 'solitary nail'. It was about 25 miles (40km) south east of the forts of the Bogue, and 20 miles (32km) north east of Macao. Theoretically it was subject to the writ of the mandarins. In practice, as Matheson wrote: 'The idea of seizure by the Chinese we consider out of the question. The only danger on that score would be from an organized band of pirates... but for some years there have been no pirates in the Canton river.'[6] Lintin had some disadvantages. The cost of insurance and storage in the three or four armed hulks anchored in an open roadstead was high, for there was no protection in the typhoon season. Other 'outer anchorages' were available, and visiting ships made use of them – Kumsingmoon off Macao and, later, Hong Kong, but despite its risk Lintin remained the principal depot until the First Opium War. There, the cargoes were transshipped into 'scrambling dragons' or 'fast crabs', the English translation of the Chinese names for the 40- or 50-oared boats rowed by ferocious Tanka rivermen, who 'fought or bribed their way inland up the river to dry land distribution points run by gangsters or Triads.'[7]

The 'Lintin System' was not the only new development which altered the nature of the China trade in the 1820s. Even more important were the changes in the source of its principal constituent. The monopoly enjoyed by the East India Company in the opium products of Bengal – Benares and Patna – broke down. The rulers of the Princely States, inspired by imitation, cupidity and competition, began to harvest increasing crops of their own brand, Malwa. The Company had no jurisdiction and could not prohibit or control growth and production. Hitherto it had been the Company's policy to restrict production in its two factories near the cities of Patna and Benares in order to keep up the price. Now this was no longer possible. Maximization of quantity, albeit at a low price, was the only answer to the collapse of the Company's monopoly and the flood of cheap opium from the Native States. As a result, the amount of opium for which it was necessary to find a market in China increased enormously, doubling between 1830 and 1840,[8] and the traditional outlets in the Gulf of Canton were not enough to cope with it.

The problem caused the Firm to revert to a form of trade attempted prematurely and not very successfully by Matheson in 1823 – direct shipment up the China coast. After one or two minor efforts, Jardine decided upon a major venture in the autumn of 1832, chartering the clipper *Sylph* for a voyage to Tientsin and beyond. For direct dealings in that part of the world, pidgin English would not suffice. It was essential to have a good linguist. Jardine selected one of the strangest characters to figure in the early history of the China Trade, the Lutheran medical missionary the Rev. Karl Frederick August Gutzlaff.[9] He was of Prussian (Pomeranian) origin, a strong Anglophile – he married three successive English wives – and was a fast and fluent speaker of several Chinese dialects, among them Fukienese, one of the most difficult of all. No better interpreter could have been secured. He was not alone in believing that European commercial intercourse was the best way of bringing true religion to the 'Heathen Chinese'. But there was the question of what sort of commerce, and the fact remained that the sale of opium was the only trade which had any chance of being effective for this purpose. Jardine wrote:

> ... we have no hesitation in stating to you openly that our principal reliance is on opium. Though it is our earnest wish that you should not in any way injure the grand object you have in view by appearing interested in what, by many, is considered an immoral traffic, yet such traffic is so absolutely necessary to give any vessel a reasonable chance of defraying her expenses, that we trust you will have no objection to interpret on every occasion when your services may be requested ... You must be well aware that in the state of our intercourse with the coast of China no other cargo holds out a prospect of gain sufficient to induce any private merchant to engage in such an expensive expedition. From all we can learn opium appears to be the only article through the medium of which we are likely to be able to gratify the cupidity of the authorities on the coast; gain sweetens labour and, we may add, lessens very materially the risk incurred in the eyes of those who partake therein.

Jardine, delicately, went on to emphasize the point about 'gain':

> Having said so much, we have only to add that we consider you as surgeon and interpreter to the expedition, and shall willingly remunerate you for your services in that capacity, and the more profitable the expedition, the better we shall be able to place at your disposal a sum that may hereafter be

usefully employed in furthering the grand object you have in view and for your success in which we feel deeply interested.[10]

Gutzlaff, evidently, had some doubts, but 'after much consultation with others and a conflict in my own mind, I embarked in the *Sylph* ... on 20 October 1832 ... She had to beat up against a strong north-eastern monsoon and to encounter very boisterous weather before reaching her destination, Tientsin and Manchu Tartary.'[11] The voyage must have been an odious experience, as anyone who has been in north China in November to December can imagine. It was bitterly cold and very stormy. They reached Tientsin but dared not anchor in the Roads because of the northerly gale. They decided to leave: 'We therefore bore away for Kin-Chow and the Great Wall. While we were anticipating the pleasure we should experience in beholding this ancient structure, we ran upon a sand-bank which was entirely unknown to us.' This was one of the endemic risks of sailing in seas which were virtually uncharted. 'The next morning a fierce north wind blew from the ice-fields of Kamtschatka down the bay; the water decreased, the ship fell over on her beam-ends, and all our lascars were disabled by cold from doing any work.' The ship was entirely covered with ice inside and out, and one of the lascars froze to death.

> Whilst we were on shore endeavouring to hire some lighters, the ship got off by the interposition of God, who had ordered the south wind to blow, thus driving more water on the bank. His Name be praised for all eternity ... After several hours of labour we succeeded in getting up the anchor and took a speedy farewell of these dismal regions ... I consider Manchu Tartary as a very hopeful field for [missionary] enterprise and humbly hope it will soon attract the notice of some missionary society.

On the way back they put in at Shanghai and Chapu which was the port of Hangchow, they did business in Chusan Island and on the Fukien coast, and returned to Lintin on 29 April 1833, after a voyage of just over six months. He concluded:

> Our commercial relations are at the present moment on such a basis as to warrant a continuation of the trade along the coast.[12] We hope that this may tend ultimately to the introduction of the gospel, for which many

doors are opened. Millions of bibles and tracts will be needed to supply the wants of the people. God who in His mercy has thrown down the wall of national separation, will carry on the work. We look up to the ever blessed Redeemer to whom China with its millions is given; in the faithfulness of His promises we anticipate the glorious day of a general conversion, and are willing to do our utmost to promote the great work.

The word 'opium' or, as was more usual 'the drug', is never mentioned by Gutzlaff in his account of the voyage which, in fact, was not financially successful,[13] although it was to be soon followed by ones which proved very remunerative indeed. The combination of the Bible and the opium chest was not quite the arrant piece of hypocrisy which it seems today. There is no need to believe that William Jardine was writing with his tongue in cheek when he talked of 'the grand object you have in view and for your success in which we feel deeply interested'. He almost certainly did believe that China would be a better place if it were opened up to the two great Western influences of Christianity and trade, and it was only through trade that Christianity could gain a foothold. 'No opium, no Christianity' might sum up the situation. As for Gutzlaff, although it was unusual for a missionary to engage personally in the trade, it has to be remembered that, being a fluent Chinese speaker, he was a very unusual missionary. Few of his colleagues could have done what he did, even if they had wished. The general missionary attitude is epitomized in a best-selling book by Archdeacon Moule first published in 1878. He referred to the Convention of Peking of 1860 by which, after the Second Opium War, the Emperor reluctantly legalized opium. He goes on:

> Opium which had formed so mighty a factor in the fomentation of war! War which had opened China! China needing the gospel in all her wide provinces! Can Christian missionaries consent to be introduced at court by the opium trade against which they must ever protest? Such conflicting thoughts must often occur to the sensitive mind. And yet the answer seems simple enough. God in his loving mercy ever delights to bring good out of evil. And Christian missionaries dare not hesitate to be the almoners of God's mercy.[14]

Whether missionaries should behave like Gutzlaff and actually connive at, or even assist in, creating the evil out of which God delights to bring good, is perhaps open to question. But it is clear that there were plenty of pious and honourable people who had what was at least an ambivalent attitude towards 'the drug'. One has to remember that opium was not banned in Britain and that, as recently as 1831, the trade had received the approbation of both Houses of Parliament.

Although the voyage of the *Sylph* was not a financial success, the next two efforts authorized by Jardine were less far-ranging and highly profitable. James Innes, who had made his mark earlier by deliberately setting fire to one of the Canton customs houses, sailed as supercargo in the 382-ton brig *Jamesina*, to Chinchew and Foochow on 8 November 1832 and sold a great deal of opium at a profit. The prices were $70 to $100 per chest above those ruling at Lintin. The Firm had taken care to make conditions for its employees as easy as possible. Innes, who was something of a character and was known as the 'laird', wrote in the journal which he kept of his voyage:

> I have ... every resource that prudence and wealth can get together. I have always considered it a wise measure of those engaging in large affairs to provide for the perfect personal comfort of their agents so as to keep their temper and mind free for thought and action. I never before now in a selfish point of view experienced the realisation of this principle ... It would have repaid Mr Matheson for all his trouble in getting good clothing, had he seen a complete covering (and a warm one) put on the backs of more than half a hundred lascars literally in rags. Even our four English cunnies [sailors] applied and got Guernsey shirts.

On 29 November in Chinchew Bay Innes 'sent ashore two Chinese servants with a list of 28 opium dealers' names to come off and do business.' He adds, perhaps with a touch of complacency:

> If a measure is doubtful the world generally judges of its prudence by its success. If the rule is to be applied here, the move to this bay among my old acquaintances (of five months) was a prudent one. Last night, two regular smugglers came off, and, after a hard set-to as to price, they this day paid 870 dollars[15] a chest and took away 36 chests. Before they were away two

more boats came and took away 40 chests at the same price, the whole run being on Benares.

Unlike his experience on a previous voyage to the same place, when a typhoon had given him 'a fair chance of instant death', he was not only 'doing good business' but enjoying 'comfort and luxury'. He continues:

> We kept St Andrew's Day yesterday very merrily; the five in the Captain's mess were (strange to say) all sons of the Saint, and what is more curious four of that five from one of Scotland's counties.
>
> Dec. 2 Employed delivering briskly. No time to read my Bible or to keep my journal.
>
> Dec. 5 Still delivering briskly. Today several small mandarin junks sailed round us once or twice when some smuggling boats were alongside ... They gave us no trouble and the opium boats came and went easily close to them.

He goes on to describe his way of doing business:

> Our shroffs [cashiers] persevered on all daylight looking at dollars. When sun went down and scales were mounted in the cuddy [mess cabin] where we weighed, I lighted up my cabin brilliantly and with open door took down weights and tallied with Mr Burnett, who stood by the scales, the shroff Olio weighing. During this, which often lasted deep into midnight, were received all owners high and low (Chinese). Some head merchant was generally extended on my couch attended by his personal servant. All had tobacco pipes, some were with abacus at table settling their balances, others buying by signs or Morrison's vocabulary small articles, or offering gold for sale. Once or twice in the evening to high and low a glass of Mareskino or Hoffman was served.
>
> Before midnight the rabble were generally as close as they could pack stowed head and feet asleep on the carpet floor. Before I went to sleep I compared balances with Burnett ... turned every Chinese rascal out of my premises, opened all cabin doors to ventilate and walked for five minutes till the cot was swung.

Innes, like almost every contemporary European, obviously regarded the Chinese as lesser breeds, but he notes their honesty '...though the

Cabin was full of articles of value (to them) I never missed a pennyworth'.

Although his experiences on a previous voyage in another ship had been much worse, Innes by no means found it all plain sailing. The coast was largely uncharted, and the winter weather violent and unpredictable. It could be very stormy and bitterly cold, though 'I have found the temperature of my cabin much improved by the hanging lamp which Mr Matheson advised me to take. After it has burnt an hour with windows shut the difference is between cold and comfort.' On 24 December the ship in the Bay of Chinchew was hit by a sudden storm which by daylight 'had assumed the aspect of a typhoon'. The *Jamesina*'s heaviest anchor was used to ride it out at 120 fathoms. Visibility was very bad. It rained incessantly and the weather was 'piercingly cold'. These disagreeable conditions lasted till 4 January. Then there was a lull with the temperature up to 60°F (16°C). There followed another few days of storm but on 10 January 'clear sunshine and hardly any wind and the sea like a lake. After the piercing north wind we have had now for nearly a month it was high enjoyment to loiter all this day on deck.' The rest of the voyage featured similar vicissitudes. On 26 January the *Jamesina* anchored at Foochow and did excellent business. 'The climate is now delightful. I loitered over a beautiful country the most of yesterday on shore.' He went on:

No portion of China we have yet seen exceeds the industry displayed here. The lowest people are well dressed with stuffed cotton clothes and the mandarins have furs. Our want now is an interpreter. We have nothing in the shape of one left but my servant boy, and he cannot speak Fukien. I would give a 1000 dollars for three days of Gutzlaff.

The *Jamesina* left Foochow on 5 February, and after selling the last of her opium, sailed down the coast before the north-east monsoon – a very different operation from beating up against it. The clipper anchored at Lintin six days later.

The diary of which only a few extracts have been quoted gives a vivid if not very literate description of one opium voyage up the China coast. It was probably a not untypical instance of many other such expeditions. The hazards for these, by modern standards small ships, were very considerable. Such charts as existed were anything but reliable and the weather was treacherous in the extreme. There were no lighthouses or beacons, no gale warnings or weather forecasts. It required a notable combination of resourcefulness, nerve, skill and cupidity to sail these largely unknown seas, treat with the opium dealers and avoid the mandarins, though in the case of the *Jamesina*, the latter do not seem to have been very effective.

Communication was not as difficult between the Firm's ships in their voyages and its headquarters at Lintin or Canton as one might have supposed. Chinese junks would convey mail and Jardine knew of the *Jamesina*'s success long before the clipper reached Lintin. Encouraged by it he sent another ship, the *John Biggar*, which also did very well, returning early in 1833 after selling $59,000-worth of opium in Amoy and its neighbourhood. Later that year the same vessel, commanded by a Captain McKay, had the advantage of the services of Dr Gutzlaff. There seemed to be a threat of trouble from the mandarins, who had anchored nearby in Chinchew Bay but the good doctor had a short way with them. As Captain McKay wrote to the Firm:

> Doctor Gutzlaff dressed in his best (which on such occasions is his custom) paid them a visit, accompanied by two boats made to look rather imposing. He demanded their instant departure and threatened them with destruction if they ever in future anchored in our neighbourhood. They went away immediately saying that they had anchored there in the dark by mistake, and we have seen nothing more of them ... A merchant came off and purchased 40 chests, paying bargain money, and engaging to clear the whole in 15 days ... We assisted in landing 22 chests and guarded them up to the old gentleman's door which was some distance from the landing place.[16]

McKay in a later letter[17] observed that Chinchew Bay was not an ideal anchorage, because the presence of an opium clipper was too obvious for the mandarins to connive at smuggling by pretending not to have seen it. The nature of the coast did not permit keeping out of view. However, the voyage was highly satisfactory. McKay returned with $214,000 worth of treasure, and considered that 'the trade at Chinchew may now be considered to be placed on a firm footing, although the mandarins may occasionally make difficulties such as we had to contend with at Lintin ten years ago.'[18]

Enough has been quoted from the contemporary records to give some idea of the hazards, pains, pleasures and profits of smuggling opium into the China coast in the 1830s. Many other voyages must have involved the same sort of experiences. In the light of these early successes, William Jardine decided to operate, as he had long contemplated, on an altogether larger and more systematic scale. The ending of the East India Company's monopoly of the China trade by an Act of Parliament in 1833, which became effective a year later, was known well in advance and clearly signalled an outbreak of competition. He wrote on 10 March 1831, when making the case for building a new clipper:

> Our idea is that the opium trade after the expiration of the East India Company's charter is likely to be so much run upon by speculators of every description for the mere sake of remittance without a view to profit that it can hardly be worth our while pursuing on the old plane unless by operating on a large scale and on the secure footing of always being beforehand with one's neighbours in point of intelligence.[19]

Speed was the key to success. Jardine took full advantage of his knowledge and resources. Two famous clippers of those days are examples.[20] There was the *Red Rover*, built in India in 1829 on the model of a famous American privateer, the Baltimore clipper *Prince de Neufchatel*, which did much commerce raiding during the war of 1812 until forced to surrender off Newfoundland by three British frigates on 28 December 1814. She was dry-docked at Deptford, and her measurements and other details were recorded. These came into the possession of William Clifton, a naval officer turned merchant marine captain, who entered the service of the East India Company in 1825 and commanded ships in the Country Trade.[21] He came to the conclusion that none of the existing craft could beat up against the north-east monsoon, but that one designed on the Baltimore model might be able to do so. In that case it would be possible to make three round-trips between Calcutta and the Gulf of Canton within a year. He secured the support of the Governor-General of India, Lord William Bentinck, who realized that the new time schedule would stimulate demand for exports to China, opium in particular, to the great advantage of the Indian revenue.

The clipper christened *Red Rover* by Lady Bentinck was a close copy of the *Prince de Neufchatel* except that she was rigged as a barque. She was launched on 12 December 1829 amidst applause and a 13-gun salute. She displaced 254 tons and measured 97 feet and 7 inches (30m) in length. On 4 January, Captain Clifton dropped his pilot at Sandheads by the mouth of the Hooghly River and, after sailing in the teeth of the monsoon, reached Macao on 17 February. Ten days later he began the return voyage from the Canton River estuary; he picked up the pilot at Sandheads on 1 April. His judgement had been amply vindicated: he had made the round-trip in 86 days and proceeded to make two more before the end of 1830. He then immediately turned round again with a view to a repeat performance in 1831. On his arrival in Calcutta in the spring, after his fourth round-trip he was presented by Lord William Bentinck with £10,000 as a token of the gratitude of the Court of Directors. Clifton had a half-share in the ship, the other half being held in Calcutta. He naturally knew William Jardine, although it was the rival firm of Dent & Co. that first acted as agents for *Red Rover* in Canton. Early in 1833 Clifton suggested that Jardine Matheson & Co. should buy the Calcutta half-share and a satisfactory deal was effected. In 1836, having made some £40,000, Clifton decided to retire and sell out to the Firm which now became sole owner. *Red Rover* continued her voyages long into the steam era. Her last voyage was from Calcutta in July 1853. She was never seen again and must have foundered with all hands in the exceptionally stormy weather of that month in the Bay of Bengal.[22]

Steam was, of course, destined to displace sail, and as early as 1829 James Matheson was interested in the idea. The firm of Mackintosh & Co. had ordered a special steam tug, the *Forbes*, for Calcutta Harbour. She displaced 302 tons and was powered by two 60-horsepower engines. She was launched at Calcutta in January 1829. On a visit to that city, Matheson conceived the idea of chartering her to tow the *Jamesina* from Calcutta to China. He backed her for $1000 to reach Lintin from

Sandheads in a month. The *Forbes* got off to a bad start, running aground on a sandbank in the Hooghly. On 14 March 1829 a second attempt was made. The *Forbes* could carry only 130 tons of coal and so the *Jamesina* was laden with another 52 tons in addition to her 840 chests of opium. The coal was not enough, and on 12 April, with only four days' supply remaining, the two parted company. The *Forbes* proceeded by sail arriving at Lintin on 19 April and the *Jamesina* followed two days later. Matheson lost his bet, but despite these setbacks the *Jamesina* was the first brig of the year to arrive with the new opium.[23] Jardine paid the freight bill of $10,000 and sent the *Forbes* back with a cargo of bills of exchange, charging a half per cent for their transmission, provided the voyage took less than a month. The tug's commander, Captain Henderson, managed to achieve this target and earned $5000 on his cargo, but he had many difficulties, a major one being the low quality of coal at Canton: 'A small proportion of the coals were good, but by far the greater were mere stones, and from their being so soaked in the open boats which brought them down from Canton, they would not burn till they were dried.'

At this juncture the one advantage of steam over sail – the ability to go against the monsoon – seemed to disappear with the advent of the *Baltimore*-type clipper which was much cheaper and just as fast. Captain Henderson found his nose put out of joint by Captain Clifton. It is perhaps not surprising that he spoke slightingly of his rival, whom he described in a letter to Jardine as 'a small vapouring little man, who never lost an opportunity of making a fuss about his arrangements.'[24] Jardine decided to commission the building of another clipper, the three-masted 251-ton barque *Sylph*, on which Dr Gutzlaff made his first missionary-cum-smuggling voyage in 1832. There was only one further venture in steam before the First Opium War of 1839. The plan was to facilitate communication between Canton and the estuary. The Chinese Admiral at the Bogue permitted his own war junk, with him in it, to be towed during a demonstration in September 1835 of the virtues of the *Jardine*, a small schooner powered by a 26-horsepower engine, but a decree from the Viceroy soon forbade 'the Smokeship' from plying in the Pearl River. Efforts to market the ship instead for the run between Singapore and Malacca failed. In Alan Reid's words, 'Despite enthusiastic sale promotion by the Agents "Of the greatest steamship of all time" and an ill-starred steam picnic when the engine room caught fire, prospective buyers were not impressed.'[25] In the end the engines were removed to power a sugar mill and the *Jardine* reverted to sail as a minor running ship at Lintin.

The second famous clipper that needs to be mentioned is the *Fairy*. She was smaller than the *Red Rover* – 161 tons and 77 feet (23.5m) in length. In general ships of 250–300 tons were meant for the Calcutta/China run, and the smaller 150–200-ton vessels operated between Lintin and Chinchew Bay. But the demarcation was not rigid. The *Sylph*, as we saw, sailed up the coast and her displacement was 251 tons. The *Fairy*, the first clipper to be built solely for Jardine Matheson, was to be a fast courier ship so that the firm could obtain intelligence from its various clients and agents in India as quickly as possible. Jardine, attentive to detail as always, gave careful instructions. The ship's tonnage was to be 125–140 'copper fastened with two suits of sails and a dandy mast'. He went on:

> Sweeps to be worked by the capstan or other machinery would be useful in the Straits of Malacca, and we wish them if practicable. The accommodations should be as much adapted for comfort as is compatible with other objects and particularly in respect of ventilation and coolness. There should be a patent water-closet, and a shower bath would not be amiss, though of no great consequence. No expensive fitting is required. The crew wanted would be two steady mates of Scotch smacks, a carpenter and five good sailors of sober habits and character, and attached to each other, who would agree to serve for a certain number of years.[26]

Not all these requirements were fulfilled. The shipbuilders insisted that 160 was the minimum tonnage for a ship to beat up against the monsoon in stormy seas. Sweeps were not practicable, and, although the patent water-closet seems to have worked, there were various other 'patent' articles and fittings which did not – or at any rate not at all easily – including kettles. 'Moral,' wrote 'the Laird' Innes, on the ship's first coastal voyage, 'when new inventions are adopted, bring the inventors with them.'[27] The *Fairy*, however, was agreed to be a beautiful little ship, both to behold and to handle. She made her maiden voyage leaving Liverpool on 20 June 1833 and anchored off Lintin on 27 November. She carried a full cargo of piece goods and one passenger bound for Canton, Jardine's nephew, Andrew Johnstone, who later became a partner in the Firm.

She was no longer needed for her original purpose. The Firm had acquired, as we saw, a half-share in the *Red Rover* while the *Fairy* was being built. Since her speed was as great as that of the *Fairy* and her tonnage greater, she was a more suitable ship for the Calcutta/China round-voyage. But the *Fairy* was well suited to assist the Firm's newest project, the stationing of a 'selling' or 'supply' ship off Chinchew Bay, the *Colonel Young* on which Dr Gutzlaff was supercargo-cum-interpreter. A 'selling' ship needed one or more 'running' ships to convey the opium and other goods from Lintin, and to bring back the payments in bullion made by the opium dealers. The *Fairy* was ideally suited for this role, but an awkward snag was encountered. Whether or not the crew which sailed her from England were of the calibre required by Jardine, they seem to have lost their nerve at Lintin, because of alarming stories about the cold, winter gales, summer typhoons and risk of piracy on the China coast. Innes, who was supercargo on the voyage and kept a diary rather like his account of the voyage of the *Jamesina* a year earlier, regarded them with contempt: 'I am surprised to see well-behaved men such fools as to quit such a service.' In view of the ultimate fate of the *Fairy* one is not quite so surprised. Despite the acid remarks of Innes about the scratch crew which had to be raised and who all spoke different and mutually incomprehensible languages, the voyage was a success. After delivering quantities of brandy, sherry and beer to the *Colonel Young* , the *Fairy* returned with $250,000 *in specie*. Innes recorded one or two items of *curiosa*. When he went to the village of Chupchow near Tysam he was invited to one of the local smoking shops. 'I found all the pipes, benches, etc. ready and was pressed to smoke, which I declined.' Europeans seem never – or at all events very rarely – to have participated in the indulgence from which they profited. He adds: 'Your political economists like to have prices recorded of various articles, so for the benefit of such I show the prices of two things here, and contrast them with the prices of the same goods in Foochow,' and he tells us that whereas a woman in Chupchow at three dollars cost three times the price at Foochow, a bullock which he bought at seven dollars was only a third of the price in that port. He does not say why – presumably supply and demand – nor does he tell us whether he bought any women at either place; it seems unlikely.

The *Fairy* continued in service until the disaster of 1836 when, on a return trip with $70,000, she disappeared. Six Manila sailors had murdered the captain, and the first and second mates rounded up the crew, sent them off on the long boat, sailed the ship to the coast of Luzon and scuttled her. They were foolish enough to try to trade gold bars in Manila, which were spotted by the Firm's agent. They were duly tried, condemned and executed for murder.

By the time that the East India Company's monopoly ended, Jardine Matheson had established a regular and highly profitable coastal trade. It was building or chartering more and more vessels of various types and possessed a fleet of a dozen ships by the time of the First Opium War. Imports of Indian opium doubled during the second half of the 1830s – in round numbers from 20,000 chests in 1833–4 to 40,000 in 1838–9. The Firm was of course not the only Canton agency engaged in the trade. Its great rival, Dent & Co., though never quite so large, operated on a very substantial scale. There was no love lost between them, nor were these two firms the only ones involved. At one stage Jardines and Dent swallowed their mutual dislike to the extent of attempting a deal in 1836 with the mandarins of Chinchew. They proposed to pay $20,000 per annum 'in order to exclude everyone but your own party,' Jardine wrote to the commander of the *Colonel Young*, 'it would have a good effect. My principal fear is that numbers may bring down the displeasure of the Government on the dealers and boatmen while competition among sellers will reduce prices very much.'[28] An agreement with Dent could help over prices, but the problem of the Chinese authorities had no easy solution. In the event the negotiations for a joint monopoly fell through, and numbers, as Jardine feared, were to bring the situation to a crisis. Nevertheless, Jardines was better placed than any other firm to deal with the problems, which were bound to follow the ending of the East India Company's monopoly and the ever-rising volume of opium imports.

FIVE

The Napier Fizzle

Less than two years elapsed between the founding of Jardine Matheson and the termination of the East India Company's monopoly of the China trade. Renewed for 20 years in 1813 it had little prospect of being continued when the period came to an end. The Act abrogating it took effect from 21 April 1834. In fact, the monopoly had by then become so diluted in practice that the transition was less abrupt than it seemed, for the Company was already in the habit of licensing certain firms to export tea to England and of using the Country traders to finance some of its needs both in India and China. The spirit of the age favoured free trade. In any case the monopoly could not exclude non-British merchants operating in Canton. Its effect was to keep out London houses which might well have done excellent business there; this was to the great advantage of non-British firms particularly American concerns like Samuel Russell & Co. The East India Company put up little resistance. Its shareholders were not the power in the land that they had been in the days of Edmund Burke. Moreover, they were far from losing everything. The Company still ruled India and still had a monopoly of Indian opium, although not of opium produced in the Princely States where its writ did not run. There was something to be said for not bothering about tea. In the words of Maurice Collis, 'Indeed the Company was more likely to make money by selling opium, without risk or overheads, in its own city of Calcutta than it had by selling tea in London after the enormous expenses of the establishment at Canton and the fleet of Indiamen had been met.'[1]

Dr William Jardine, long before then, had been the leading figure among the Country traders in Canton. He was convinced that British commerce would never flourish unless the British government took a really tough line with the Chinese authorities. He was at loggerheads with the Select who wanted a quiet life and were terrified of any interruption of commerce. He was also in disagreement with a minority of the Country traders led by his great rival, Launcelot Dent of the firm bearing that name. Dent shared the East India Company's view and tended to be an 'appeaser'. Events played into Jardine's and Matheson's hands, although it took time and a tragi-comedy of errors before they got their way.

The first step towards their success was the disappearance of the Select. Something had to be done to replace the East India Company as the intermediary between the British traders and the authorities in Canton. Palmerston, who was foreign secretary, decided, without much thought and with little understanding of the peculiar conventions which swayed the Chinese authorities, to send out a representative of the government. From his point of view it was a logical step. The East India Company's rule was now restricted to the Indian subcontinent. There was a vacuum in Canton. It would, no doubt, have been possible to create some chamber of commerce to perform the function, but the British merchants saw clearly enough that such a body would have no more clout than the Select, probably less.

A powerful article in the *Chinese Repository* of December 1833 stated the case. It may have been written by Jardine.[2] It certainly accorded closely with the views that he later expressed. The gist of it was that for 100 years the East India Company had met with complete failure in its protests against the Eight Regulations which were themselves roughly the same as those applied to Arab traders 1500 years earlier. The Company's conduct was one of subservient timidity. The author of the letter did not fail to refer to the traumatic incident in 1784 regarding a gunner on a Company ship, the *Lady Hughes*. Firing a saluting gun he accidentally killed a Chinese sailor alongside the ship. The Chinese authorities, whose legal system dictated 'a life for a life', threatened to stop all trade unless the gunner was handed over. The Company, with scandalous cowardice, did so. After a secret trial the young man was executed by strangulation. This affair had never been forgotten. The author went on to press the case for a government representative to replace the president of the Select with a mandate to take a hard line in dealing with the Imperial officials. True, there would be great difficulties in making any contact at all, given the rule that representatives of trade could only petition the mandarins via the Co-hong. But this ridiculous protocol could not survive. There were economic forces too powerful in Britain to be restricted: 'our capital, our manufacturing interest, our power-looms which cry out "Obtain for us but a sale for our goods, and we will supply any quantity".'[3]

War was undesirable. It might produce, the author argued, an internal Chinese revolution which like all such convulsions would damage commerce. But the threat of war was necessary. 'It is well known that the Tartar Manchu dynasty floats upon a smooth but dangerous sea, and that its existence depends upon the habit of tranquil obedience to its authority. Sensible of this, the high authorities view with abhorrence anything that savours of perturbation.'[4] The one aspect of British power which the Chinese respected was the British navy. What was needed was not occasional demonstrations but an island harbour and preferably one far away from Canton to the north, whence it would be easy to launch 10,000 men against Peking. 'The basis of the new Commissioner's demand should be open trade with China...The scrupulous deportment of past embassies should be wholly laid aside.'[5] As William Jardine wrote on 29 February 1832:

> Great Britain can never derive any important advantage from the opening of the trade to China while the present mode of levying and extorting money from the Hong Merchants exists. We must have a code with these Celestial Barbarians, before we can extend advantageously our now limited commercial operations. We have a right to demand an equitable commercial treaty, so say we residents. But I am afraid that our friends at home differ from us.[6]

But the Chinese and European worlds were divided by a yawning ideological gulf. Foreign traders existed on sufferance. Chinese merchants, who dealt with them, might or might not make fortunes, but they were an inferior and dubious class bowing to the mandarinate which 'squeezed' them remorselessly. How could British merchants break through this elaborate, corrupt, bureaucratic red-tape system and establish a new world governed by the principles of Adam Smith? Hope among the merchants of Canton centred on the government's choice of the Chief Superintendent of Trade to replace the president of the Select Committee. Palmerston appointed Lord Napier of Merchiston, a descendant of the famous inventor of logarithms. He was Scottish, which was, no doubt, an asset, for most of the British merchants hailed from north of the border. An ex-naval officer of some distinction he had retired to his estates and become a model landlord. He was 48 years of age. Although he knew a lot about ships and sheep, he knew nothing whatever about China. His peerage, deemed at Whitehall to be an advantage, meant nothing to the Imperial authorities at Peking or Canton, who took no cognizance of degrees of rank among the Barbarians.

There was, moreover, a major problem of protocol – and protocol was a vital issue in Imperial China. Napier, unlike the president of the Select Committee, was not a taipan. He was an appointee of the British government supported by two assistants as Second and Third Superintendents, old hands from the East India Company. He was not actually, as he sometimes seems to have believed, a representative of the Crown in the strict sense of the words, like a colonial governor; but his position was far nearer to that than the position of the president and raised the whole question of the future relationship between the British government and the Chinese Empire. The Son of Heaven, ruler of the Middle Kingdom, recognized no other country as a sovereign independent state. Living in the cloud-cuckoo world engendered by millennia of self-sufficiency the Emperor regarded – or affected to regard – all countries as tributary vassals. Concessions to foreign merchants or to their representative chief through a limited guild of Chinese merchants were harmless. They could always be modified, amended or withdrawn. It was quite another matter to deal with emissaries of foreign powers except as bearers of tribute. There would be no problem if Lord Napier was a rather grand merchant and behaved as such. He was not and did not.

Before his arrival a curious episode occurred which, if he had known about it, would have been a forewarning of what to expect from Chinese officialdom. The Viceroy, Lu K'un, decided, for reasons that remain obscure, to pay an 'unofficial' visit to the East India Company's factory on 2 May 1834 and made his intention known to the Hong merchants. The factory was in the process of being converted into a hotel and offices for individual merchants on the departure of the Company, but some of its servants were still there. It was possibly one of them who wrote the account in the *Chinese Repository*, which is the basis of the entertaining description in *Foreign Mud*.[7]

Arrangements for the reception were made by the Hong merchants of whom Howqua was the chief and by far the richest, but the hosts were the Barbarians. The visit was scheduled for the morning. Chairs were arranged in the main drawing-room according to Chinese usage, one facing south,[8] two facing east and two west. The visit was scheduled for 9am but no mandarin ever condescended to be punctual when visiting inferiors. That would be loss of face. The first grandee arrived at 1pm in a sedan chair borne by eight servants taking the centre place in a long procession of acolytes. This was the Tartar General. He sat down to await the Viceroy, meanwhile summoning Howqua to his presence for conversation. Then came a Manchu lieutenant-general. The four sat and talked. The one official who might have been expected before the Viceroy was the Governor but the previous holder had been sacked and his successor had not yet arrived. Finally at 3pm the Viceroy arrived in a sedan chair with a retinue similar to the Tartar General's, for they were equal in rank. After much affectation of mutual reluctance, the Viceroy agreed to behave as host and take the chair facing south; he put the Tartar General on his left which is the seat of honour in China. All five conversed freely, ignoring everyone else. The Hong merchants brought them birds' nest soup as a starter. The five grandees then repaired to the dining-room and did justice to an ample meal. When it was over they departed without having spoken a word to their European hosts; nor did they send any message of thanks afterwards.

Mortifying though this experience must have been for the British, it was slightly less painful than the behaviour of the new Hoppo two or three years later. Apart from the unusual visit just described, which was

'unofficial', the Hoppo had never invited himself to any of the factories. For him to make an official visit on his own was unprecedented,
and it is by no means clear why he came. The English merchants gave a
grand breakfast in his honour – the best silver and plate and a gigantic
collation. Attended by his interpreters, secretaries and servants he sat at
the head of a table groaning with rich viands. The British merchants
were ranged on his left as observers separated from the table by a rail.
Dish after dish – beef, fowls, hams, plum pudding – were successively
placed before him. He examined each closely, and wearily waved them
aside untouched. The hosts began to be impatient. Some quietly
absconded. At last he asked for tea, and having sipped a cup made his
formal leave.[9] The gulf was unbridgeable.

Lord Napier's instructions from Palmerston were obscure and
ambiguous. Probably the Foreign Secretary did not quite know what to
do next. They read as if he was thinking aloud. Napier was to try to
extend trade to other parts of China. It was therefore desirable to establish direct communications with Peking. But he must bear in mind
'that peculiar caution and circumspection will be indispensable on that
point lest you should awaken the fears or offend the prejudices of the
Chinese government, and thus put to hazard even the existing opportunities of intercourse, by a precipitate attempt to extend them.'[10] Yet
in spite of these emollient orders, Palmerston added another which was
sure to cause trouble: 'Your lordship will announce your arrival at
Canton by letter to the Viceroy.'

The only way of breaking the centuries-old Chinese rule against
contact between officials and foreigners was force or its threat, but the
three superintendents were particularly enjoined not to call on support
from the armed services or endanger existing relations with the
Chinese government. To those few who knew about China, it was as
certain as anything could be that a letter from a 'Barbarian Eye' – the
translation of the curious phrase used to describe a foreign envoy –
would under no circumstances be even opened by the Viceroy or by
any mandarin. To do so would be to break all the rules which governed
Chinese officialdom; it would incur the fury of the Emperor and entail
ruin of one's career. The letter would be returned unread.

Palmerston's instructions gave no guidance as to what Napier should do in the circumstances of that inevitable rebuff. But the Foreign Secretary, like almost everyone else in Britain, was wholly ignorant of China at this time. Nor was he much wiser six years later. The Chinese were, he said, 'Just as reasonable as the Rest of the world.' Dresses vary, but strip them off, and you will find the same animal Form when you come to the naked man, with very little Diversity of structure.'[11] However true this may have been anatomically, it did not correspond to political and psychological reality, as in the end Palmerston himself came to realize.

What Napier should have done, if he was to conform to Chinese usage, was to wait in Macao and send a message, in the form of a petition to the Viceroy via the Hong merchants, that a foreign envoy was seeking permission to open negotiations with the Viceroy. The petition would go to the Viceroy who would refer it to Peking. If the Emperor was willing as a favour, not as a matter of right, to allow the envoy after suitable promises of submission and obedience to take up residence in Canton, he would send what was called a Red Mandate to Macao. Only when this had been received, should the envoy continue on his journey. This procedure had been followed in the case of the Macartney mission in 1793, though not by Lord Amherst in 1816. True, both those efforts had failed, but the Emperor was much more offended by the latter than the former. The process had the disadvantage of being extremely slow, and this was no doubt one reason why Napier bypassed it. But he had a further reason. His instructions from the Foreign Secretary, though ambiguous and obscure in many respects, were quite clear in one; Napier was to go to Canton and make contact by letter with the Viceroy when he got there.

Napier arrived with his wife and daughters at Macao on 15 July. To signal the new commercial arrangement he decided to disassociate himself from the old order by staying at the house of Jardine Matheson rather than the grand residence of the East India Company. But he took as advisers, on Palmerston's orders, two old hands of the Company, former members of the Select Committee, John Davis and Sir George Robinson, with titles respectively as Second and Third Superintendents. A Captain Elliot RN was to be Master Attendant in charge of all ships and crews within the Bogue. A Mr Astell was appointed Secretary. Napier had as his Chinese Secretary and interpreter the Rev. Dr Robert Morrison, who was a famous missionary and the leading sinologist of the day. He was not very successful in the former capacity. In a long career he converted only ten people, but he was a leading authority on the Chinese language. It was unlucky that he was to die worn out by age and illness soon after the arrival of the mission in Canton. Had he lived he might possibly have persuaded Napier to avoid some errors. The Foreign Secretary's choice of appointments as Napier's second and third in command is a clear sign that he was not at this stage in favour of a forward policy. The Company's attitude had been in general to avoid confrontation, not perhaps at all costs but certainly at most. Davis and Robinson were most unlikely to advise in favour of a show-down. Indeed they must have warned Napier of the difficulties into which he would run if he obeyed Palmerston's order to enter into direct negotiations with the Viceroy. Napier was not deterred. He fixed 23 July as the date of departure from Macao in the frigate HMS *Andromache*, which had brought him there. The frigate arrived at the Bogue at midnight. At noon next day the party proceeded by cutter to Canton. It was a tedious fourteen-hour journey. They landed at 2am on 25 July, and were escorted by William Jardine to the English factory where they were to reside during their mission.

News of the arrival of Napier at Macao had soon reached the Viceroy. He issued on 21 July an edict to the Hong merchants on whom all responsibility for the behaviour of foreigners was placed and ordered them to warn the Barbarian Eye that he could not depart to Canton until the formalities already described had been obeyed. A delegation of the Co-hong sailed at once for Macao by the inner channels. Too late: the *Andromache* was already on her way to the Bogue by the outer passage. But Napier would probably have disregarded the edict anyway. The day after Napier's arrival Howqua and Mowqua, who was the second most important Hong merchant, went to the factory and delivered the edict. Napier was polite but firm. He came, he said, to inaugurate a new trading system. The merchants departed unhappily, well aware that there was trouble ahead and it would, as was invariably the case in Canton, fall on them rather than anyone else, given their theoretical responsibility to the authorities for curbing the irregularities of the Barbarians. That night Napier dined with William Jardine.

On 27 July, Napier, having had his letter translated by Dr Morrison, sent his secretary Astell bearing it to the Petition Gate. This was not in itself an unprecedented action. The Chinese officials recognized that there were occasions when a petition could not be sent through the Co-hong, as for example if it contained confidential remarks which the merchants ought not to see, but such occasions were very rare, and in any case the envelope must be marked 'petition' not 'letter'. Astell, accompanied by some of the merchants, duly went to the Petition Gate. He was kept waiting for a quarter of an hour before a mandarin appeared, looked at the letter and said a superior officer would soon arrive. Another hour elapsed – no doubt to teach the Barbarian a lesson. It must have been a disagreeable experience. The Canton climate in July and August is one of damp, stifling heat, and a xenophobic crowd soon gathered, displaying hostility by word and gesture. At the end of the hour a series of mandarins arrived and departed, declining to look at the letter on the same excuse as the first one.

The Hong merchants now endeavoured to persuade Astell to entrust it to them, but Astell saw that this would give the whole game away. At that juncture a much grander mandarin appeared. He condescended to look at the letter, though not to touch it. As soon as he saw the word 'letter' he evinced, or affected to evince extreme astonishment. To receive it would be out of the question and a fatal error. He was followed by the Adjutant of the Tartar General, but he too refused. Then Howqua intervened after a word with the Adjutant and suggested that he and the Adjutant should jointly receive the letter, which he called a petition, and lay it before the Viceroy. Astell saw that this apparent compromise was not what it seemed. He would have been witnessed by a large crowd handing the letter to Howqua, and it would look as if the British had after all accepted the rule that foreign petitions should go through the Co-hong. This would entail a disastrous loss of face. Deadlock had been reached and Astell had to return with the unopened missive to the English factory.

The Viceroy now decided to put pressure on the Hong merchants to ensure that Napier left as soon as possible for Macao. He would squeeze them until the Superintendent departed. In the edict which thus admonished them, the word 'Napier' was represented by two ideographs which were a pun on his name and could be translated as 'Laboriously Vile'. These, it need hardly be said, were not the ideographs used by Morrison to express the sound of the name in the unopened letter to the Viceroy. He at once noticed the difference when translating a letter from Howqua asking for an interview on 29 July. The same uncomplimentary ideographs were used there, and he felt obliged to inform Napier. It is hard to see what motive Howqua could have had for this insult. It is more likely that his secretary had simply copied from the Viceroy's edict. Whatever the cause, the episode did not improve Napier's temper which was further inflamed by the news which Howqua brought, that the Viceroy was unyielding on the question of 'petition'.

Napier had thus failed in his main purpose. His letter had not been served on the Viceroy. But the Viceroy was scarcely better placed to serve his orders on Napier. They took, of course, the form not of direct communications – that would be a loss of face – but edicts to the Hong merchants. It was up to them to induce the Barbarian Eye to leave. Naturally they wanted to show the edicts to the Chief Superintendent, but Napier decided that two could play at the game of non-reception, and when Howqua arrived at the English factory on 31 July with no fewer than three edicts, each successively more harsh than the previous one and culminating in an order of expulsion – 'These are the orders. Tremble hereat! Intensely tremble' – Napier refused him permission to read them out. Howqua was therefore reduced to circumlocutory observations about the August climate being better at Macao. But there was a solution. The Hong merchants could show the edicts to Jardine in the almost certain knowledge that he would pass their contents on to Napier. They did and he did, but the reaction was not what they wanted or expected.

The attitude of Jardine and the Firm was made clear enough in a letter which he wrote from Canton to his colleague, Thomas Weeding, in London in June 1834 before Napier arrived:

The appointment of Lord Napier ... has created a great sensation here and in Macao ... The authorities here have not made up their minds as to the reception to be given to the Superintendent. They are waiting with much anxiety and much will depend on his own conduct. They will probably send the Hong Merchants to him in the first instance, to whom, I trust, he will behave with great courtesy but not permit them to say a word on business. A reference will then be made to Peking by the Viceroy and others; and, should this be the case, the First Superintendent should order the Frigate he comes out in to prepare for a trip to the Yellow Sea and proceed to the Imperial Palace there to state our grievances to the Son of Heaven himself and demand redress. If this is done in good manly style I will answer for the consequences. It may do good but cannot do harm.[12]

Jardine was a strong advocate of the forward policy, but to send a frigate to the Yellow Sea would be a drastic step, and Napier had no authority to do anything of the sort. In August Jardine wrote to John MacVicar in Manchester:

You will find from the *Canton Register* that the British trade with China is everything but suspended. Cargo boats have been refused but no official edict has yet proclaimed the stoppage.

The question at issue, divested of all nonsense, is simply this: shall Lord Napier address letters to the Viceroy or shall they be petitions addressed to His Excellency the Viceroy through the Hong merchants as the Select Committee did?

His Lordship is firm in his refusal and the Viceroy threatens to convince him of his errors by stopping the trade for ever. We wait the result in fear and trembling as ordered by the authorities to do.

The last observation was clearly ironic. Every Chinese proclamation, however little expected to be obeyed, ended with phrases of this sort as translated into English. Jardine continued:

Matters have been badly arranged at home and I am afraid that Lord Napier has not sufficient authority. A reference to Peking might do good. We can scarcely expect the parties here to give up power, peculation, etc. without a struggle.

We are much surprised here at the Company's finance operations and really at a loss to discover what induced all you merchants and agents to be silent. It is likely to turn out a vile job as might be expected.[13]

The last paragraph is presumably an allusion to the lack of free trade agitation against the East India Company. Napier soon came to depend more on the advice of his fellow Scots countrymen in Canton than on that of the survivors of the Select. William Jardine and James Matheson had a clear policy. They could see no way of opening China to world trade, short of force or the threat of force. Jardine recognized that Napier had no proper backing from London; he might well have to endure, given the situation in Canton, a disagreeable rebuff. But it would be an occasion of *reculer pour mieux sauter*. In the end the British government would have to intervene and a slap in the face would make public opinion more ready to accept intervention. The question was when and on what issue. Opium-smuggling would not be a good one. But Jardine Matheson was better placed than many British firms to ride out the Viceroy's threat of cutting off the Canton trade. On this issue there was a conflict between the firms which traded principally or exclusively in Canton and those, like Jardine Matheson, the biggest operator of all, which also traded outside the Bogue, largely in opium and in areas beyond the effective writ of the Chinese government. The former would be badly hit by any stoppage in Canton; the latter could manage without too much difficulty.

These mercantile divisions did not follow obvious or predictable lines. Dent & Co. was a leading 'appeaser', although it had interests outside the Bogue second only to those of Jardine Matheson. But there was a deep personal animosity between Launcelot Dent and William Jardine. Politics, too, may have played some part. Dent was a Tory, William Jardine and James Matheson were on the other side, and later became successive MPs for Ashburton in the Whig interest. On the whole their party, with its free trade-backing in Scotland and the north country, tended to favour a show-down, while the Tories were more cautious and reluctant, partly influenced by the tradition of the East India Company, a stalwart Tory stronghold ever since the failure of Fox's India Bill in 1784. These conflicts added another dimension to the already complicated problems with which the Chief Superintendent had to deal. All the evidence suggests that he was converted early on to the Jardine view. His despatch of 9 August was optimistic and ambivalent, but on 14 August – by which time he had received the gist of the edicts from Jardine – he sent a despatch in very different terms. The edicts, as Jardine knew, would have the opposite effect to that expected by Howqua and Mowqua, who, like Rosencrantz and Guildenstern, seem to have been at this time inseparable figures on the Canton stage. Far from weakening Lord Napier's resolve to stay in Canton, the edicts made him more determined than ever to remain; the honour of his Commission was at stake. He pressed the Foreign Office for an ultimatum to an 'imbecile' government, 'too contemptible to be viewed in any other light than that of pity and derision.' Force would easily prevail. 'Three or four frigates or brigs with a few steady troops, not sepoys, would settle the thing in a time inconceivably short.'[14] He scoffed at a government so feeble that it had ordered his expulsion but done nothing about it. 'Suppose a Chinaman, or any other man were to land in Whitehall, your Lordship would not allow him to "loiter" as they have permitted me.'[15]

Canton was not Whitehall. The Viceroy had to get rid of Napier, but he preferred to manage the matter as quietly and smoothly as possible, although in the last resort he would have to call Napier's bluff. Any major row would cast doubt in Peking on his ability as a diplomat. The last thing he wished was to draw undue attention at Court. Already he was afflicted with a visit from three officials of the Censorate, who had arrived to investigate charges against the Hoppo. The Viceroy's own affairs could scarcely bear examination, nor indeed could those of almost every high official in Canton. The Viceroy managed to buy off the Censors by a bribe in gold so enormous that its purchase raised the open market price by nearly four per cent. But they had not yet returned to Peking, and the situation was far from safe.

Meanwhile Napier had become more optimistic. The frigate *Andromache*, in which he had arrived, was now at anchor, after a cruise in the China Sea, outside the Bogue at Chuenpi. She had been joined by another frigate, the *Imogene*. Their accidental presence might strengthen his hand. He optimistically, but of course vainly, hoped that he might make contact direct with the Court through the Peking officials. There was no chance of this, but his spirits were raised when Howqua and Mowqua informed him that the Viceroy had authorized three high-ranking mandarins, among them the Prefect of the quarter in which the factories were situated, to call on him if he was willing to receive them.[16] Napier was delighted. He had never even seen a mandarin. Perhaps the presence of the frigates was having an effect. The meeting was fixed for 11am next day, 23 August. It was to be a mixed success.

Early that morning servants of the mandarins arrived with ceremonial chairs and placed them in the main hall so that the three mandarins would face south and the Hong merchants would sit in two rows running at right angles facing each other east and west. One of them had its back to the picture of King George IV. Apparently, Napier and his officers were meant to stand. Napier was naturally furious. Such a calculated insult could not be suffered. He at once had the chairs rearranged. He would sit facing south across a table with a mandarin at each hand. Facing opposite and north was his secretary, Astell, flanked by the third mandarin and Mr Davis, the Second Superintendent. No one would have his back to the King. The Hongs sat in one row facing the mammoth portrait. Howqua and Mowqua arriving before the mandarins – not a difficult problem since they were to be two hours late – were dismayed. Their pleas fell on deaf ears. Napier was adamant and angry, and his temper was not improved by the late arrival of his visitors, who were merely following the normal Chinese usage of superiors when dealing with inferiors.

The mandarins showed no sign of discomposure at the changed seating plan, whatever they thought privately. After Napier had scolded them for being late, discussions became polite and amicable in form but uncompromising in substance. The Viceroy would not receive the letter, nor would Napier convey its contents orally. Wine was consumed, smiles and bows exchanged, courtesy preserved. But the impasse remained. Napier may well have deluded himself that he had somehow gained a point or two. If so, he was wrong.

His next step was disastrous. Like many Europeans he believed or had been led to believe that the Cantonese population, insofar as it had an articulate opinion, was in favour of open commerce and was only inhibited by Manchu tyranny. The Co-hong naturally held and encouraged that view but they were hardly typical. However, Napier, who was by now ill of a fever, decided to push his case by having a proclamation fixed at street corners on 26 August, attacking the policy of the Viceroy to whom he attributed 'ignorance and obstinacy', and regretting the steps towards the stoppage of trade. The Viceroy was understandably enraged. Abandoning the elaborate, polite circuitous language of the edicts he approved though did not actually sign a counter-proclamation on 28 August:

> A lawless foreign slave, named Laboriously Vile, has issued a notice. We do not know how such a barbarian dog can have the audacity to call himself an Eye ... It is a capital offence to incite the people against their rulers and we would be justified in obtaining a mandate for his decapitation and the exposure of his head as a warning to traitors.

On 2 September the Viceroy issued an edict. Trade, already partly stopped since 16 August, would henceforth cease entirely until Napier left. We have no knowledge of the considerations which decided the Viceroy to risk the repercussions of a public row and call Napier's bluff. One can only be surprised that action had not been taken earlier. For bluff it undoubtedly was. Napier was in no position to defy the Viceroy. The new edict was not conveyed as hitherto via the Co-hong and Jardines but posted on the factory gate. The news was brought to Napier during dinner on 4 September, and he decided, probably on advice, or certainly with no discouragement from Jardine, to order up the *Andromache* and *Imogene* from Chuenpi to Whampoa with instructions to shoot it out if necessary with the batteries of the Bogue forts, but only if they fired first. His instructions from Palmerston entitled him to call on naval power only in extreme emergency, but the circumstances hardly justified this description. Napier may have believed that his colleagues and the British merchants were in danger of losing life and limb. Jardine, his closest adviser, cannot have been alarmed. No British resident had ever been hurt in Canton, nor had their goods or treasure been stolen or confiscated. Chinese soldiers, when involved at all, had been there to protect the merchants against the Canton mob. The people who suffered in the event of a clash with the Barbarians were invariably the Chinese merchants or underlings who had dealings with them. Jardine, however, was pursuing a consistent policy and one which events fully justified unless British traders were to withdraw entirely. The arrival of the frigates would either force the Viceroy to give way or, if he refused, would result in Napier's withdrawal. This would be a rebuff to Britain and in the end would produce the change in public opinion needed to justify a major expedition against China in order to open up the country to western trade.

The rest of the story of the Napier 'Fizzle', as it was unkindly termed, can be briefly told. The frigates, after a fair amount of shooting, but very few casualties, forced the Bogue and sailed to Whampoa. The Viceroy blocked the channel at both ends, so that the ships were at his mercy, though he deemed it prudent not to press his advantage too far. Napier now had no option but to go. He had been ill for some time with a fever, possibly malaria, for weeks on end. Since the thermometer in Canton by night can be as high as 90°F (30°C) indoors at that time of year, one can imagine how he must have felt. The Viceroy would not let him leave in a frigate, but insisted on a Chinese boat with Chinese escorts. The journey took seven days, the nights being made hideous by the endless beating of gongs and exploding of firecrackers. There were long bureaucratic delays at intermediate ports of call. Napier, at last, rejoined his wife and three daughters at Macao on 26 September, an exhausted and very sick man. A fortnight later he was dead.

SIX

The Emperor Intervenes

The shots exchanged between the naval frigates and the forts of the Bogue in 1834 can be seen in retrospect as the beginning of the Opium Wars. But it was to be another five years before the crisis came to a head and three more until the Emperor was forced to concede terms which gave the European traders most of what they wanted. By 1843 the firm of Jardine Matheson could feel that its principal objects had been secured. If it failed to prosper now it would be the Firm's own fault, not that of the restrictions of the Celestial Empire.

It was clear after the Napier tragi-comedy that persuasion and diplomacy would get nowhere. But where did the Canton foreign merchants want to get to? They were already making vast profits from opium smuggling. Was there much to be gained by a row with a regime under which they flourished? The answer, oddly, was yes. The opium trade was the object of much criticism at home, and the most that any government could publicly state was that Britain had no duty either to interfere with it or support it. British traders were not entirely happy at making money out of a racket. The only really disreputable commerce, which had produced great profits in the recent past, was the slave trade, and public opinion had in the end caused its suppression. The possibility that similar feelings might affect the opium trade could not be excluded. What Lord Melbourne called 'this damned morality' was on the rise, not the ebb. Only a few years were to elapse before it affected the great Firm itself, effectively bringing an end to the Matheson opium connection on grounds of conscience.[1]

The European traders were, moreover, conscious that there might be limits to the incompetence and corruption of the Imperial regime. It could not be denied that the trade was entirely illegal. Sooner or later the Court at Peking might decide to enforce the law by practical measures instead of issuing high-flown edicts which no one took seriously. This fear was to be fully justified. There was a further consideration. Vast though the precarious profits from 'the drug' might be, would not the profits from legitimate trade be even larger, if China lowered or removed the barriers which prevented it? On this score the Canton traders were over-optimistic. The immense potential market of 400 million people which they expected to exploit was to prove more difficult to penetrate than anticipated, even after the restrictions had been abolished. That, however, was a problem for the future. The immediate task was to achieve a breakthrough; the snag was that it could only be made by war or the threat of war, and no British government was going to send ships and troops on a campaign which critics would certainly 'smear' as a surrender to the opium lobby, as long as shipments of China tea continued to arrive smoothly and provide a healthy revenue for the Exchequer. The fact that the regular arrival of tea depended on regular delivery of opium did not worry Whitehall. Ironically the very success of firms like Jardine Matheson in selling contraband opium contributed to the British government's failure to open the China market to legitimate goods and commodities. In the end it was the Emperor who unintentionally solved the problem for it.

Napier's despatches in favour of a forward policy, which arrived at the Foreign Office well after his death, had little effect. The Whig Government, which Napier thought he was addressing, had resigned – in effect been dismissed by William IV – in November 1834, and there was a short-lived Conservative minority government in office from then until April 1835. The Duke of Wellington was Foreign Secretary. He was even more inclined towards inaction than Palmerston. James Matheson decided to accompany Lady Napier and her daughters on the voyage back to England, hoping to call at the Foreign Office and press for a more positive policy. He was reinforced by a petition signed late in 1834 by 64 Canton merchants and addressed to His Majesty in Council urging the appointment of a replacement to Napier with authority and sufficient backing of force to exact reparation for the humiliating treatment given to that unlucky figure – an insult to the flag and to the nation.

The full details of the Napier 'Fizzle' did not reach Whitehall until March. Meanwhile Matheson had arrived and made his visit to the Foreign Office where he met with a frosty reception from the Duke of Wellington. One can easily imagine what the attitude of that famous Tory soldier and aristocrat would be to a volatile and voluble *parvenu* adventurer who spoke with a Scottish accent, and, like most of his compatriots, was, from the Duke's point of view, on the wrong political side. We only have Matheson's version of the interview. He made no headway at all. The Duke, he wrote to Jardine, was 'a cold-blooded fellow...a strenuous advocate of submissiveness and servility'.[2] Nor would a change of government help. He told Jardine in an undated letter written after Palmerston had returned to the Foreign Office:

> The fact is, Jardine, people appear to be so comfortable in this magnificent country, so entirely satisfied in all their desires, that so long as domestic affairs, including markets, go right, they cannot really be brought to think of us outlanders. Until therefore there is a stoppage of trade, or something to touch the pockets of the merchants and ship-owners, expect no sympathy here. The more successful you are in China in keeping things quiet, no matter at what sacrifice or in what manner, the less sympathy you will have here. Lord Palmerston means to do nothing.[3]

The Duke of Wellington had summed up the situation in a somewhat gnomic observation which he jotted down on 24 March after receiving a full report of the Napier affair. 'That which we require now is not to lose the enjoyment of what we have got.' The Duke did, however, have some degree of second thought, for in the same paper he noted: 'I would recommend that till the trade has taken its regular course, particularly considering what has passed recently, there should always be within the Superintendent's reach a stout Frigate and a smaller vessel of war.'[4]

Palmerston was to be the Whig Foreign Secretary for the next six years, from April 1835 until September 1841. In spite of James Matheson's verdict he was, though cautious, more sympathetic than

Wellington to the arguments of the Canton merchants. He liked the flamboyant gesture and he was not averse to 'gunboat diplomacy'. The Tories depended for electoral support on the squirearchy and the landed interest, who were by no means keen on free trade and knew nothing about China. The Whigs depended on the 'field of cotton', not 'the field of corn'. They were sensitive to pressure from the manufacturers and merchants of northern England and Scotland, who believed that there was a market for exports in China comparable to that of India. (The election of 1835 had greatly reduced the Whig majority of 1832, but they still had a margin of 100 over their rivals.) The election of 1837 left them with a lead of only 30. Without the support of the north including Scotland they would be in a minority. The electoral situation in the United Kingdom should not be forgotten in any analysis of the causes of the First Opium War. William Jardine and James Matheson were Whigs. Their voices were more likely to be heeded by Palmerston than by any Tory tenant of the Foreign Office.

Meanwhile affairs stagnated in Canton. Napier's successors, first John Francis Davis, who resigned after six months, and then Sir George Robinson, were happy to do nothing until they received categorical instructions. They resided at Macao, drew large salaries and occasionally signed ships' papers. The Canton merchants were worse off than they had been under the East India Company. There was now no corporate representative to parley with the Co-hong. True, a chamber of commerce was formed with Matheson as its first chairman, but it was rendered ineffective by the internecine strife which raged between his firm and Dent & Co. The feud is said to have originated in an episode connected with the failure of a number of Calcutta firms in 1830. This was a result of the collapse of the price of indigo following the news that Prussian blue could be used as a satisfactory and much cheaper substitute. One of the principal dealers in indigo was Palmer & Co. with whom both Jardine Matheson and Dent & Co. had dealings. Apparently a Jardines clipper brought the news of the failure of the firm to Canton. Jardine kept it to himself and made dispositions which limited his losses. He did not pass the letter on to Dent who was badly stung and never forgave him.[5] During the Napier crisis Jardine came to believe that Dent had intrigued with the Chinese authorities against the

Chief Superintendent. In October 1834, after Napier's death, Jardine wrote to Thomas Weeding:

> You will see allusions made to a certain party here inimical to his Lordship's measures, and doing everything in their power to induce the Chinese to resist, by false representations to Howqua respecting the extent of his powers from home, his rank, etc., etc. These points can never be proved; but from many conversations with Howqua and Mowqua I have every reason for believing that such was the case.[6]

The disappearance of Dent's papers after the firm's bankruptcy in 1867 makes it impossible to say for certain whether the accusation was justified. But, given Dent's views on the forward policy favoured by Napier and backed by Jardine, one may guess that it probably was.

The apathy of the two Chief Superintendents continued until 1836. Robinson even moved out of Macao, deeming the place too unsafe against Chinese troops, and in November 1835 had taken up residence in a ship off Lintin Island, the haven of drug-smuggling. All that the Canton merchants could do was to bombard Whitehall with petitions, memorials, pamphlets and long letters. A persistent theme was the need to have a base of operations less precarious than Macao, preferably more than one. Amoy, Ningpo, Chusan or Hong Kong were suggested. Palmerston may have read Gutzlaff's *Essay on the Present State of Our Relations with China* and perhaps the pamphlet by one Hamilton Lindsay who had taken Gutzlaff with him in an expedition up the coast as far as Weihaiwei in 1832. Both emphatically supported the strong line. Palmerston seems to have become irritated by Sir George Robinson's verbose letters in favour of doing nothing. In June 1836 he decided to dismiss him and appoint Charles Elliot, a junior member of the Commission, in his place. Robinson retired in December and Elliot took his place.

Elliot was, like Napier, a naval officer and a Scottish Whig grandee. He was not in line for a title and estates, but his connections were even more influential. His father, Sir Hugh Elliot, was a brother of the 1st Earl of Minto and had been a career diplomat and Governor of Madras. His first cousin, the 2nd Earl of Minto, was First Lord of the Admiralty from 1835 to 1841, and his daughter married Lord John Russell. Lord Minto's younger brother, Rear Admiral George Elliot, was commander-in-chief at the Cape Station from 1837 to 1840, and was later to be given charge of the naval forces in the Opium War. Charles Elliot was an intelligent man but he was over-confident, opinionated and impractical. *The Times*, in anticipation of a similar verdict by Ernest Bevin on his colleagues in 1945, describes him as 'unfit to manage a respectable apple-stall'.[7] This may be too harsh, but he was undoubtedly impetuous and lacking in judgement. He was unlucky too, for his appointment coincided with a momentous decision in Peking, which no one had expected and which was to throw Anglo-Chinese relations into confusion. The Emperor at last decided that the opium traffic must be stopped and the law genuinely enforced.

There were two reasons for perturbation in Peking. First there were the adverse effects on health, efficiency and morality which was becoming more and more obvious as more and more opium poured in. It may be true that only some two per cent of the whole population was affected, but the proportion within the élite upon whom the Imperial government depended was very much higher. Opium was rotting the minds and bodies of the governing class itself. Those high officials who pressed memorials upon the Emperor to this effect were known as the 'Moralists'. Their solution was to extirpate the trade entirely.

The second reason was based on an economic argument. The drain of bulk silver known as '*sycee*' to pay for imports of opium was believed to have had the effect of depreciating the copper currency in which cash transactions were made. China had a type of bimetallic currency in which legally 1000 copper cash exchanged for one silver tael, but by 1838 the rate had risen to about 1650. In fact the 1000 rate had never been a reality in the history of the dynasty. It was the figure for government accounting purposes, and the government was well aware that the actual rate fluctuated. Nevertheless, official policy was to try to keep it reasonably close to the legal figure. In the eighteenth century it varied between 750 and 900. It was 1000 in 1808 and steadily fell thereafter.

Actually the fall had nothing to do with the export of silver. It is fully explained by the declining production of the Yunnan copper mines which obliged the government to mint cheaper coins. The debasement of the currency resulted in the annual minting of eight times as many coins in the period 1800–30 as in the early eighteenth century. Bad money drives out good; silver became more scarce and so more expensive in terms of copper coins.[8]

But the Chinese officials who favoured the economic argument against the opium trade attributed the trouble exclusively to the export of *sycee*. Regarding this as the great danger and believing that a ban on opium-smoking was only possible by a reign of terror, they wished to legalize the trade but make it a monopoly under the Hoppo who would obtain the drug by bartering goods instead of exporting silver. This group was known as the 'Legalists' and the Emperor considered their case seriously. Among other advantages a state monopoly would have much increased his income, for smuggled opium, of course, paid no duties. But he was conscientious and worried about the depraving effect of opium on his subjects. The Moralists won the day. The trade would be extirpated. The question was how.

The Emperor began by ordering the Viceroy and the Governor of Canton to enforce the laws against Chinese dealers and smugglers more effectively. At first this seemed to work. The 'smug boats' almost vanished from the river. Although the Viceroy, Teng T'ing Chen, who had replaced Lu after the latter's death in 1835, sent his own boats to Lintin to take delivery of shipments and distribute them appropriately, he had to make some show of severity and he issued an edict deporting Jardine and eight other British merchants. They ignored it and nothing happened. Not surprisingly, Jardine did not take the new policy seriously. It was certainly true that trade was interrupted. 'The drug here is completely at a stand,' he wrote from Canton in January 1837. In June he described it as entirely closed down and in November he wrote: 'The drug market is getting worse every day, owing to the extreme vigilance of the authorities.' The British merchants were well informed about the debate in Peking through the Co-hong. Jardine had hoped that the Legalists would win, though he was well aware of the difficulties which would arise even in that event. But the Firm was not unduly worried by the decision to prohibit the trade. This had been proclaimed so often before and there had been so many stoppages which soon ended that the two partners regarded the affair as a mere repetition of an old theme. What they never expected was that the prohibition would really be enforced and that the Emperor meant business.

As late as December 1838, on the eve of his final retirement from the Firm, William Jardine believed that the storm would blow over, but he noted in a letter to Jamsetjee Jejeebhoy that, although what he called the 'persecution' of the opium dealers was not much worse than on previous occasions, it had now spread to every province in China, 'a circumstance never before known to have occurred'.[9] His spirits, and those of other merchants, had been raised by a short-lived boom in opium in the summer of 1838. Armed European schooners had taken the place of the smug boats and defied hostile junks. Their employment was too expensive for any but the biggest firms. Jardine Matheson and Dent & Co. cornered the market and pushed up the price of Patna from $300 a chest to $580 in the first fortnight of May. The Imperial edicts were, wrote Matheson, regarded as waste paper.[10] But he was soon disillusioned; the official anti-opium policy was pursued with renewed vigour in September. Chinese smugglers and dealers were terrified. By the end of the year some 2000 arrests had been made for trafficking and smoking. There were numerous executions. In Canton province the Viceroy ordered house-to-house searches by night and the closure of divans and dens. On 16 December Jardine wrote: 'Not an opium pipe to be seen ... not a single enquiry after the drug.'[11] Up and down the coast the situation was just as bad. It was virtually impossible to land supplies or do business with local dealers.

Nevertheless, both William Jardine and James Matheson remained on the whole optimistic. There was a widespread but erroneous European belief that the Chinese people were chafing under Manchu tyranny and longed to overthrow the dynasty. The Manchu rulers were not popular, but it was quite another matter to eject them at the behest of the red-headed Barbarians. Both partners saw hope that these draconian measures might produce enough discontent to cause an insurrection. In any case they were on past precedent unlikely to be enforced consistently or for any length of time. The Imperial Court would soon weary of the whole business.

Jardine and Matheson were too sanguine. The Emperor not only meant to enforce with severity his current measures, he was even at this moment engaging on a new, even more drastic initiative. The most persuasive of the Moralists was the provincial Governor-General, Lin

Tse-shih. He was a learned scholar, poet and calligrapher, descended from a distinguished but impoverished Foochow family. His career was one of rapid unimpeded success in the government service. He had never had a setback. He was able, thoughtful, calm and wholly incorruptible. He did not belong to the hard-line party among the Moralists such as Huang Cheh-tzu, who favoured the death penalty not only for dealers and smugglers but all smokers as well. This would extinguish the demand, even if it meant many thousands of executions. Lin considered that this was too harsh. Addiction was a psychological problem. There should be sanatoriums in which addicts lived under the threat of death. It was wrong to execute them but right to terrorize them into rehabilitating themselves.

This was one side of the coin. The other was the question of supply. Here Lin went to the heart of the matter. Canton was a sink of corruption and must be cleaned up. The traffickers in the south were the source of all the trouble, and foreign smugglers should be treated as effectively, if not in quite the same way, as native Chinese. They had been dealt with too tenderly for too long. The Emperor accorded no fewer than nineteen audiences to Lin and was fully persuaded. On 31 December 1838 he appointed him Kinchae or Imperial Commissioner with vast plenary powers to root out the opium trade. It was only the fifth time that such an extraordinary appointment had been made in the history of the dynasty. When the Viceroy of Canton saw the news in the *Gazette* he fell into a swoon which lasted an hour.

Commissioner Lin was aware that a tough policy with the Barbarians might involve war, not in the modern sense between states, but rather of rebellion by tributary Barbarians against the Middle Kingdom. He wished to avoid it by a policy of cajolery, moral persuasion, economic pressure and intimidation. It was not his task to exclude foreigners entirely. The Emperor's income depended on foreign trade through Canton. But, if it did come to war he was confident of the result. Like all the Confucian officials he had no concept of the colossal technological superiority of the British, indeed any Western navy and army. A mere squadron of the navy that had won Trafalgar, defeated Napoleon and obliterated the Turkish fleet at Navarino as recently as 1827, could smash the entire Chinese navy with ease. Lin maintained that British ships might manage well enough on the oceans with their deep draught but would be no good in the shallows of the Chinese rivers and coasts. As for a military expedition their men wore clothes tightly bound which handicapped leg movement. They would fall an easy prey to Chinese troops in a land battle. Of the immense power of British musketry and artillery, compared with Chinese weapons, he had no idea whatever. Nor had the Emperor, or any of his advisers.

What, meanwhile, had the new Chief Superintendent, Elliot, been doing since the confirmation of his appointment at the end of 1836? Palmerston had been unlucky or inept with all his appointments to the post. Napier was too rigid, Davis and Robinson too inert. Elliot was by turns over-confident, vacillatory, nervous and inconsistent. Dryden's lines could be applied to him not unfairly:

> Stiff in opinions always in the wrong;
> Was everything by starts and nothing long.

He began by disregarding the clear orders of the Foreign Office and 'petitioning' the Viceroy through the Hong merchants to proceed from Macao to Canton. Permission was graciously granted. He took up residence and the Union Jack was hoisted over the British factory on 12 April 1837 for the first time for 30 months, but he had conceded of his own free will the very point for which Napier had died. He was now a taipan as far as the Chinese authorities were concerned and could be treated as such. The Viceroy was triumphant and the Canton merchants were in despair, believing that Elliot must have had orders from an appeasing Foreign Office to make such a cowardly *volte face*. This was not so. Palmerston, when informed by Elliot after the usual time lag, gave peremptory orders that he was not to do it again. He would have been better advised to sack him. The result, amidst increasing chaos in the trade, was that Elliot could not communicate at all with the Canton officials, and was powerless to protect the traders or reform abuses. On 2 December he hauled down the flag and departed disconsolately to Macao. There was no point in remaining unless he had adequate naval force behind him. Meanwhile the Viceroy gave orders for the dispersal of the store ships at Lintin and Kumsingmoon.

The Foreign Office's attitude was beginning to harden by the end of 1837. The China trade was important nationally and it had already been much disrupted. Moreover there was considerable pressure in Britain for something to be done. The propaganda campaign of the Canton merchants has already been mentioned. In February 1836 the Manchester Chamber of Commerce sent a memorial to the Foreign Secretary on the subject. Matheson, during his stay in England, had already made representations to Palmerston whom he found rather more sympathetic than Wellington. Both Matheson and, even more, Jardine were by now very well-known figures in the business world, widely respected if not always liked. A powerful blast from a quarter which politically could not be ignored was likely to have some effect especially since it was followed by similar pressure from Liverpool and Glasgow. Matheson worked on the President of the Chamber, John MacVicar, a somewhat abrasive Mancunian merchant and calico man-ufacturer for whom Jardines acted as agent in China, though they had no intention of reciprocating by having him as agent in Britain. The search for a suitable agent was among Matheson's tasks during his visit. The memorial pointed out the dangers to which unprotected British merchants in China were subjected, and the precariousness of a trade which was of the greatest importance. It provided employment for 100,000 tons of shipping, a market for British manufacturers and for the products of India (the memorial naturally did not say that opium was the main one) to the extent of £3 million per annum. This enabled 'our Indian subjects to consume our manufactures on a largely increased scale'. Moreover the China trade could be greatly extended. 'We cannot contemplate without the most serious alarm the uncertain and unprotected state in which this most important trade has been placed particularly since the failure of Lord Napier's "Mission".'[12] James Matheson chimed in with an influential pamphlet, *Present Position and Future Prospects of Trade in China* (1836). As Greenberg puts it, 'by 1836 the weight of the "home" manufacturing interests of Britain was thrown behind a "forward" policy in China.' This was perhaps the most important consequence of 1834. The abolition of the Company's charter had brought together the Country traders and the Manchester manufacturers.[13]

Elliot's appeal for naval support had some effect. The commander-in-chief of the East Indies Station, Admiral Sir Thomas Maitland, sailed in his flagship early in July to Tong Ku (usually called Urmston) harbour a few miles south-east of Lintin early in July. He had no very clear instructions other than a general charge to show national solicitude to British subjects. Elliot now had a final go at the Viceroy. He arrived in Canton, raised the flag on 26 July and presented a letter. It contained an assurance that the naval presence was in no way meant to intimidate; it was as usual returned unopened. Elliot retired to Macao after lowering the flag on 31 July. An alleged insult to the British flag at sea a few days later prompted Admiral Maitland to make a demonstration off Chuenpi, which was followed by a climb-down and apology with much courtesy by the Chinese Admiral. Encouraged, Elliot sent a second letter to the Viceroy. It had the same response. The services and the officials of China were worlds apart. There was a complete impasse.

By the early 1830s William Jardine had been in the China trade for 30 years and had made a fortune. His plan had been to retire in 1837 when Matheson returned to China, buy an estate in Scotland and start on a new course as a Whig Liberal Member of Parliament. But he decided to postpone the move in view of the uneasy situation in Canton created by the Napier 'Fizzle'. It seemed clear that Elliot was for different reasons likely to be as ineffective as Napier. There was no point in further delay. Early in 1839 and a few weeks before the arrival of Commissioner Lin, a great farewell party was given by the foreign community in his honour. No fewer than 166 guests sat down for dinner, each with his own servant standing behind him. Among the numerous toasts was one drunk 'to his health and a charming wife', to which Jardine replied that the best he could hope for was 'fat, fair and forty'. The feeling between Jardines and its great rival was so bitter that no one from Dent & Co. accepted an invitation to the dinner,[14] or contributed to the leaving present of silver plate worth £1000.

On 26 January, on the eve of his departure in the *Bolton* from the Macao roads after similar jollification, Jardine wrote a farewell letter to James Matheson whom he was destined not to see again:

I shall say nothing about dinners, speeches, dancing in the streets, etc. Young Jardine[15] will tell you all that nonsense. One thing I beg to assure you of: I am thoroughly convinced that you will carry on the business of the House quite as well as ever I did. You only require confidence to be fully equal, if not superior to me, in managing the business of the House. Time will be required to gain the thorough confidence of the Chinese. I mean a short time. In the meanwhile I have perfect confidence in your management and feel quite easy on that subject.[16]

The departure of 'the Iron-headed Old Rat' may have been welcomed by the Chinese authorities, but it meant the arrival in London of their most formidable and determined adversary, and it was in London, not Canton, where the future fate of China was to be settled. Jardine proceeded home in a leisurely way, stopping at Bombay to take his leave of his Parsee friends and 'constituents', including Jamsetjee with whom good relations had long ago been restored. Another of these, Cowasjee, was in financial trouble. 'Jardine, on his own and on Matheson's behalf, contributed a third share of a fund being raised to set him up again.'[17] He went by the overland route to Suez and did some sightseeing in the Mediterranean, but when he was in Genoa during August alarming news reached him in letters from Canton. The opium trade was at a standstill and the whole position of the British merchants in grave danger. Clearly, he must go to London as soon as possible and use his influence to stiffen Whitehall into positive action. He arrived early in September.

SEVEN

The Opium War

Commissioner Lin had arrived in Canton on 10 March 1839, heralding his arrival with seventeen orders for arrest. His policy had two prongs. One, which is not relevant to this history, was an even more determined drive to suppress smoking by enlisting the support of the village notables. It had long-term consequences for Chinese rural society leading to a great increase in the power of the 'gentry' as against the government-appointed magistracy, but this was of no concern to the maritime European merchants. What did affect them was the second prong authorized in the Imperial edict appointing Lin. He was to clear up 'the source of this fraud' in Canton:

> This does not only refer to that province's opium brokers and fast crabs, or its opium houses, warehouses, divans and other glaring aspects of corruption. It also means that he must, according to place and circumstances, radically sever the trunk from its roots.[1]

This was exactly what Lin intended to do. The 'roots' were partly in India which he could not touch, but also in the store ships packed with chests of opium off Lintin Island and elsewhere, and in the factories of the foreign merchants who negotiated business from the factories in Canton. Here he could do something. He could threaten the Hongists with strangulation if they did not induce the Europeans to turn in their supplies for destruction at the Bogue and sign bonds promising under pain of death never to traffick in opium again. He could hold as hostages for the same purpose individual taipans. Now that Jardine had left, Dent, being the senior merchant, was regarded as the British 'headman'. Lin could go further and treat the whole foreign community as hostages. On 18 March he ordered the delivery of 'every particle of opium' and the signing of bonds by all merchants. On 19 March he forbade all Europeans to leave Canton.

The 'Old China Hands' were not unduly alarmed, but they decided that something had better be done, and offered through Howqua to hand over 1037 chests valued at £140,000. Lin refused with contempt. He knew, he said, that 'the Barbarian, Dent', alone, had 6000 and demanded that Dent should come and see him. Dent was ready to go. He believed that he could talk Lin round, and he did not anticipate any danger. Since Lin had been thoughtful enough to hire two cooks who could prepare foreign food, it certainly looked as if no physical harm was meant, but Dent might well have been detained as a hostage. His colleagues urged him not to go without a safe-conduct. This was refused and Lin threatened to arrest him. After some haggling with the mandarins during Saturday 23 March it was agreed that Dent should present himself to Lin at 10am on Monday. Meanwhile Elliot, hearing the news that foreigners had been forbidden to leave, hastened from Macao. He arrived at 6pm on Sunday 24 March in a state of much alarm. Seeing that there was no flag flying over the British factory he ordered the Union Jack to be hoisted, but in the general confusion his own official flag could not be found, and he was obliged to tie on to the broken flagstaff the small ensign of the gig which had conveyed him over the last few miles of the journey from Whampoa, 'for I well know, my Lord,' he wrote to Palmerston, 'that there is a sense of support in that honoured Flag, fly where it will, that none can feel but men who look upon it in some such dismal streights [sic] as ours'.[2]

It is a moot point whether the 'streights' were quite as dismal as Elliot thought. Lin might have held some of the leading taipans as hostages, but it is unlikely that he would have maltreated them, let alone killed them. It would probably have been a matter of intimidation mixed with diplomacy. Maurice Collis in *Foreign Mud* suggests that Lin thought in terms of gradual pressure:

He was not suddenly going to overrun the factories with an armed rabble and deal in a brutal manner with those in his power. And in as much as his method was diplomatic by nature, it would enable the British to counter with diplomacy, to bargain, to threaten on their side, and to make offers, as for instance to curtail the drug traffic in return for concessions in the legitimate trade. In short it is doubtful whether the situation was as alarming as it seemed to Captain Elliot. There were expedients of all sorts yet to be tried.[3]

And he points out the evidence submitted by some of the witnesses to the Select Committee on China Trade in 1840, which confirms this view. Dent's partner, Inglis, for example, believed 'that a bargain could have been made, had the matter been handled with skill and nerve.'

Obviously one is in the realm of speculation here. What is certain is that the arrival of the Chief Superintendent and his subsequent conduct played into Lin's hands in the short term, although in the longer run it led straight to the war which dealt a fatal blow to the old order in China. Elliot promptly forbade Dent to keep his appointment with Lin next day. He would never allow him, he said to Dent's surprise, in the tone of a man priding himself on his chivalry, to be a scapegoat for the community. He would take him into his official protection, and he summoned all the merchants to the hall of the British factory telling them to keep calm and not to panic. At this moment news came that Lin had ordered all Chinese servants to leave the factories on pain of death if they refused. He had also cut off supplies of food and water. Then the beating of gongs signalled the arrival of troops in Thirteen Factory Street and on the Square. An arc of densely packed junks was drawn along the river front. Lin had decided to forget about Dent and to treat Elliot as the 'headman' responsible for all the British merchants. The factories would remain blockaded until the opium had been disgorged and bonds signed. The Chief Superintendent had put his head in a trap. It was folly to have gone to Canton at all without the backing of a far larger naval force than he had at his disposal.

Folly tends to produce further folly. Elliot panicked. In fact the condition of life in the factories under Lin's embargo was by no means disagreeable. Matheson, anticipating trouble, had stocked up with plenty of salt beef and flour. There was a well which produced rather stale water. One could wash in it, but water was not the favourite drink of the inhabitants who could still draw on great reserves of beer, claret, Madeira, etc. The Hong merchants, having persuaded Lin that it would be better to avoid 'incidents' with the Barbarians, substituted their own servants for soldiers unaccustomed to dealing with foreigners. They smuggled fresh vegetables and other provisions into the factories. A Parsee friend loaned his Indian cook to Matheson. Apart from an unfortunate fall downstairs by David Jardine after dinner, injuring his back, the Princely House survived comfortably enough living on curry and claret. The servantless firms, too, were quite happy. It was all rather like a picnic. In London at the end of the year, the so-called 'siege' of the factories was blown up by Jardine's propaganda machine into something like the 'Black Hole of Calcutta'. In reality the only danger to the besieged was obesity from too much food and too little exercise.

Elliot decided to surrender abjectly and completely. He ordered the British merchants to hand over all the opium under their control wherever placed. He guaranteed indemnification, although he had no authority whatever to commit the British taxpayer to compensate smugglers for the loss of contraband to the tune of £2 million. Palmerston was furious when informed months later, although he soon saw how to exploit the situation. Elliot then sent for the stock lists of the merchants and, without consulting any of them personally, added the figures up to a total of 20,000 chests, thus making himself responsible for nearly 1000 more than were actually held. Being a naval officer, not a man of business, he made no allowance for recent sales or for duplication caused by a mortgagor and mortgagee including the same item in their returns.[4] In any case he was being *plus royaliste que le roi*. Lin could guess that 1037 was far too low, but he had no way of knowing the real total. The Hong merchants were astonished at Elliot's naivety. Matheson reported them to Jardine as saying, 'What for he pay so large? No wantee so much. Six, seven-thousand so would be enough.'[5]

Lin would lift the blockade only by stages until the 20,000 chests were all delivered, and insisted on signature of the bond. Matheson prudently signed 'for himself and partners only' leaving Jardine's nephew, Andrew, who was not yet a partner, free to continue the trade from Macao or Manila, if practicable. The chests were duly delivered at

Chuenpi and the opium was destroyed – quite a formidable operation. The British merchants were not at all sorry about the affair. They had found it difficult to sell the drug. They were now guaranteed reimbursement, and the market would be all the better next year, for they were convinced that there was no risk of the trade coming to an end. The British government would be bound to intervene. Nor was Matheson worried when orders of expulsion were served on him, on two of his nephews and on Andrew Jardine. Canton was impossible for the time being. He wrote to William Jardine on 15 May 1839:

> I suppose we shall move to Macao in about five days. If not permitted to go there, we shall live afloat in one of our outside vessels to give advice and know what is going on. The affairs of our constituents will, I am persuaded, be conducted with the same regularity as if we were on the spot.[6]

By the end of the month, along with the whole British community, he was based on Macao while Andrew Jardine was despatched to Manila whence he could superintend the despatch of opium to the China coast. Elliot also retired to Macao putting an embargo on all trade with Canton after the winter tea supplies had been shipped. He was convinced by now that the problem could only be solved by force, and in a despatch to Palmerston written during the blockade of the factories he advised a course of action which would bring to an end 'this defiance of every obligation of truth and right toward the whole Christian world' – a curious description of Commissioner Lin's behaviour in enforcing his country's laws against smuggling. The Chinese were, he said, not acting in ignorance of the evils they had committed 'but in ignorance of the Power of Her Majesty's Government to resent them'. To bring them to their senses British forces should occupy Chusan Island, blockade Canton, Ningpo and the Yangtse from its mouth to its junction with the Grand Canal. An ultimatum should be sent to Peking demanding full financial compensation and free entry for British ships and cargoes into Canton, Ningpo, Amoy and Nanking.

The arrival of this despatch in London coincided with the arrival of William Jardine from Genoa, already aware of the news. Along with John Abel Smith, a partner in Magniac, Smith & Co. whom Matheson in 1835 had appointed as the Canton Firm's London agents, he was determined to see Palmerston. Abel Smith was a friend of the great man and in a position to introduce Jardine who was now quite a celebrity and known to be a potential Whig candidate for Parliament. After some delay they were received by the Foreign Secretary on 27 September 1839. Jardine had no use for Elliot but his advice was very similar. He and Smith were accompanied by Alexander Grant, until recently Commodore of the Jardine fleet, and they brought maps and charts which they left with Palmerston.

> The conference ended in His Lordship retaining the charts etc., saying they were to hold a Cabinet meeting on Monday next, and he hopes to see us again in the course of the ensuing week... It is difficult to form an opinion as to the real views of the Government, though it is still more difficult to believe they can remain quiet, pocket the insult, and purchase a continuation of the legitimate trade at two million sterling.[7]

Palmerston had decided by mid-December that he must demand reparation and send a force to back the demand. He asked Jardine to submit a paper about the best course of action. Jardine and Smith were happy to oblige. On 19 December Jardine wrote to Matheson:

> My advice is to send a naval force to blockade the China coast from the Tartar Wall [the Great Wall] to Tienpack, or from 40 to 20 degrees north; the force to consist of two ships of the line, two frigates and two flat-bottomed steamers for river service with a sufficient number of transports to carry...six or seven thousand men. The force to proceed to the vicinity of Peking and apply directly to the Emperor for an apology for the insult... payment for the opium given up, an equitable commercial treaty, and liberty to trade with the northern ports... say Amoy, Foochow, Ningpo, Shanghai and also Kiaochow, if we can get it.[8]

Jardine thought that the first two demands would be accepted, but a commercial treaty and liberty to trade with the northern ports might not. In that case Britain should seize some islands as hostages until the demands were met, in particular 'Chusan Island which being near Peking would be a source of great annoyance to the Emperor'. On 6

February 1840 Jardine had a further interview with Palmerston and took the opportunity to press for Chinese payment of the Co-hong's debts incurred as a result of the interruption of trade.

It was another fortnight before Palmerston declared his hand. It is not surprising that he had hesitated for nearly five months after receiving the news of Captain Elliot's surrender to Commissioner Lin. Elliot had pledged indemnity to the opium traders, admittedly without authority, but it would be very awkward to repudiate him. On the other hand there was no chance of persuading Parliament to vote £2 million to compensate the loss of merchants engaged in an illegal and obnoxious traffic in drugs. Palmerston's solution was to send a force to China mounted from India with the Governor-General, Lord Auckland, as titular commander-in-chief. Its purpose would be to extract a sufficient indemnity to cover not only the opium losses, but the Co-hong debts and the entire cost of the expedition itself. It would also seize Chusan and open up a group of northern ports. The strategy would closely resemble William Jardine's advice, although the naval force would be rather larger and the idea of blockading the coast from 40 to 20 degrees north was rightly dismissed as impracticable. Palmerston sent his instructions to Lord Auckland on 20 February 1840 before making any statement to Parliament which did not debate the matter until 7 April, and only then on the demand of the Opposition leader, Sir Robert Peel, who had decided to move a vote of censure against the Government. Its majority was precarious and there seemed a good chance of success.

Peel was, however, in a dilemma. It would have been convenient to take the high moral line, denounce the drug trade as vigorously as the slave trade, and accuse the Government of encouraging a nefarious contraband traffic. The difficulty was that in 1830 there had been a report from the Select Committee on the East India Company which discussed the opium question and recommended on grounds of revenue that there should be no interference. The Tories, in office at the time, had raised no objections. It would be hard to argue that the moral case was different ten years later. To rest the attack on that basis would give Palmerston an easy come-back. On the other hand it would be a pity to forego the chance of turning out the Government. The trading interest was by no means unanimous for the Whigs, and if Peel could not use the ethical argument, others certainly would. He decided to attack the Government for incompetence rather than immorality; the stoppage of trade might have been avoided if Elliot had been given clear and full instructions – Palmerston's were few and brief – and diplomacy could have prevented a confrontation which was bound to result in a costly war.

The three-day debate is well worth studying as an epitome of early Victorian attitudes to 'the flag', commerce, religion, foreign policy and national pride. It was opened with a speech from the Tory Opposition of remarkable obscurity and prolixity by Sir James Graham, to whom Thomas Macaulay, Secretary for War and Colonies, replied with characteristic eloquence. He referred to Elliot's first step on arriving at Canton – the hoisting of the flag. 'This was an act which revived the drooping hopes of those who looked to him for protection. It was natural that they should look with confidence on the victorious flag... which reminded them that they belonged to a country unaccustomed to defeat.' It reminded them too, he went on, of their country's fame 'in redressing the wrongs of her children', and he quoted the humiliation of the Bey of Algiers for insulting the British Consul and the revenge for the horrors of the Black Hole taken at Plassey. It was sturdy, patriotic, even jingoistic oratory, and Macaulay took the opportunity to state officially for the first time that war impended in China.

On the second day of the debate the most notable speech in opposition came from Gladstone, then a high Tory. He had not been in Parliament at the time of the Report of the Select Committee on the East India Company and so was not inhibited by the considerations which influenced Peel. He took a strong moral line, all the stronger, no doubt, because his sister was an opium addict.

A war more unjust in its origin, a war more calculated to cover this country with permanent disgrace, I do not know and have not read of. The Rt. Hon. gentleman opposite spoke of the British flag waving in glory at Canton. That flag is hoisted to protect an infamous contraband traffic; and if it were never hoisted except as it is now hoisted on the coast of China, we should recoil from its sight with horror.[10]

It was a matter on which for once, in a way, Gladstone and Disraeli were in agreement. Jardine, well known as a pillar of the opium trade, was satirized by Disraeli in *Sybil*, some years later. Charles Egremont, an idealistic Tory, is standing for the seat which is his family's stronghold. Egremont refers to the Opposition:

> To tell the truth, I quite gave up the thing the moment they started their man. Before that we were on velvet; but the instant he appeared everthing changed, and I found some of my warmest supporters members of his committee.'
>
> 'You had a formidable opponent Lord Marney [Egremont's elder brother] told me,' said Sir Vavasour. 'Who was he?'
>
> 'Oh! a dreadful man! A Scotchman richer than Croesus, one McDruggy fresh from Canton, with a million of opium in each pocket, denouncing corruption and bellowing free trade.'
>
> 'But they do not care much for free trade in the old borough?' said Lord Marney.
>
> 'No, it was a mistake,' said Egremont, 'and the cry was changed the moment my opponent was on the ground. Then all the town was placarded with "Vote for McDruggy and our young Queen", as if he had coalesced with Her Majesty.'[11]

The vote of censure was defeated. Palmerston could out-gun most people, even Peel, in an issue of this sort. Peel's line on the third day was not to deny that a punitive expedition was now necessary, but to condemn the alleged apathy and inefficiency which had brought matters to this sorry pass. The administration had got itself into a tangle which could easily have been avoided. The House could have no confidence in a government which had behaved so ineptly and had given such perfunctory orders to its representative in Macao. Palmerston was in his element, dealing with these charges by a mixture of ridicule and flag-waving.

> I gave the Superintendent instructions, and have been blamed because they were not long enough. Gentlemen who make long speeches think, I suppose, that I should write long letters. They imagine that precise instructions contained in a few but significant words are not proportioned to the length that they had to travel; they imagine that when you write to China your letter should be as long as the voyage.[12]

In any case what instructions should he have given? Palmerston had the clever politician's gift of attributing to his opponents silly ideas which they never held. Did they wish him to tell Elliot to expel every smuggler and remove every clipper? The law would not permit it. Was he expected to police the Canton River and the Yellow Sea 'for the purpose of preserving the morals of the Chinese people, who were disposed to buy what other people were disposed to sell them?' Parliament would laugh out of court the request for a grant for such a purpose. As for the argument that the opium trade could be stopped by banning the cultivation of the poppy in India, he pointed out, rightly, that the Government could not interfere in the Princely States, and that ample supplies could be secured from Turkey.[13] Palmerston read out the petition from the China firms whose top signatory was Jardine, though he did not, of course, mention the secret advice that he had received from that quarter. As a final trump card he produced a 'memorial' from the American traders in Canton to Congress earlier that year, in January. The gist of it was that a joint naval demonstration by Britain, France and America would reopen trade almost certainly without bloodshed. Palmerston was sustained throughout by his knowledge that a charge of ineptitude leading to an armed expedition would cut no ice at all with a large section of the House, which regarded such an expedition, bloodless or not, as the only solution to the problem. Palmerston had played his cards well. He won but with little to spare. The Opposition motion was lost by nine votes.

Meanwhile much had happened in China. Matheson was soon able to get the trade going again. The price of opium shot up after the destruction of the 20,000 chests. For whatever reason the vigilance of the authorities on the China coast slackened, and Andrew Jardine from Manila had no great difficulty in making satisfactory shipments. The figures speak for themselves. The Firm's net profits which had been as high as £309,000 in its first financial year 1832–3 fell to £63,000 in 1837–8 and £53,000 in 1838–9, but rose to £235,000 in the following year and stood at £203,000 the year after that. But life was not easy. Scarcely had Matheson and his colleagues, along with the other British merchants, repaired to Macao than the place became too hot to hold them. In July 1839 an affray in Hong Kong by some drunken sailors resulted in the death of a Chinese. Lin demanded a member of the crew to be handed over for trial and certain execution. Elliot refused. Lin now threatened Macao, which could easily be captured from the land by Chinese troops. The entire British community, wives and children included, took to their ships and resided off Hong Kong.

Matheson sent instructions to Otadui & Co., the firm's agents in Manila, for supplies:

> Poultry and pigs with provender, as many as are likely to come over alive. To crowd them too much will be a useless waste ... some salt provisions will not be amiss – also some of your best beer – about half what you last sent arrived broken and leaky – send also some moderately good French claret and some seltzer water. We shall not grudge ... 5000 dollars for the purpose of this letter, but you need not be extravagant, and gradual sendings will be better than too much at once.[14]

The partners knew how to look after themselves, but Matheson's early optimism began to disappear. Elliot seemed to be almost more anxious than Lin to suppress the opium trade, and 'had adopted', so Matheson wrote, 'the novel course of assisting the [Chinese] Government in this against his own countrymen'.[15] Early in September the first shots of the Opium War were exchanged when Lin ordered armed junks to forbid access to Kowloon for food and water. Elliot, with two small ships, opened fire, severely damaged the junks and broke the blockade. Matters were now heading for a crisis. Lin demanded that the 60 merchantmen anchored at Chuenpi outside the Bogue should enter the Canton River to resume normal non-opium trade or depart, under the threat of destruction if they disobeyed. Elliot saw that the crunch had come. To accept the demand would be to place hostages of the greatest leverage in Lin's hands, and he could not disregard the threat of destruction by fireships. He had at his disposal a second-class frigate, *Volage*, with 28 guns, and a third-class, *Hyacinth*, with eighteen. A large Chinese fleet of fifteen men-of-war and fourteen fireboats was sighted on 2 November 1839 approaching the mouth of the river. Elliot sent an ultimatum: withdraw or else ... It was refused. The Chinese fleet anchored outside the Bogue. The two frigates opened fire and swept the decks of the junks. One blew up, three sank and another two or three were waterlogged and beached. The whole fleet could have been destroyed but Elliot, who was averse to bloodshed, believed that the lesson was learned and he returned to Macao. He was wrong. He did not reckon with the almost limitless Chinese power of self-deception or the capacity of the Emperor's envoys to conceal the truth from their master.

A pause ensued in Chinese affairs. The Firm traded as vigorously as ever, but there could be no settlement of the dispute until the British expedition arrived – in June 1840 at the earliest. Charles Elliot and his first cousin, Admiral the Hon. George Elliot, who commanded the fleet, were given joint plenipotentiary powers to obtain reparations from China for 'insults and injuries', indemnity for the confiscated opium, payment of the Co-hong's debts and security for traders and their property. Parliament was not, however, told that the indemnity was to cover the entire cost of the expedition as well as the lost opium, nor was anything said about the cession of a strategic base; indeed Palmerston had not yet made up his mind on this point.

The history of the war can be briefly summarized. The naval force of sixteen ships of war, four armed steamers and 28 transports carrying 4000 soldiers assembled off Macao late in June 1840. A small force was detached to blockade Canton. The rest sailed north, to the indignation of the less percipient Canton merchants, who felt that retribution should be inflicted where the 'insult' had occurred. Jardine was too intelligent to be influenced by sentiment of that sort. He had seen from the start and had advised Palmerston that, given the centralized Chinese system, the only effective action would be to threaten the capital itself. It was no use dealing with a remote provincial government. Canton was far too distant and the likelihood of the Emperor being correctly informed of any setback there was nil. The first step was to seize the island of Chusan which was bombarded into surrender after nine minutes' fire. The fleet then moved towards the Peiho River. By the beginning of August pandemonium reigned in Peking. The letter to the Emperor was reluctantly accepted. An envoy of great grandeur and wealth, Ch'i-shan (anglice 'Kishen') was appointed to negotiate. He did so with such skill that the Elliots withdrew to the south, believing that the 'peace party' was winning in Peking. This was a serious error. As soon as the pressure on the capital was relaxed, Imperial policy changed. Although by now aware of British naval power, the Chinese authorities still believed that European clothing made it impossible for them to fight on land; so the struggle was not yet lost. Lin was dismissed in September 1840 for failure to prevent the barbarian incursions, and exiled in July 1841 to the remote and frosty northern province of Ili. But he was a survivor and was to be reinstated into government service in 1845 and died a natural death five years later. He was replaced in Canton by Kishen who pursued a circuitous policy of prevarication pending the arrival of the Chinese army.

Charles Elliot, who was now in sole charge, his cousin having been invalided out, saw through this screen of duplicity, albeit belatedly. He attacked the Bogue forts on 7 January 1841 and destroyed them with ease. Canton was now at his mercy, and Kishen promptly came to terms under the Convention of Chuenpi: an indemnity of $6 million, the cession of Hong Kong, the reopening of trade, letters instead of petitions. The Convention, however, had no binding power until rati-fied both by the Chinese and the British Governments. The two negotiators thought that they had done well for their respective author-ities in the circumstances and expected to be praised. The reaction from Peking and London was one of indignation. The Emperor and Palmerston were equally angry with their subordinates. The Emperor had decided even before the Convention of Chuenpi that the Barbarians should be exterminated. His edict to this effect, arriving just after Kishen had given away Hong Kong and $6 million, produced con-sternation in the unfortunate Viceroy. When in February the Emperor was informed of the Convention he promptly repudiated it, dismissed Kishen who was sent in chains to stand trial in Peking, and gave renewed orders for military action. As for Elliot, he was to receive one of the most devastating letters ever written by a minister to an appointee. It was dated 21 April 1841. Elliot, said Palmerston, had failed to secure an adequate indemnity – neither the cost of the expedition nor the Co-hong's debts were covered – he had abandoned Chusan instead of keeping it as a security, he had acquired Hong Kong, although it was not clear that the Emperor had actually ceded it – the British might be in the same position as the Portuguese in Macao. In any case it was 'a barren island with hardly a house upon it. Now it seems obvious that Hong Kong will not be a Mart of Trade any more than Macao is so.' Finally Elliot had not succeeded in obtaining 'an additional opening for our Trade to the Northwest'. Palmerston ended: 'You will no doubt by the time you have read thus far have anticipated that I could not conclude this letter without saying that under the circumstances it is impossible that you should continue to hold your appointment in China.'[16] Queen Victoria was equally angry. She wrote on 10 April to her uncle, the King of the Belgians: 'the Chinese business vexes us much and Palmerston is deeply mortified at it. All we wanted might have been got, if it had not been for the unaccountably strange conduct of Charles Elliot ... who completely disobeyed his instructions and tried to get the lowest terms he could.'[17] In his place Palmerston appointed Sir Henry Pottinger, a soldier and diplomat, who had been made a baronet for his services in India.

The letter of dismissal did not arrive until August 1841, along with Pottinger. Meanwhile, Elliot, aware of Kishen's disgrace, began to suspect that the authorities in Canton were spinning out time. There was no sign of the promised reopening of trade, and it became clear that hostilities impended. Elliot decided to get his blow in first and at the end of February he sent his warships up to Whampoa, including that novel armed vessel, the iron paddle-steamer, *Nemesis*.[18] The Bogue forts were again knocked out on 26 February, the Chinese Admiral was killed, and Lin's recently purchased man-of-war, *Cambridge*, was blown up by a rocket. By the end of March, Canton was at the mercy of British naval guns, but Elliot, naive and gullible as ever, also humanely anxious to avoid slaughter in a defenceless city, accepted a truce proposed by the Canton authorities in return for a reopening of trade. His decision dismayed the service chiefs and the Canton merchants. It soon became obvious that the Chinese government regarded the truce merely as a means of averting war until its troops were ready. Elliot sensed this on a visit to Canton in April. He postponed action until the last possible moment, but on 21 May he ordered the British to leave Canton, after a Chinese attempt to destroy his ships at Whampoa by fire-boats. Hostilities were resumed. The navy sank 71 junks and landed a force of 2400 men who took up position on the foothills of the White

Cloud mountain. By 26 May their batteries dominated the city. Nevertheless, for yet a third time Elliot, to the fury of both navy and army, especially General Hugh Gough, who commanded the latter, consented to a truce. The conditions were withdrawal of the Imperial forces to a distance of 60 miles and payment within a week of $6 million. But the Chinese had saved 'face'. It was easy to convince the Cantonese that the withdrawal of troops and fleet was a victory and – more important – to tell the Emperor that his forces had repelled the Barbarians.

Elliot was now at a loss what to do. He had become convinced that Canton was irrelevant, that a foray to the north to pressurize Peking was needed and he made plans for it, but he was out of sympathy with Palmerston's enthusiasm for northern ports. The truth is that Elliot was at heart a 'mandarin'. Just as the real mandarins looked down on the Co-hong, so Elliot disliked the Jardines, the Mathesons and the Dents of this world. And he thoroughly disapproved of the opium trade. Those involved were indirectly responsible for a war which evoked his humanitarian distaste. He regarded them as greedy troublemakers. He drifted into a Sargasso Sea of incertitude.

The arrival of Sir Henry Pottinger on 9 August 1841 changed all this. Pottinger had very explicit instructions from Palmerston, who, however much he had bantered Graham and Peel about short letters, took care that no similar criticism could be repeated. Pottinger did not share Elliot's aversion to the opium traders. One of his first actions on being appointed had been to consult Jardine in London, with whom he dined amidst charts and maps, their only companion being Alexander Matheson until they were joined at 10pm by Abel Smith. He was therefore well briefed before his departure. On 21 August, a naval force under Rear Admiral Parker sailed, accompanied by transports full of soldiers, from Hong Kong to Amoy. The troops were commanded by General Gough. The island was occupied on 26 August. Chusan was recaptured by 6 October. Chinhai was taken on the 10th and Ningpo three days later. Garrisons were left for the winter. It was too late in the year to proceed any further.

Pottinger's plan, inspired by Jardine, was to move ships up the Yangtse, cut China in two and blockade supplies of grain to Peking rather than, as Palmerston had preferred, advance up the Peiho River to Tientsin. For safety's sake he needed further reinforcements, and the army which was to launch the attack in May 1842 amounted to 10,000 men of whom 4000 were British, the rest Indian. On 4 June 1841 the Whig government lost a vote of censure. The ensuing general election resulted in a conclusive victory for Peel, who formed a government on 30 August. Palmerston's successor was Lord Aberdeen, but the affairs of China were transferred from the Foreign Office to the Department of War and Colonies headed by Lord Stanley, who, as the 14th Earl of Derby, was later to be Prime Minister three times. Lord Haddington succeeded Lord Minto at the Admiralty, and in October Lord Ellenborough became Viceroy of India in place of Lord Auckland. Pottinger's change of plan from the Peiho to the Yangtse was inspired not only by Jardine but also by Ellenborough, who as Viceroy was titular commander-in-chief and had great influence on Stanley. The latter had no experience of Eastern affairs and looked to Ellenborough for a lead. The Duke of Wellington, Minister without Portfolio, strongly endorsed the view that an expedition to Peking would be far too dangerous.[19]

In the spring of 1842 the Chinese launched their only counter-offensive in an attempt to recapture Ningpo and the other occupied cities. Although the commander I-ching, a cousin of the Emperor, was so confident that he instigated a scribal competition for the most elegant account of the forthcoming victory, disaster ensued. I-ching consulted an oracle for the auspicious day to launch the attack, and drew a divining slip which referred to 'tiger' omens. Clearly, a tiger hour on a tiger day in a tiger month during a tiger year was the right moment; this was between 3 and 5am on 10 March 1842. But as Professor Wakeman points out[20], it was 'also incidentally the height of the spring rainy season'. Nor were matters helped by the fact that I-ching's chief of staff in charge of reserves, who might conceivably have recaptured Chinhai, was an opium addict and was in a coma when his reinforcements were required. As in all these encounters, the Chinese losses were immense and the British negligible. Pottinger's campaign began on 7 May 1842 and finished on 20 August. By then Chapu, Shanghai and Chinkiang were captured. Peking was effectively blockaded and Nanking, the old capital, was wide open to attack. The Imperial Court surrendered. On 29 August the Treaty of Nanking was signed on Sir Henry Pottinger's ship, *Cornwallis*. It conceded almost everything the British demanded and represented the seemingly final triumph for the Canton traders.

There was to be an indemnity of $21 million to cover the confiscated opium, the Hong debts and the cost of the expedition. Canton, Amoy, Foochow, Ningpo and Shanghai were to be open to foreign trade and foreign settlement. Officials from each country were to be treated on an equal basis – no more petitions. There was to be a British Consul and a ship of war at each 'Treaty Port'. The Co-hong monopoly was abolished, which meant that the Consoo system of security for bad debts was abolished too. There were to be known fixed and uniform duties on exports and imports. Hong Kong was to be ceded and to come under British sovereignty. Not a word was said about opium which still remained in theory an article of contraband. This was a matter of form rather than reality. No serious attempt was ever again made on either side to enforce the law. On 21 April 1843, Alexander Matheson wrote to the London office:

> The Plenipotentiary [Pottinger] has published a most fiery proclamation against smuggling, but I believe it is like the Chinese edicts, meaning nothing and only intended for the Saints in England. Sir Henry never means to act upon it and, no doubt, privately considers it a good joke. At any rate, he allows the drug to be landed and stored at Hong Kong.[21]

Three months later, on 31 July he wrote again:

> The drug trade continues to prosper. On the new tariff coming into operation, all the opium vessels under the British flag left Whampoa, but they are not interfered with outside the Bogue. Sir Henry Pottinger will do nothing adverse to the trade as long as it is not forced on his attention at the five ports ... The only object now to be desired is the legalisation of the drug trade, and of that there is no hope during the lifetime of the present Emperor. The next thing to be desired is that it should be carried on by parties of respectability and not be driven into the hands of desperadoes and pirates as would inevitably be the case were Lord Ashley and his friends to succeed in carrying their measures. No one is more conscious of this than Sir Henry Pottinger who, of course, communicates his sentiments to Sir Robert Peel.[22]

The Treaty of Nanking, extended and reinforced by that of Tientsin in 1858, shaped the political and commercial relations of the Western world with China for almost a century. In the long run it was fatal to the Ch'ing dynasty, although this was not obvious at the time. The Emperor regarded it as a defeat. In June 1842, two months before the signature of the Treaty, he issued an edict reviewing past events and future policy, in which he said:

> If I should be content with peace for the time being, and ... let the evil of the opium go its way without any prohibition, that would mean that I am betraying my ancestors who entrusted to me the care of the Empire and that I am unable to afford due protection to the lives of my subjects. Thinking about these points, how ... dare I not strictly prohibit it?[23]

The Treaty enabled him to save face as regarded opium, but it was a heavy blow to Imperial prestige. As his principal negotiator, put it:

> In settling the barbarian affairs this time we are governed at every hand by the inevitable and we concede that the policy is the least commendable. What we have been doing is to choose between danger and safety, not between right and wrong ... But the spirit of the invaders is running high. They occupy our important cities ... should we fail to take advantage of the present occasion, and to ease the situation by soothing the Barbarians, they will run over our country like beasts, doing anything they like.[24]

Viewed from Peking the Treaty of Nanking was a setback rather than a disaster. There were more serious problems in prospect for a regime concerned above all else to suppress rural unrest in the interior and preserve the loyalty of the scholar landed élite through which it controlled at several removes the vast Chinese peasantry ever pressing upon their means of subsistence. Eight years later over-population and religious fanaticism led to the Taiping Rebellion. A civil war of immense ferocity broke out. In comparison, the activities of the barbarian merchants in a few coastal ports seemed relatively trivial, even if tiresome.

Viewed from London, Macao and Hong Kong, the Treaty of Nanking was a notable triumph for Western ideals and practice. It was widely accepted in Britain that the opening up of China to trade was for the good of China as well as the West. There was consensus about the purpose, though some dissent about the methods. No dissent troubled Jardine Matheson, for whom the treaty was a particular triumph. Seldom has a private business had more effect on public policy. When Palmerston, no longer in office, heard the news of the Treaty, he wrote to the Firm's London agent, John Abel Smith, on 28 November 1842:

> ... To the assistance and information which you (my dear Smith) and Mr Jardine so handsomely afforded us it was mainly owing that we were able to give to our affairs, naval, military and diplomatic, in China, those detailed instructions which have led to these satisfactory results.
>
> It is indeed remarkable that the information which we procured from yourself and various other persons whom we consulted in the autumn of 1839, which was embodied in the instructions we gave in February 1840, was so accurate and complete that it appears that our successors have not found reason to make any alterations in them. It has turned out that the decisive operation has been in the Yang tsi Kiang, which we suggested to our naval Commander as far back as ... February 1840; and that the conditions of peace are precisely those which we instructed our plenipotentiaries Elliot and Pottinger to obtain.
>
> There is no doubt that this event, which will form an epoch in the progress of the civilisation of the human races, must be attended with the most important advantages to the commercial interests of England.[25]

Palmerston's opinion of the ethics of British intervention would be hotly disputed by modern Chinese historians and by many Europeans too. But his assessment of the part played for good or ill by William Jardine, James Matheson and their associates is fully justified. It was crucial. For over ten years they had advocated through their paper, the *Canton Register*, through petitions to the House of Commons and through private conversations, at top level in the Foreign Office, precisely the political and strategic policy which Palmerston adopted and which the successive Tory Cabinet implemented. During the war they had leased well-armed opium ships to the Royal Navy, lent their captains as navigators and their agents like Morrison and Gutzlaff as translators. They supplied charts, information and advice. Their hospitality in accommodation, food and drink was always available – an important boon in this remote and unfamiliar world. Above all, the silver from opium sales, which flourished throughout the war, was exchanged for bills drawn on London to pay for naval and military expenses. Jardine Matheson was not the only firm to render these services; Dent & Co. and others did so too. But Jardine Matheson was the largest and the most vigorous. On paper and in theory, the treaty had given the opium traders almost all they wanted. It remained to be seen how far practice would correspond to theory.

EIGHT

Hong Kong and Scotland

The Convention of Chuenpi, later to be repudiated by both London and Peking, was signed by Elliot and Ch'i-shan on 20 January 1841. One of its clauses contained the offer of Hong Kong, though it was not clear what the judicial situation would be. The Chinese view was that Hong Kong would be like Macao, leased as a trading centre. Elliot was clear that it had been ceded to the British Crown. The matter was put beyond doubt by the Treaty of Nanking nineteen months later. Meanwhile the armed forces and the British traders treated the island and harbour as an undisputed British possession. Neither Palmerston nor his merchant advisers had favoured the acquisition of Hong Kong. Their preference was for the island of Chusan, and Palmerston at one stage took the view that the establishment of 'Treaty Ports' on suitable conditions would solve the commercial problem without the need for any territorial annexation. But the cession of Hong Kong did not displease James Matheson. He wrote to Jardine, now in London, on 22 January 1841:

> ... those imperfectly acquainted with the circumstances are much dissatis-fied with the arrangement, but we are well pleased with it. We think that the possession of the island will be such a check to the Chinese as to prevent a recurrence of the indignities and impositions we have hitherto been exposed to at Canton ... There will be no Mandarin interference or control on the island which will be entirely British and will be occupied in a few days ... So independent will Hong Kong be that it will even be allowable to store opium on it as soon as we build warehouses there.[1]

On the face of it Palmerston's objection to the acquisition of Hong Kong was not unreasonable. A barren, dry, rocky, mountainous, wind-swept island, 90 miles (144km) south east of Canton, it was far away from the Yangtse estuary, which was likely to become the most important trading area in China. It is eleven miles long and from two to five miles broad, divided upon its long east-west axis by a range of hills which shuts out the cooling south-west breezes, rendering the then only inhabitable northern coastal area facing Kowloon intolerably hot during the long summer months. Air-conditioning, refrigeration and many other boons of twentieth-century technology have combined to ease day-to-day life, but it remains true that a visitor who has any choice should avoid June, July and August. Hong Kong did, however, possess one great asset: the best, though almost wholly landlocked, deep-water harbour on the China coast. But even this was, and still is exposed to ferocious and devastating typhoons. It is not surprising that the only indigenous inhabitants in 1841 were some 2000 fishermen and their families living on the margin of subsistence. For Europeans it long remained an insalubrious station which people who had made enough money were only too glad to quit.

Why did the British Government abandon the plan to acquire Chusan which commanded the Yangtse and settle for Hong Kong instead? Palmerston, who had objected so strongly to Hong Kong, was no longer in office and Jardine Matheson and its associates continued to favour the annexation of the northern island, though Matheson himself saw advantages in the apparent *fait accompli* of the cession of Hong Kong. The answer is probably a combination of drift, muddle and general lack of forethought. Hong Kong, after all, had been ceded. Why hand it back even if Elliot's action had been contrary to instructions? And Chusan, a prosperous well-cultivated island of a million inhabitants, might be considerably harder to hold, if they became resentful, than Hong Kong with its 2000 impoverished fishermen. Palmerston himself, to judge from his letter to Abel Smith, seems to have been gratified by the result.

On 26 January 1841, James Matheson was present at the hoisting of the British flag over Hong Kong on Possession Point. He then sailed round the island with Commodore Bremer RN, Admiral Elliot's second-in-command. The Firm lost no time in building a large mat shed 'godown' (warehouse) above the foreshore and installed a manager who slept on the Company's receiving ship, the *General Wood*, moored in the harbour. Opium and other cargoes were considered to be safer there than on land. In August, Sir Henry Pottinger replaced Charles Elliot as Superintendant of Trade, but he brought with him the news that the Convention of Chuenpi had been repudiated by the Foreign Office. There followed a period of much uncertainty, to the dismay of James Matheson. He was by now convinced that Hong Kong ought to replace Canton whose volatile mob seemed an endemic threat to Western traders. While these doubts prevailed, he wrote on 21 August 1841:

> ... there is no inducement to lay out money on buildings, whereas if a positive declaration were made...a town would soon spring up and a considerable Chinese population flock to it.[2]

Four days later he again wrote to William Jardine:

> I fear that Elliot's unpopularity will in some degree descend upon his pet child...but I have earnestly to beg you will (my dear Jardine) use your influence if not for its retention, at least for the retention of some place near this river [the Pearl River], where alone the British people are known, and multitudes of natives are ready to become our subjects and trade with us in place of being scared away as at Chusan and elsewhere.[3]

In the same letter he lamented that the Firm had not yet been able to do any trade other than opium at Hong Kong. But for the harbour, he thought, it might have been better from a commercial standpoint to have chosen some other place on the Macao side of the river:

> But I know not where else we could have got a harbour equally good, more especially for large vessels. Were we able to settle this in right earnest under the acknowledged and irrevocable protection of the British Government it could hardly fail to become a considerable Emporium. Our outlay in building an extensive godown, etc. ... will amount to about 20,000 dollars, so I am not disinterested in advocating its retention. Many prefer Cowloon Peninsula, but we ought to have both.

The acquisition of Kowloon had to wait until the Treaty of Tientsin in 1858 after the Second Opium War. Meanwhile Matheson's anxiety about the future of Hong Kong was partly relieved. Sir Henry Pottinger might have been expected to dislike the 'pet child' of his disgraced and unpopular predecessor. On the contrary, he was from the start an enthusiast for Hong Kong. On his voyage from Bombay to Macao he was accompanied by James Matheson's nephew, Alexander, who had gone back from China to Britain in 1840 to get married and had tragically lost his wife only a few months later. They landed on 9 August 1841, and Alexander at once offered Pottinger the hospitality of his uncle's grand house close to the shore where General Gough, who commanded the army in the war, was also staying. James gave a dinner to introduce Pottinger to 'the commercial community on all of whom he has made a favourable impression', so James wrote to William Jardine.[4]

Whether convinced by the arguments of the Mathesons and other merchants of Macao or determined on his own account, Pottinger proceeded to Hong Kong with a clear plan. Hong Kong was an asset both as a naval base and a mart; it should not be abandoned.

When he landed Pottinger found that there was already a shanty town at what became Victoria, consisting of a higgledy-piggledy assemblage of bamboo huts and mat sheds. The first land sales were made in June 1841 at Macao, some five months after the Union Jack had been hoisted at Possession Point. The Emperor's repudiation of the Chuenpi Convention was known, but not Palmerston's parallel action which was a much more serious affair. Always quick off the mark Matheson had erected his mat shed godown only a month after the flag had been hoisted and well ahead of the official land sales. It was situated on the centre of the northern coast near the present site of Flagstaff House, and was soon rebuilt in stone, the first solid building on the island. At the land sales, Captain Morgan, Jardine Matheson's agent, bought the three lots on which the new godown stood, together with a substantial area at East Point (in early days called Matheson's Point). The central lots were on land surrounded by the military and in 1843 the Government decided to requisition them in exchange for cash compensation and first choice of lots elsewhere. Morgan wrote: 'The Point is best for our purposes altogether. I have no doubt we can sell our other godowns to the Government for at least 100 per cent profit.'[5] The Firm chose two lots in West Point, meanwhile developing East Point as quickly as they could, having decided to make it their headquarters, rather than Macao or Canton.

Although Pottinger strongly supported the annexation of Hong Kong, it was by no means certain during the year and a half following the hoisting of the flag that the British Government would agree. James Matheson had good reason to write as he did to Jardine in August 1841.[6] The Foreign Secretary, Lord Aberdeen, regarded the acquisition of any Chinese territory with misgiving, because of 'the certain expense, the nature of our Relations with that Strange Empire, and the probable embarrassment it would create with other Powers.'[7] Stanley at the Colonial Office was equally reluctant but feared that they might have to give way over Hong Kong – 'all classes, Military, Civil and Mercantile, are conspiring to force us into its adoption'.[8] Both were writing in October 1842 before the news of the Treaty of Nanking had arrived. Earlier in the year Aberdeen had ordered all building operations, except purely temporary ones, to be stopped. These orders sent at the end of January did not reach Pottinger until April. He decided to ignore them. He was the man on the spot and he was backed by Ellenborough, Governor-General of India. When in August he sent the terms of the Treaty of Nanking to Aberdeen, he frankly admitted that the retention of Hong Kong was 'the only single point on which I intentionally exceeded my modified instructions'. And he justified it as giving 'an Emporium for our trade and a place from which Her Majesty's subjects in China may be alike protected and controlled'.[9] Aberdeen made no comment in reply. Pottinger had got away with it, as pushy proconsuls in the Victorian era so often did. Silence meant consent, and Hong Kong was now a British colony. To ascribe this outcome solely to William Jardine and James Matheson would be absurd. Many other people were involved, above all the Superintendant of Trade and first Governor; and many other pressures were exerted in Whitehall and Westminster. Nevertheless, the merchant firms which had operated from Macao and Canton did play a major part in the series of events which led to the acquisition of one of

Britain's strangest and most exotic imperial possessions. Among those firms the most powerful, wealthy, enterprising and influential was undoubtedly Jardine Matheson & Co.

The Firm does not seem to have entertained any serious doubts about the future status of Hong Kong. Like the other representatives of the Western mercantile interest, its agents rapidly settled in. Major-General Lord Saltoun[10], who succeeded his commander-in-chief, Sir Hugh Gough, after the Treaty of Nanking, wrote a vivid account of early British life on the island, in the autumn of 1842. After observing that he had been told that in September the previous year there were only four houses, he went on: 'and now they have a street nearly a mile and a half long, most of the houses finished and inhabited, good shops of every kind, a bazaar and a covered market place'. He was renting a house from Jardine Matheson.

> I am going to the upper end of the bay to call on Mr Morgan who manages for the great house of Jardine and Company and acts as my landlord. He lives at the upper end of the anchorage in a sort of palace he has there ...
>
> This house of Jardine, they say, has made an immense fortune since the war began by smuggling this poison [opium] into China ... As they receive payment in money only they run very little risk and are supposed to have realised a very large fortune. They have their vessels, beautiful sailing ones called clippers, in all directions.[11]

Life was not uncomfortable. There was plenty of wine when he dined with Sir Henry Pottinger. They had roast turkey, a present from the Morgans imported from Manila and fattened in Hong Kong. There was also a sheep club to which people subscribed for the import of sheep from Bengal and Sydney. 'We graze them here on the hill and feed them with grain which makes them very fat and good.'

In March 1844, Jardines' headquarters office was moved from Macao to the 'palace' at East Point. Alexander Matheson wrote:

> ... We are now fairly settled here and I think we shall in a short time find it fully as comfortable and far more convenient for business as Macao. We have our shipping almost within hail of our office, so that not a moment is lost in despatching vessels either for the coast or to Whampoa, and the commanders have no excuse whatever for being absent from their ships at

night. As yet very few Chinese merchants have settled here, but there is little doubt that they will do so in time.[12]

The Firm's principle office was to remain in Hong Kong from that day to this. Before considering what happened next we should return briefly to the two founders.

Neither William Jardine nor James Matheson saw China again. Jardine, after he had briefed Palmerston in the autumn of 1839, was given a grand public dinner by the London East India merchants among whom he was widely respected. Magniac, Smith gave him an office in 3 Lombard Street. In 1841 he bought out the Smith interest and the firm became Magniac Jardine. Under another change of name, Matheson & Co., it operates from the same address today, continuing to do the London business of the Hong Kong firm. Jardine bought an estate in Scotland, at Lanrick in Perthshire. He would have preferred Castlemilk in Dumfriesshire, which was close to his birthplace, but the Perth property seemed a better bargain. When in London, he lived in a house in the fashionable area of Upper Belgrave Street. He joined the Oriental Club and busied himself much with discussion of affairs in China.

On 6 February 1841, he was elected to Brooks's, one of the two oldest and most prestigious clubs in London.[13] He was proposed by E.J. Stanley, Chief Whip of the Whigs and later Lord Stanley of Alderley, and seconded by Edward Ellice, another Scot and a prominent Whig politician. Jardine had long cherished the idea of a parliamentary career when he retired, partly for its own sake and partly for the help it might be to the Firm to have a spokesman for the China trade in the House of Commons. He obtained the Whig nomination for the borough of Ashburton in the general election of July 1841. This Devon town depended partly on the manufacture and exports of woollens to China – always a precarious trade, and hit especially hard by the current commercial crisis in Canton. In their Cantonese days the Dents had enjoyed ridiculing Jardine's ambitions. But he had the last laugh. The Tory candidate, an associate of the Dents, realizing that he had no hope, ran out at the last moment and Jardine was returned unopposed. With rare exceptions the China interest favoured free trade. The Tories, who had won the election, were dead against it. Sir Robert

Peel's conversion was yet to come. By no means all Whigs were free traders, but all free traders were Whigs, or Radicals, who voted on the Whig side. Jardine was an emphatic opponent of tariffs and restrictions on commerce.

Unhappily it was to be the last laugh for him in another sense. He had little time in which to enjoy his position as MP and Scottish landowner. He died on 27 February 1843, in his 59th year after a long and painful illness, at his house in London. He was buried at Lochmaben where he had been born. It was a sad ending to a remarkable career.

Fate was kinder to James Matheson. For reasons of health and a desire to enjoy his immense fortune, he followed Jardine back to Britain late in 1842. Like his partner he had parliamentary ambitions. The vacancy at Ashburton created by Jardine's death provided the obvious opportunity. On 1 March 1843, as he put it in his election address, a 'unanimous resolution passed at a Crowded and Influential Meeting of the Electors of this Borough emboldens me to announce myself as a Candidate for your suffrages at the approaching Election'. In the address printed next day, he wrote:

> I present myself to you as the friend and former partner of your late lamented Member, Mr JARDINE – my Political opinions are favourable to every measure of practicable and progressive Reform, and I profess myself the zealous and ardent friend of Civil, Religious, and Commercial Freedom.
>
> My Mercantile Connexions will, I trust, enable me to promote the Prosperity of THE STABLE TRADE OF YOUR TOWN. ...
>
> It is my intention to pay my Personal Respects to every Elector previously to the day Election, which is fixed for Tuesday, the 7th Instant.[14]

He was duly elected and sat until the General Election of 1847 when he transferred to Ross and Cromarty – a more appropriate seat for a Scottish landowner, as he had been since 1844 when he bought the Hebridean island of Lewis for over half a million pounds. He sat for Ross and Cromarty until 1862. Meanwhile he had been made a baronet in 1851 for his services to the relief of famine on the island.[15] He married but had no children. When he died in Mentone at the age of 82 in 1878, the baronetcy became extinct.[16]

The control of the Firm now devolved, as was intended, upon the nephews of the two founders. The immediate successor to James Matheson was his nephew Alexander. But although there were other Matheson nephews, he was destined to be the last of the family to be a partner. For the time being his cousin, Donald Matheson, was in charge of affairs in Hong Kong, and William Jardine's nephew, David, played the same part in Canton, while Alexander, based most of the while on Macao, had overall control. He was a somewhat testy figure. Alan Reid quotes an indignant letter from him to Donald in 1844, denouncing Pottinger's successor, Sir John Davis, for naming the streets in Victoria after friends who had never been to China, or even out of England:

> ... and not even a lane has been called after a merchant, tho' the merchants have been the makers of the place. Just fancy 'Shelley Street' named after a swindler, etc., etc. How much more natural Jardine Street, Dent Street, Gibb Street, etc. would have sounded. No! the devil of a dollar shall I lay out in Hong Kong except for the sake of a profitable investment.[17]

But irritability can be forgiven in a man who had lost his wife tragically young, felt alone in the world and suffered from frequent bouts of ill-health. He left China in 1847 and although he retained his position as senior partner until 1852 he did not return.

His arrival in London coincided with a major financial crisis caused by over-investment in railways, foreign as well as British, and violent fluctuations in the price of wheat. Alexander investigated the finances of Magniac, Jardine. He decided that the past investment policy of John Abel Smith had put the Firm's whole position at risk and that it could not cope with the calls likely to be made on it without a major injection of capital. The threat of bankruptcy was averted by financial support from Alexander himself, his uncle James, and Andrew Jardine, nephew of William – and David's elder brother – who had inherited a large legacy from his uncle. Between them they salvaged and reconstructed the business which now became Matheson & Co. in 1848 under the management of Hugh Matheson, another of James's nephews and younger brother of Donald. He was only 27 and was destined to have a highly successful business career, achieving among other things the foundation in 1873 of the Rio Tinto Company.

Hugh and Donald were sons of James Matheson's brother Duncan who was an advocate at the Scottish bar and deputy sheriff of Edinburgh. The family background was devoutly Evangelical. When Hugh embarked on his career as an apprentice in the mercantile firm of James Ewing & Co. of Glasgow, his father wished him success adding, 'You know, however, that this blessing is only to be attained by constant and regular supplication to the throne of grace'.[18] Hugh was a devoted and pious Christian all his life. In 1843 he was offered by his rich uncle James an opening in Jardine Matheson, but the opium aspect stuck in his throat – the trade was becoming much criticized in Britain – and he refused, although he fully understood that it was sure to lead to 'a great position and a large fortune'.[19]

His views may have influenced his elder brother who developed increasing doubts about the morality of the commerce which he supervised in Hong Kong where the opium aspect was more blatant than almost anywhere else. Hugh made an extended visit to China in 1845–6, and no doubt the subject was much discussed. Donald decided in 1848 that his conscience forbade him to remain as a partner. Alexander from London crossly warned him that this meant the end to any financial interest in the Firm, but he was not deterred. He returned to England and eventually inherited his uncle James's Scottish estates. In 1892 he became Chairman of the Executive Committee for the Suppression of the Opium Trade.[20] He died in 1901.

Donald's resignation and Alexander's retirement effectively ended the family connection with Jardine Matheson & Co., but the Mathesons continued to be highly active in the allied but separate firm of Matheson & Co. at 3 Lombard Street. Alexander in 1851 bought extensive estates in Ross for £773,000. These included Lochalsh and Attadale which had been in the family from the twelfth century until they were forfeited after the execution of the clan chief following an unsuccessful rebellion in 1427. In 1854 he remarried – this time very much into the aristocracy, his wife being a sister of the 8th Lord Beaumont. He sat as Member for Inverness Boroughs from 1847–68 and at the General Election of that year succeeded his uncle James for Ross and Cromarty until 1884. He was made a baronet in 1882 by Gladstone. The title is still extant. He died in 1886; his latter years were clouded by financial worries and he was obliged to sell much of his land although he held on to Lochalsh and Attadale.

The future of Jardine Matheson lay with the collateral descendants of William Jardine. He had four nephews by his elder brother David to whom he always felt a deep debt of gratitude for the help given during his years as an aspirant medico. He certainly repaid it handsomely. The eldest nephew Andrew (1812–89) left China in 1843 and became a partner in Magniac, Jardine and from 1848 in Matheson & Co. True to family form he bought a Scottish estate – Corrie in Annandale, Lanark. The next brother David, taipan in 1852 after Alexander Matheson's retirement, died young but rich at the age of 38 in 1856. Joseph, the third brother, was a partner, although not taipan, from 1845 to 1860. In 1854 he bought the estate of Castlemilk near Lockerbie in Dumfriesshire, which his uncle had coveted. He died in 1861. None of the three older brothers married, and in due course the entire interest in Jardine Matheson, together with great landed estates in the Lowlands of Scotland, passed to Robert, the youngest nephew who was born in 1825 and lived until 1905.

These were not the only nephews. The oldest of all was Andrew Johnstone (1798–1857), son of William's sister Jean. Like his uncle he became a ship's doctor on the China run. He began to trade on his own account in 1824. He was briefly a partner in Jardine Matheson in 1835–6. By then he was rich enough to retire and purchase the estate of Halleaths near the town of Dumfries. He was keen on sport and racing. In 1841 he won the Goodwood Cup with Charles XII for which he paid the very large sum for those days of 3000 guineas. He was described as much attached to horses and women, but he never married. His younger brother John, however, did, and numerous Johnstone descendants played their part in the Firm or its associates. So did the descendants of his sister, Margaret. She married into the Keswick family whose heirs now control Jardine Matheson.

The list of nephews is still not exhausted. There were the two sons of William Jardine's second sister Margaret. They were confusingly surnamed Jardine, because she had married into an entirely separate branch of the family, the Jardines of Balgray. David, the elder brother (1819–53), known as 'the other David' to distinguish him from his cousin, who became taipan, founded the firm of Jardine, Skinner in Calcutta. His younger brother Robert (1822–73) was a partner and so was their cousin John Johnstone. The firm was quite independent but, along with Jejeebhoy & Co. and Remington & Co., both of Bombay, it was one of the three most important Indian 'correspondents' of Jardine Matheson and it played a vital part in the development of the opium trade and other activities during the nineteenth century.

NINE

The Second Opium War

From 1842 onwards Hong Kong rapidly developed into a major entrepôt. The next three decades saw a great increase in the opium trade in which Jardines continued to have the lion's share. Opium, as we saw, found no mention in the Treaty of Nanking. The omission was not accidental. The Emperor, whose decision to enforce his own decrees against 'the drug' had indirectly led to the war, could not afford the loss of face which he would suffer, if, as the British emissaries suggested, he legalized the trade. The British Government could hardly insist. After all, whatever the reality behind the war, it was outwardly a campaign to obtain general free trade, the 'open door' and the safety and security of British subjects, not to promote the sales of opium. But if Whitehall was not in a position to force the Chinese authorities to legalize the sale of opium, there was no intention whatever to discourage the British and Indian end of the operation, or to make British merchants comply with Chinese law. It would remain as it always had been – a contraband trade in which men of enterprise participated at their own risk.

The opinion of the partners in Jardines about legalization seems to have been fluid. In the autumn of 1842 Alexander Matheson was against it. But in July 1843 he was for it, although without hope of any step being taken in the Emperor's lifetime.[1] He believed it would lower delivery costs and 'dampen the speculative excitement which was attracting many small dealers to Hong Kong'.[2] By the end of 1843 he had changed his mind yet again. He still believed that legalization

would lower delivery costs, but he was not so sure that this would necessarily benefit Jardines, given its already commanding position. It
might increase competition. The Firm was all for competition when it
had been trying to break the East India Company's monopoly ten years
earlier. It was less keen if it threatened its own. The Firm did not want
to see 'men of small capital' arriving, who had hitherto been put off by
the heavy expenses of a contraband trade which only well-capitalized
concerns, like Jardines and Dent could afford. Then there was the possibility that if the trade was made legal, a condition might be its
centralization on Hong Kong, thus depriving the two big firms of their
profitable duopoly of the coastal trade. So there was a distinct sense of
relief when the Imperial Commissioner Ch'i-ying during the negotiations for a supplementary treaty in 1843 refused even to consider
legalizing the opium trade, because the Emperor would never agree.[3]

Opium remained one crucially important side of the triangular trade
which financed the British import of tea and provided a large proportion of the revenues of both the Indian and British Governments. In
1844, the import of Bengal opium was reckoned at 22,000 chests, Patna
opium at 26,000.[4] In 1850, Patna alone amounted to 29,500. Five years
later Patna had reached a high point of 48,380.[5] Full and exact statistics
are not easy to ascertain, but all authorities agree that opium was for
many years to come by far the most important item in the Chinese
import trade.

The period also saw the heyday of the opium clipper. These superbly
equipped and elegant vessels were the apotheosis of merchant sailing
craft before the advent of steam. They must have been a wonderful
spectacle. Their crews, paid at double the rate of other merchant
marine officers and seamen, were highly capable and took immense
pride in their ships and in themselves. The sails were immaculate, the
decks were scrubbed white and clean, the brass fittings and cannons
gleamed in the sunlight. The latter were not there merely for show. The
opium clippers were heavily armed to cope with pirates and other
potential predators. Sailing in the China seas remained for many years
a hazardous business. There was the risk of terrifying typhoons. Piracy,
based on intelligence communicated from the Hong Kong Chinese
underworld through the crews of junks anchored off-shore, was a

perpetual threat. Charts were few and far between and so inaccurate that it was a moot point for the captain whether he was better off with one than without.

The task of the opium clippers before 1842 was to anchor by the receiving ships off Lintin and transfer their cargoes, which would then be picked up by Chinese junks and landed as contraband at various suitable places along the China coast. The clippers did not on the whole trade directly with the coast, though there were exceptions. After the cession of Hong Kong, East Point took the place of Lintin, and an old Indian 'Country ship', *Hormanjee Bormanjee*, stowed the opium and the bullion received in payment. The next stage in the operation was to get the opium (or other goods) to the Chinese dealers. This was done by transferring the goods from the East Point receiving ship to the opium clippers, which would then deliver 'the drug' to receiving ships stationed near, but not actually inside, the five Treaty Ports. This procedure was adopted in deference to successive proclamations against smuggling issued by governors of Hong Kong from Sir Henry Pottinger onwards. The wording of these was designed to placate opinion at home and also to smooth diplomatic relations with the Imperial Court. An ironical episode involving Jardine Matheson shows the unreality behind the proclamations.[6] One of its schooners, the *Vixen*, set sail from Chusan in April 1843. Captain Hope RN who was the commanding officer on the island, believed the ship to be heading for Shanghai laden with opium, although Shanghai had not yet been officially opened to foreign shipping, and opium would have been contraband even if it had. He tried to intercept the schooner but failed. He did, however, chase four other British ships out of the mouth of the Yangtse. An uproar ensued among the Western traders in Macao and Hong Kong at unwarranted interference with the delivery of opium. Meanwhile the *Vixen* returned to Hong Kong without having gone near to Shanghai, and an official enquiry was unable to prove that she had been carrying opium. Pottinger was able to reprimand Hope for *trop de zèle* without seeming to connive at illegality. Moreover, Hope was not only reprimanded but in June abruptly recalled to Singapore from Hong Kong after delivering a vigorous defence of his conduct. The moral of all this was not lost on those most closely concerned.

Whatever the letter of the law, the navy would be ill-advised to take the edicts of the governor too literally. Rigid enforcement of the rules against opium smuggling was not the path to promotion.

The Firm also drew a moral from the episode, and that was the need for discretion. James Matheson wrote from Britain in 1843 to the commander of his opium fleet, Captain McMinnies, adjuring him not to boast about his 'victory' over the navy and

> ... to make every effort ... to please the mandarins, such as moving from one anchorage to another when they require it, and not approaching too near their towns. The opium trade is now so very unpopular in England that we cannot be too cautious in keeping it as quiet and as much out of the public eye as possible.[7]

Matheson, fresh from a by-election campaign and entry into Parliament, was better placed to gauge English opinion than any of his compatriots on the China coast. He was quite right. The trade in a commodity, described as long ago as 1783 by Warren Hastings as 'a pernicious article of luxury', was indeed unpopular. Gladstone's speech in the vote of censure on Palmerston in February 1840 has already been quoted. Matheson may have been present in the House of Commons in 1843, when Lord Ashley (later Earl of Shaftesbury) moved a resolution declaring that the opium trade 'was utterly inconsistent with the honour and duty of a Christian Kingdom'. Matheson need not have worried. Lord Ashley succeeded in many of the idealistic causes which he took up in a long life of reforming zeal, but this was not to be one of them.

The Indian Government, relying for a sixth of its revenues on opium duties, was not going to stop production of the drug in a hurry. Nor was the British Government, receiving a similar proportion of its income from duties on tea, keen to suppress the opium trade upon which the import of tea depended. There was far more money at stake – government money moreover – than in reforming the conditions under which children worked in mines, factories or chimneys. And it was not the British who were being corrupted and demoralized but the far-off subjects of what Lord Aberdeen had called 'that Strange Empire'.

The opium trade now entered a period of regular routine after 1846. Jardines and Dent possessed a duopoly which effectively controlled prices. In general the two firms were anything but friendly. Nevertheless, since the 1830s they had allowed a certain amount of sporadic co-operation between their captains at the coastal stations. It is true that if a captain found himself with too much opium on his hands he was often inclined to undersell his rival, and indignant letters would flow freely. But it paid Jardines and Dent, however much they disliked each other, to combine against smaller firms trying to horn in on the trade. Their ships would anchor near an interloper, undercut his prices even at the cost of temporary loss, and effectively drive him away. The two great firms also had the asset of long experience, knew the Chinese dealers well and were trusted by them. They could prevent most dealers from negotiating with anyone but themselves, and they dominated the trade until 1850. In that year, however, an important change began to have effect. The Peninsula and Oriental Steamship Company extended its services to the China coast, and, although the opium clippers of the two firms continued to operate successfully for several more years, their duopoly no longer prevailed.

It was clear that Shanghai would be much the most important of the Treaty Ports, and Jardine Matheson was as quick as any other company to install itself there. The city had a long history as a place of trade and shipping, which dated back to the thirteenth century. It had been a safe harbour for many years. It was well placed to communicate with the canals and waterways spreading inland from the Yangtse estuary to which it was linked by a tributary river. By sea it was easily accessible from Canton, Tientsin and Yokohama – a centre of trade and distribution for most of East Asia. Shanghai was close to the most fertile food-producing area of China – the rice fields of the Yangtse delta which supplied the capital via the Grand Canal. It was a measure of the total defeat of the Ch'ing regime that it was forced to concede extraterritorial rights to foreigners in this of all cities, destined to become the metropolis of China.

Shanghai was not only unique among the Treaty Ports for its wealth and its fertile hinterland. It was also unique in respect of the legal and institutional status of its European residents. In the other ports the

form was for the European consuls to secure leases for their governments from the Ch'ing regime. These could then be leased by the
consuls acting for their own governments to their own nationals. In
Shanghai, however, foreigners were allowed to negotiate perpetual
leases directly with Chinese landlords. Such leases had to be reported
through the relevant consul to the *taotai* (administrator of Shanghai)[8]
who would then make a direct grant of land title. Although the British,
Americans and French had at first claimed separate areas, the British,
being devotees of free trade, had no objection to citizens and consuls of
other countries residing in the 138 acres of their own area. The effect of
this mélange of lessees was to lead over the years to the unique phenomenon of an 'international municipality' jointly administered by the
relevant consuls. The International Settlement, as it came to be called,
had no other parallel in the other Treaty Ports, where each consul
administered his own area separately. It was an eccentric, essentially
British anomaly, but that did not stop it working remarkably well until
it was relinquished in 1943 as a response to the rising pressure of
Chinese nationalism to which it naturally seemed an affront.

On 17 November 1843 the port was officially declared open to trade
under the Treaty of Nanking. The British Consul was Captain (later
General Sir George) Balfour. Before the end of the year seven ships had
arrived, the largest being, naturally, Jardines' *Eliza Stewart*. It is equally
natural to learn that Alexander Dallas, Jardines' first representative in
Shanghai, bought as his headquarters Lot No. l on the waterfront next
to the British consulate. He was one of only 25 people listed as British
subjects in Shanghai in December 1843. He was a Matheson nominee
and a man of energy and perseverance, one of the first partners not to
be related to the founders of the Firm. It was a tough assignment at the
start. He had to work at first in the insalubrious confines of the old
Chinese walled city, where he lacked banking facilities, wharves, drinking water and even ink.[9] He did not get on well with his consular
compatriot. Relations between merchants and officials in the Treaty
Ports were often uneasy. The traders expected the consuls to give positive help. But the consuls, often army men – there was no regular
consular service – tended to look down on commerce, dislike the
opium traffic and regard their chief duty as the enforcement of the

Treaties, which indeed it was under their instructions. They did not feel inclined to bend the rules for businessmen. Despite these difficulties, trade in Shanghai roared ahead and Jardines with it. There were two important advantages over anywhere else on the China coast, in addition to the economic and geographical assets mentioned earlier. Both stemmed from the deterioration of Anglo-Chinese relations in Canton. There, trade was becoming less and less easy during the 1840s. This in itself drove business away to the second largest entrepôt where there was none of the history of conflict and violence which had been such a feature of the intercourse between the Chinese and the Barbarians up and down the Pearl River and its tributaries. A second advantage arising partly from the first was the increasing number of Cantonese merchants, bankers and compradors migrating to Shanghai. It cannot be over-emphasized how dependent Jardines and all the European firms were upon Chinese intermediaries to cope with the problems of language, law and custom in this alien culture. From long experience the Cantonese Hongs knew the form and were able to oil the wheels in Shanghai, making great fortunes for themselves in the process.

Canton was itself a Treaty Port, the biggest of all. In theory the snags which beset European trade before the Opium War should have disappeared. In practice they did not. The provisions of the Treaty of Nanking were simply disregarded. Canton was like nowhere else in China. Its mandarins were more corrupt, its merchants more wily, its populace more xenophobic and its location further from the capital than any other major city. The Chinese have always hated foreigners. The peculiarity of Canton was that there were far more foreigners to hate. The authorities were terrified that concessions to Europeans would provoke riots and violence which in their turn would provoke armed intervention from abroad with disastrous results.

The foreign residents in Canton remained confined to the Thirteen Factories area on the north bank of the river. Attempts to lease or buy houses elsewhere, although quite legitimate under the treaty, were frustrated by various procrastinatory devices. In all the other Treaty Ports the Consul resided in the city. In Canton this was forbidden. The entry of foreigners had become a symbolic issue. They were allowed to go only into the hinterland to walk in the countryside and shoot wildfowl.

But this was a mixed blessing. There were liable to be acrimonious encounters with the local inhabitants, to which British arrogance and Cantonese hostility alike contributed. A series of riots, beatings and brawls culminated in early March 1847 with an 'incident' when six Englishmen, who for once had done nothing provocative, were stoned on an excursion to Fatshan, fifteen miles out of the city. The Governor of Hong Kong, Sir John Davis, who was regarded by the merchants with contempt as an appeaser, decided that the time had come for action. Early in April he sent a punitive expedition to spike the guns on the Bogue – all 827 of them and to occupy the factories area. Despite these achievements the most he could get out of the Imperial Commissioner Ch'i-ying was a promise to implement the Treaty of Nanking and open the city gates in two years' time. When in 1849 the new Governor of Hong Kong duly demanded entrance, Ch'i-ying's successor, Hsu, refused point-blank and proceeded to raise a defensive militia. Clearly, armed force was the only way of persuading Canton to abide by the treaty, but in 1849 Palmerston was not ready to use it. Jardines found itself conducting trade much as it had all along, and the other Canton merchants were in the same boat; but at least there was now no danger of a clampdown on 'the drug' which was being sold in ever increasing quantity. But the Chinese authorities in Peking remained adamant that negotiations, not only in Canton but in all the Treaty Ports, must be conducted through the Imperial Commissioner in Canton.

In 1850, there began one of the most cataclysmic episodes in Chinese history. The Taiping Rebellion, or revolution, started in the province of Kuangsi. The leaders of a Hakka-based group known as 'the God-Worshippers' under the influence of a half-mad fanatic, Hung Hsiu-ch'uan, proclaimed the heavenly Kingdom of Great Peace (Tai-p'ingt'ien-kuo). He declared that he was the younger brother of Jesus Christ and preached a creed of extreme evangelical and puritanic Christianity combined with a mission to overthrow the Manchu empire. Like many previous messianic and millenarian movements, it stemmed from economic disruption, partly a product of the Opium War, from racial antagonism – the Hakka were an alien expatriate ethnic group – and from the chronic Chinese curse of population pressing upon the means of subsistence.

The Taipings set out on an extraordinary crusade which carried them from Kuangsi into the rich Chinese heartland of the Yangtse tributary network. Sacking and abandoning city after city, they captured in March 1853 the old capital of Nanking and set up a Utopian communistic regime which forbade alcohol, opium, tobacco and sex (even between husband and wife) on pain of death. The last prohibition, never observed by the leaders, was soon relaxed. The élite rulers lived in luxury, enjoying harems, fine clothes and high cuisine. The Taiping regime was neither the first nor last egalitarian experiment in which some people soon became much more equal than others. The rebels made a thrust for Peking, but it was a half-hearted effort and petered out at Tientsin. Had they put their full weight behind it, they might well have overthrown the Ch'ing dynasty and established a new empire. In the event they were content to consolidate their position in the Yangtse valley. They reached the apogee of their power in 1856, controlling all the strategic cities along the river from Chinkiang in the east to Wuchang in the west, and dominating the provinces of Kiangsi, Hupeh, Anhwei and Kiangsu. In June they inflicted a crushing defeat on the Imperial forces outside the walls of Nanking.

The little colony of merchants in Shanghai did not at first feel threatened, but rumours of war caused Jardines' taipan, Alexander Dallas, to recommend defensive measures at a public meeting on 12 April 1853. It was decided to mark the boundaries of the International Settlement with a broad ditch connecting the Soochow Creek in the north with the Yan-king-pang in the south. It became known as Defence Creek. The Taipings were not a threat for the moment, but an indirect consequence of their rebellion was to stimulate other revolutionary movements which took advantage of the prevailing anarchy. One of these, the 'Small Swords', a branch of the Triad Society, seized the old Chinese walled city in September and was not dislodged by the Imperial troops for seventeen months. These events and the capture of Nanking caused the settlers to form first, the British Volunteer Company, equipped at their own expense, which merged later with other foreign residents to create the Shanghai Volunteer Corps, described as 'probably the first truly international force in the world'.[10] Its earliest engagement, oddly enough, was against neither the Small

Swords nor the Taipings, but the Imperial forces which were out of control and behaved outrageously. Hence in April 1854, in the 'Battle of Muddy Flat', a tiny contingent of Europeans and Americans defeated a force of 10,000 Chinese and sent them packing. It was a lesson not lost; Chinese troops never again assaulted the Settlement's perimeter.

Meanwhile the situation in Canton remained highly unsatisfactory from the point of view of the American and European traders. Their British supporters were keen for drastic action, but the dismissal of Palmerston in 1851 from the Foreign Office deprived them of their most powerful ally. Matters drifted for the next five years. Then the scene suddenly changed. A plausible *casus belli*, the seizure on 8 October 1856 by the Chinese authorities of the *Arrow*, a *lorcha* (a vessel with foreign hull and Chinese rig), flying the British flag and anchored in the river at Canton, was exactly what was needed. It is true that the *Arrow* had a dubious claim to fly the flag and the action by the Chinese authorities in pulling it down (if they did – another point of dispute) was not nec-essarily illegal. Moreover, Commissioner Yeh, the effective ruler of Canton, had a case for believing that the *Arrow*'s all-Chinese crew included three notorious pirates – a class of persons whom, with every sanction of Chinese law, he had been strangling or decapitating by hundreds ever since he took office. But the 'insult to the flag' was too good a chance to miss. Harry Parkes, Consul in Canton and nephew of the Rev. Karl Gutzlaff's wife, was a blue-eyed blond and frail-looking young man of 28, but a tough operator as far as China was concerned. He spoke the language fluently and believed that one should never concede any point of phrase, form or ceremony, however trivial it seemed in European eyes, when dealing with the mandarins who 'had been trained to believe that details of form were a clue to the reality of power'.[11]

Parkes urged his immediate superior, Sir John Bowring, Governor of Hong Kong, to demand an apology and the return of all the crew of the *Arrow*, not simply the nine non-pirates. Bowring, a Benthamite radical in whose arms the great man had died, entirely agreed. There were rad-icals then, as still exist today, who excuse every sort of corrupt tyrannical regime in Asia, Africa and elsewhere on grounds of hardship, poverty and lack of political or constitutional tradition. Bowring would have none of that. To him the Chinese Empire was a worthless, degenerate and obscurantist tyranny. He shared the view of most of those on the Western side who were concerned at all, especially the merchants in Hong Kong, Canton and Shanghai, that trade would never flourish properly while the Emperor refused to receive envoys in Peking and insisted that all communications should be petitions to Commissioner Yeh in Canton, described succinctly by Douglas Hurd as 'a fat, sour, intelligent man with a taste for astrology'.[12]

The case for the Western traders was vociferously pressed in Britain, and eighteen months earlier by a happy chance for them the alliance of Parkes and Bowring had been reinforced by the most powerful supporter they could have hoped for. The whirligig of politics which had removed Palmerston in December 1851 from the Foreign Office brought him back as Home Secretary a year later, but he could not interfere much in foreign affairs, even then. There was another whirligig and he became Prime Minister in February 1855 at the age of 70. Bowring and Parkes could now rely on support at the highest level. The China merchants were moreover an important influence in the political world of London. Twenty or more MPs of different political persuasion were on their side. This mattered much in a period of hung parliaments, close votes and weak party discipline.[12]

Bowring, strongly supported by Parkes, decided not only to demand reparation for insult to the flag but to reopen the whole question of the Treaty of Nanking and to insist on the European right of entry into the walled city of Canton. This was contrary to his instructions which were to let sleeping dogs lie, but Bowring was not the man to be deterred by such considerations. 'Cannot we use the opportunity and carry the city question?' he wrote to Parkes, on 16 October. 'If so, I will come up with the whole fleet. I think we have now a stepping stone from which with good management we may move on to important sequences.'[14]

The history of what followed has been told many times. It is enough to say that Bowring got his way. The Commissioner's half-hearted apology was not accepted. Rear-Admiral Sir Michael Seymour took appropriate naval action and, accompanied by the American Consul who was drunk and waving the Stars and Stripes, led a body of marines into the bombarded city through Yeh's headquarters on 29 October. But what could one do next? To capture and hold the city required a major military, not merely naval, effort. There followed many months of desultry warfare. The Indian Mutiny swallowed up any forces which might have been used against Canton. Lord Elgin, son of the acquirer of the famous marbles and appointed as plenipotentiary to deal with the China question over the head of the now mistrusted Bowring, had to sit on the sidelines. He accepted this perilous office on 12 March 1857. Some days earlier, the Government had faced major battles in both Houses on votes of censure against their approval of Bowring's actions. They won by 36 votes in the Lords, but lost by sixteen in the Commons in the early hours of 4 March. They were defeated by a curious alliance of Tories and Radicals. Palmerston at once advised a dissolution of Parliament. Disraeli, the only prominent Conservative to have misgivings about the vote of censure, found his fears fully justified. Palmerston was returned with a much increased majority early in April 1857. He could claim a mandate for a tough line with China.

Meanwhile, life in Canton and Hong Kong had been anything but peaceful for Jardines, Dent, Russell and the other European and American traders. The naval intervention prompted Commissioner Yeh to burn down the 'factories' on 15 December 1856. The financial losses were immense. Of course Yeh denied responsibility, but there can be no doubt that he connived, even if he did not order the act. A fortnight later there was a mutiny by the Chinese crew of the small steamer *Thistle* on her way from Canton to Hong Kong. Eleven Europeans, who had the misfortune to be on board, were decapitated. The murderers bore the badges of Yeh's militia. By now all trade in Canton had ceased.

Trouble then spread to Hong Kong. The island was packed with smugglers, opium dealers, Taipings, Triads and a host of dubious characters. It had all the formal structure of a British colony, but the colonialists, few of whom could speak a word of Chinese, were ignorant of what was happening. Bowring became, after his first characteristic euphoria, uneasy about the dangers for a handful of Britons among some 80,000 Chinese. It was known that Yeh had close and sinister contacts with the fishermen in Kowloon. Arson and assault multiplied in the streets. On 15 January 1857 Bowring, his wife and family, along with leading members of the British community were smitten by arsenic poisoning traced to the bread they had eaten. Luckily the poisoner had overdone his act. He put in so much arsenic that the consumers vomited at once and soon recovered. The art of arsenic poisoning lies in administering small but increasing doses over a long period of time. Whether Yeh had instigated this attempt is obscure. He denied it, but few Westerners believed him. The baker who fled to Macao was apprehended and put on trial, but acquitted through lack of evidence that he had personally inserted the poison.

There was general agreement that nothing could be done about China while the Indian Mutiny was raging. Lord Elgin was himself responsible for a crucial decision to divert troops intended for Hong Kong to Calcutta instead. The question that vexed the British Government, the Governor of Hong Kong and the merchant community was where to make their attempt to 'open up' China, when there was the force to do so. The Government thought that a direct démarche should be made to the seat of Chinese authority in Peking, and instructed Lord Elgin accordingly. Local opinion held precisely the opposite view. The Cantonese believed their city to be impregnable. Only by shattering this delusion could the Westerners cajole the Imperial Court into the concessions needed to gain access to the market in China (whose potential was greatly exaggerated by almost everyone concerned). The merchants were trading successfully in all the other Treaty Ports. A démarche to Peking, almost certain to be rebuffed, could lead to a general war which would adversely affect the whole of the China trade. A brisk and conclusive action confined to Canton was safer, less expensive and less disruptive. Eighty-five Hong Kong Western merchants pressed this argument on Lord Elgin in a memorandum of 9 July 1857. They were headed, not surprisingly, by Jardines, and they were strongly supported by Bowring and Admiral Seymour.

Elgin gave way to their opinions. By the end of the year the threat to British rule in India had vanished, and an adequate force was available to capture Canton. It was a joint Anglo-French affair. A Catholic missionary, the Abbé Chapdelaine, had been murdered in Kuangsi early in

1856. It was alleged that his heart was cut from his body, cooked and eaten.[15] So the French Government too had an insult to avenge. An ultimatum was presented to Yeh: free admission of British subjects to Canton and compensation for damage, or else ... Yeh remained obdurate. The ultimatum expired on 26 December. Three days later the allied forces had conquered the invincible city. Yeh was taken prisoner and deported to Calcutta where he died after a year in the comfortable villa chosen as his residence. His second-in-command, Pih-Kuei, soon known as 'Pickwick', claimed to be an opponent of Yeh. He was installed as Governor acting upon the 'advice' of a tribunal of three allied officers. The trio was dominated by Parkes, the only fluent Chinese speaker, and effectively ruled Canton for the next three and a half years. The streets were policed, law and order were restored. Trade barriers were lifted.

The effect was soon seen in Jardines' profit and loss account. In 1856–7 the Firm made a profit of HK$1,430,000. The following year, during which the factories were burned and trade extinguished, the profit was only HK$61,000. In 1858–9, after the restrictions were lifted, profits jumped to HK$949,000.

This change was gratifying, but neither the merchants of Hong Kong nor the British Government believed that matters could be left as they were. Canton must be held until a new treaty could be negotiated to replace that of Nanking. The only way to do this was to send an expeditionary force to threaten Peking itself. Accordingly, an Anglo-French force sailed to the Gulf of Pechihli, bombarded on 20 May 1858 the forts at Taku which were intended to bar access to the Peiho River, and occupied Tientsin on the 26th. The result was apparent Imperial capitulation, and the Treaty of Tientsin which tripled the number of Treaty Ports, gave foreigners the right to travel inland, opened the Yangtse as far as Hankow (after the Taipings were defeated), and imposed indemnities of 16 million taels. The treaty also provided for tariff duties of five per cent plus a maximum of another two and a half per cent to cover the abolition of the innumerable and complicated internal transit levies. Finally it legalized the opium trade.

The treaty still needed effective confirmation. There was plenty of co-operation between the Chinese merchants and compradors in Canton and Shanghai, and the Westerners in both ports. They had a common interest which was far from being shared by the Emperor and his princely Manchu advisers in Peking. The court still refused the Western demand for representation in the capital and still insisted upon ambassadors coming as tribute envoys, who should be supplicants to a regime superior to any other on earth. Treaty ratification was expected in June 1859. Sir Frederick Bruce, Lord Elgin's brother and successor, was sent with a naval force to settle the matter, but received a major rebuff outside the now heavily reinforced Taku forts. He lost four gunboats, 89 men were killed and 345 wounded. This defeat could not be tolerated. Lord Elgin was recalled.

There had been a brief blip in British politics. Palmerston was ousted early in 1858 for being too conciliatory to France, but he was back again fifteen months later after winning his second general election in June 1859. The vicissitudes of British politics had little effect on events in China. Derby had bitterly opposed the capture of Canton, as had Lord John Russell and Gladstone. But Derby made no attempt to reverse the forward policy in China during his brief 1858–9 ministry. Palmerston's cabinet contained both Russell and Gladstone, but no change of course occurred. Events in such a distant place, where an exchange of correspondence took at least 22 weeks, acquired a momentum of their own. One should not under-estimate the pressure of the 'Chinese lobby'. In Hong Kong the Western merchants headed by their foremost firm, Jardines, were vociferous for a more vigorous policy. Elgin, a Scottish landed aristocrat, who had little love for self-made Scottish entrepreneurs, was by no means sympathetic to them. On 24 January 1858 he had written in his diary after the fall of Canton: 'I learn from Loch[16], who has just returned from Hong Kong, that the thirst for blood is not yet slaked among the meek Christians of that locality.'[17] He firmly repudiated the advice of an earlier Governor of Hong Kong to make Canton a heap of blazing ruins. 'No human power shall induce me to accept the office of oppressor of the feeble.'[18] Elgin and his masters in Whitehall were anxious to avoid China becoming a new India in the event of a complete collapse of the Manchu dynasty, while at the same time they were determined to bring it into the comity of nations and thus open up trade. Elgin was, however, more realistic than most about how much trade there really was to open up. He had disinterred a suppressed memorandum of 1852 in the Hong Kong archives by one Mitchell, a government servant who pointed out that it would be a slow business to expand exports to China, not because of restrictions, but because British textiles, on which the powerful cotton interest of Manchester pinned their faith, could not effectively compete with native industry. He also observed that the economies of northern and southern China were largely complementary and needed few imports, although they would always accept some in order to sell tea to Britain. In March 1858 Elgin pointed this out in a reply to an address of welcome by the merchants of Shanghai. It did not go down well, but it was more realistic than the dreams of the Western merchants. There were indeed to be trading opportunities, but they had to be worked for, and many firms fell by the wayside in the process. China was no Eldorado.

In 1860 Elgin's second expedition brought Imperial resistance to an end. There were atrocious actions on both sides. The Chinese authorities ambushed and kidnapped a party of allied envoys outside Peking. Of a party of 37, 22 were either beheaded or tortured to death. Parkes and Loch survived after 20 days in constant expectation of execution. In retaliation, which Elgin had decided must be spectacular for such abominable cruelty and treachery, the allies burned down the Emperor's Summer Palace, already looted by French and British troops. Thus what seems by all accounts to have been one of the wonders of the world, an assemblage of some 200 halls and pavilions of enchanting and delicate design in a park of 80 square miles (207km²), was systematically destroyed on 18 and 19 October 1860. Elgin was carried into Peking in a red sedan-chair escorted by 500 soldiers. He was received by Prince Kung, the Emperor's younger half-brother. A new Convention of Peking was signed, and the Treaty of Tientsin was at last ratified with the addition of British annexation of Kowloon.

As far as Jardines was concerned, the trading situation was now in the clear. Their main objectives had been achieved. The only threat that remained was the Taipings, whose capital, Nanking, was inconveniently close to Shanghai. Already great numbers of refugees had poured into the settlements. This process, with all its consequences of overcrowding, disease and insanitary practices, was enhanced in May 1860 when the rebels broke through the Imperialist cordon round Nanking and on 2 June captured Soochow, allegedly slaughtering over a million people. This seemed a direct threat to Shanghai. There was a tentative push by only 3000 men on 19 and 20 August, which was repulsed by Anglo-French forces, but the danger remained.

The Western powers, hitherto neutral or even slightly friendly towards the Taipings, began to change. The principle 'my enemy's enemy is my friend' no longer made sense after the Manchu capitulation of 1860. Even the missionaries, do-gooders and 'progressives', who then as now were always keen to support 'freedom fighters', began to have doubts about the Christian and libertarian ideals of the long-haired fanatics who had devastated great areas, starved and slaughtered millions with every accompaniment of horror – crucifixion, torture, mutilation and burial alive. A more important consideration was trade. The Taipings were against opium just when the demand rocketed in the early 1860s. Apart from that specific point, in order to flourish trade needs law and order. After the final ratification of the Treaty of Tientsin this seemed far more likely to prevail if the Ch'ing forces, who had a notable revival, defeated the rebels. Moreover, the Taipings were torn by furious feuds, vendettas, intrigues and heresy hunts, and were on the wane.

Wu Hsii, a Shanghai *taotai*, had pressed for Western intervention ever since the fall of Nanking in 1853. He was a typical example of the new alliance between Ch'ing bureaucracy and commerce. He was a business partner of the immensely wealthy Yang Fang (Takee), Shanghai comprador of Jardine Matheson in the 1850s. Partly at their instigation and with their financial support the Shanghai merchants in September 1861 clubbed together to pay for a private army of Chinese mercenaries officered and armed by Westerners with the object of warding off a renewed threat to Shanghai. This was named with optimism, which turned out to be largely justified, 'The Ever Victorious Army'. It was under the Imperial Government, for the British remained ostensibly neutral, but British officers could not have served nor British weapons been used if the Foreign Office had objected.

After the EVA's first commander, Frederick Ward, an American soldier-of-fortune, had been killed and another of that ilk, Henry Burgervine, had been ousted for drunkenness, the command fell to Major Charles Gordon, later to be of Khartoum fame. To the end of his days, after all the vicissitudes of his extraordinary career, he was still known as 'Chinese' Gordon. He had artillery and an armed flotilla with a fire power superior to anything in China. During 1862–4 city after city fell to his 3000 strong brigade. It was disbanded before the crowning victory of the Ch'ing regime, the fall of Nanking in 1864. This was the effective end of the Taiping Rebellion. It had been conducted with appalling brutality on both sides, no quarter given, no prisoners taken, men, women and children massacred. It is claimed that over 20 million perished – more than all the deaths in the First World War.

TEN

New Challenges

The Taiping Rebellion had less effect on the fortunes of Jardines than might have been expected. It was largely confined to the vast interior of China and impinged little upon the coastal ports, where the Firm's business was transacted. Its defeat was welcomed by all the Western firms as a restoration of order, but the events in Canton and the ratification of the Treaty of Tientsin were more important. So were developments in Shanghai, where Chinese and Western interdependence greatly increased in the 1850s. In 1854, the *taotai* of that city, a Cantonese, Wu Chien-Chang (Samqua), negotiated with the foreign consuls a new institution, a foreign inspectorate of customs. The Chinese bureaucracy hired Westerners to be Imperial civil servants. The object was to substitute for the hopeless corruption and incompetence of the Ch'ing officials a system with a far lower tariff, but one which was actually collected and paid into the Imperial treasury. It was a great success and was soon extended to the other Treaty Ports. In the words of the *Cambridge History of China* there was a 'common interest centred around the suppression of rebellion and the regulation of trade expansion, which would spell profit to foreign merchants, revenue to Chinese authorities and survival to the dynasty.'[1] It was a major factor in producing the revenue needed to crush the Taipings.

Jardines, along with its Western competitors, operated as far as China was concerned in a more favourable legal, political and economic climate than ever before. The 'drug' was no longer contraband. The increased number of Treaty Ports made trade easier and conferred the advantages of 'extraterritoriality' on an increased number of traders. But these changes did not necessarily mean a rise in profit for an individual business. There was keener competition, and the message, which Lord Elgin had tried to convey to unwilling ears in Shanghai in March 1858, was beginning to persuade the commercial community that China was not a country which offered the opportunity of huge and easy gains.

The profit account for Jardines reached its highest point between 1832 and 1887 in the financial year 1856–7 with profits of HK $1,430,000. In the quarter century after the ratification of the Treaty of Tientsin in 1860, the figures fluctuated from a high of HK $965,000 in 1861–2 to a loss of HK $33,000 in 1866–7, and HK $200,000 in 1868–9. These were the only two years when the Firm went into the red. The average profit between 1861–2 and 1871–2 was HK $297,000. Over the next fifteen years it was rather higher at HK $341,000. From 1886–7 the ledgers and journals are missing for the next 21 years. After that the profits became much larger, but the figures are probably not comparable, as Jardine Matheson in 1906 ceased to be a partnership in the old sense and became a limited liability company.

The twelve years which followed the Treaty of Tientsin, or rather its ratification at Peking in 1860, were an important transition period for Jardines. It was during those years that the Firm gradually moved out of the purchase and sale of commodities such as opium, cotton, tea and silk, on which its fortunes had hitherto been largely built. Instead it became more and more involved in dealings on commission, and in shipping, banking and insurance. This was not a change peculiar to Jardines. The other Western hongs were doing the same thing in varying degree. LeFevour quotes the senior partner in Russell & Co.,[2] the biggest of the American firms, writing in 1872: 'When the period of transition is over, no doubt, most of the larger firms with capital and credit will have transferred themselves from produce to industrial and commercial enterprise and will become in fact private bankers.' And in the same year a Jardines partner wrote from Shanghai to James Whittall, the taipan in Hong Kong: 'I believe legitimate development is towards a permanent revenue by commission accounts and the avoidance of large scale operations on our sole interest.'[3]

There were many reasons for the change. For one thing, commission and ancillary services were a good deal safer than sale and purchase of commodities, which involved speculative risks. These might be very profitable, but they might also be ruinous. Another reason was the greatly increased activity of Chinese merchants who had a knowledge of conditions in the interior markets which Westerners, even making use of their compradors, could hardly hope to rival. Moreover, Chinese merchants operated with much lower overheads, compared with the high commissions exacted by the compradors on foreign merchants. This was particularly true of the new ports opened by the Treaty of Tientsin and of three of the older ports, Amoy, Ningpo and Foochow.[4] In Canton and Shanghai, however, Western interests were well entrenched. At the latter, a roaring trade continued to be done in opium. Now that it had been legalized, the receiving ships could openly anchor off the Bund. In 1863–4 Jardine Matheson's opium account had 7,325,590 taels to its credit when the gross business of the Firm totalled 12,237,395 taels.[5]

Yet this long-lasting foundation of the Firm's prosperity was to crumble away within ten years. The reason was not any worry about the morality of the trade. On the contrary, its legalization made it, if anything, more respectable – or, at any rate, marginally less disreputable. No doubt it was not entirely pleasant for the partners who had made their pile, returned to Scotland – or England – and moved into public life, to be associated with a commerce much denounced by British moralists. But they and their predecessors had, with an occasional exception, hardened themselves to this sort of criticism for half a century. The reason for the Firm's withdrawal from the trade had nothing to do with ethical considerations. It was the emergence of a formidable competitor who could undercut their prices.

The Sassoon family, Baghdad Jews in origin, migrated to Bombay in 1825. They had prospered by handling financial affairs for the Turks. The Sultans were by no means intolerant towards those of the Jewish faith whom they regarded, of course, as 'infidels', but on balance preferable to Christians. It is not clear exactly why David Sassoon moved to India. Whatever the reason, he and his family of eight sons prospered immensely. At an early stage the Sassoons took an interest in opium. They established themselves in Canton in 1845 and in Hong Kong soon after the colony's foundation. David Sassoon's sons lived unostentatiously and kept what nowadays would be called 'a low profile'. Colin Crisswell suggests that 'judging by their subsequent way of life in Britain, this was probably not by inclination but as a result of social prejudice against them in the higher reaches of Hong Kong society.'[6] Most accounts agree that in Hong Kong, far more than in Shanghai, social life was stuffy, not to say snobbish. This may partly have been due to the hierarchical structure of a crown colony. But in any case the somewhat exotic offspring of an Oriental merchant, who could not even speak English, were likely to be less acceptable than the scions of the middling Scottish gentry. No Sassoon was elected to the Hong Kong Club. But the family more than made up for any social rebuffs when they established themselves in Britain towards the end of the century, moving easily in the rather raffish world centred on the Prince of Wales and making a series of grand marriages.

The Sassoons could not make a great impact on the opium trade while it depended upon the clipper fleets of Jardines and Dent. In the 1850s they were beginning to compete through the extension of the P&O's steamship service to the coastal ports. After 1860 two major changes occurred. Opium sales and the growing of 'the drug' in China were legalized, subject to a fixed duty of 30 taels per chest. This meant a new form of competition: Chinese-grown opium would compete with the products of India. The second change was in communications. Steam conquered sail. The Jardines/Dent duopoly of the clippers, which smuggled opium to the receiving stations on the coast, became irrelevant. Henceforth the Western merchants were trading on a 'level field'. This meant that the Indian end of the long line which connected the poppy fields of Bengal with an opium den in Shanghai needed the most careful attention – a great deal more than the established Western firms had been in the habit of giving it. As LeFevour puts it:

> The most pertinent result of legalisation was the importance given to the organisation of the trade in India. After 1860 all dealers in China, regardless of experience, faced the same tax and the growing competition of the Chinese drug, so that prices and costs in India became crucial to continued success in the trade.

It was here that Sassoons had the edge and in effect forced Jardines and Russell out altogether (Dent had already gone for other reasons). Jardines had always dealt with the actual producers of Indian opium, Malwa, Patna or Benares, at arm's length. The Firm had no less than 150 'correspondents' in India between 1840 and 1870. The most important were the two Bombay firms Jejeebhoy & Co. and Remington & Co., and the Calcutta firm, Jardine Skinner. Their job was to act as brokers and to send agents to estimate supplies, especially of Malwa; information about crops in the Princely States was more difficult to obtain than in Bengal where the government-controlled monopoly entailed official reports and reasonably reliable information. The upshot of the intelligence from the major correspondents was the monthly *Jardine Opium Circular* sent out from China to 'friends on the opium list'. It described current markets for each type of opium with special reference to Woosung-Shanghai which was the major import centre for Malwa from Bombay. The circular gave average prices, current exchange rates and estimated stock in China. By 1850 Woosung-Shanghai had become by far the most important centre of Jardines' opium business. Average monthly sales were some 350 chests out of a total for all stations of 600.

In spite of its multitude of Indian correspondents, the Firm had never gone closely into the agrarian village production economy on which the sale of opium ultimately depended. Its agents gathered information but did not buy, or make advances for, crops directly to the growers or dealers. This system worked satisfactorily when Jardines and the other older Western hongs in effect controlled access to the China coast. It was a different story in the 1860s. Sassoons was a firm originating in Bombay and far nearer to the Indian base of the whole trade than Jardines had ever been. A warning note was sounded in 1862 by G.M. Robertson of Jardine, Skinner, who reported that during the Second Opium War Sassoons' associates (E. Gubbay & Co, E.D.I. Ezra & Co. and S. Isaac, all of Calcutta) were in effect trying to corner the market by buying at high levels and holding their stock in China for a considerable time before selling.[7] In 1862 the Firm wrote to Jardine, Skinner: 'There is a steady increase in opium deliveries. I cannot impress upon you too strongly the vast importance of carefully watching the proceedings of [the Sassoons] and speculators whose activities are seriously upsetting prices here.'[8]

The real strength of the Sassoons was based on their close involvement directly with the Indian dealers who bought the raw opium. The Sassoon group was prepared to advance as much as three-quarters of the costs to those willing to consign shipments on a regular basis. Moreover they were ready to buy unharvested crops of Malwa opium poppy from the producers. This was something that Jardines had never done. The Firm had relied on its Indian middle men and it soon became apparent that it had been out-manoeuvred. The Sassoons, by a close control over prices and costs, had by 1871 acquired control of 70 per cent of Indian opium of all varieties and could undercut everyone else. By then the only considerable opium firm in India with which Jardine dealt was the Parsee house of Eduljee & Co. in Bombay. The Firm encouraged Eduljee to organize a syndicate among Parsee firms in rivalry to the Sassoons. It did not work, and in November 1872 Eduljee & Co. collapsed. This was the end of Jardines' major operations in opium. 'The trade altogether has gone to the dogs,' wrote a Jardine partner on 2 August, to Remington & Co., 'and my surprise is the infatuation still shown on your side.' He added that the Firm 'now looked to opium only for freight, charges, insurance and storage'.[9]

The Firm's departure from the opium trade, however reluctant, was no bad thing in the long run. It forced Jardines to continue and enhance a policy of diversification which had begun in the 1860s and was to be a major element in its commercial success from then onwards. Jardines was both cautious and adaptable. It took few risks but was always alert for opportunities in the rapidly changing conditions of the China coastal trade. Opium had undoubtedly been the foundation of its fortunes. Cotton, often mentioned as the other 'great staple' of the Chinese import trade, was, in fact, trivial by comparison. But the Firm glided quite easily into other activities and survived the fluctuations of 1860–70.

Its great rival did not. Dent collapsed in 1867. This was partly a result of the fall of the Overend & Gurney bank in 1866, which precipitated a major financial crisis in the City of London and had a knock-on effect all over the world. Dent failed with debts of HK $5 million. Why it went down, whereas Jardines pulled through, is impossible to answer. The documents and accounts of Dent disappeared along with the business. We know that it was affected too by the decline of the opium trade. In an effort to diversify it bought two large and expensive steamers for the newly opened Yangtse. These were not profitable and tied up a good deal of capital. The same was true of its investment in real estate. John Dent, head of his firm, lived in an extravagant style. He spent HK $10,000 on a horse which he hoped would win the Hong Kong Cup from Robert Jardine, and he successfully seduced David Jardine's Chinese mistress. Relations between the two major Western hongs could scarcely have been worse. When Heard & Co., another tottering firm which finally collapsed in 1875, made an approach to Jardines on behalf of Dent it got a dusty answer.

Jardines probably survived because it was more cautious, less heavily invested, and owned fewer eggs in one basket than its rival. But this is a guess. The line between bankruptcy and profit in the China trade was narrow and precarious, and even a small error of judgement could tip the balance towards irrecoverable disaster. Jardines must have been near the edge too. Its worst years were in 1866–7 and 1868–9, and were almost certainly a by-product of the fall of Overend & Gurney, but it did not crash. It was and remains a great survivor. As individuals the Dents, too, survived. John Dent's sons, Alfred and Edward, set up a new partnership in London. Having burnt their fingers in China, they moved their commercial activities to an even more remote part of the world, Borneo, and set up the British North Borneo Company, which governed that territory for 70 years. Alfred was knighted and began to take an interest in China again, becoming chairman in 1889 of a newly formed pressure group in London called the China Association. There is something almost symbolic of a long-past history that he was soon kicked upstairs to the honorific post of president, the kicker being none other than William Jardine's great nephew William Keswick, back from Hong Kong where he had been the Firm's taipan from 1874 to 1885.

Two developments in the 1860s took place, neither of them welcome to Jardines: the formation of the Hong Kong & Shanghai Banking Corporation, and the advent of a new and formidable competitor in

Shanghai, John Samuel Swire of Butterfield & Swire. Hitherto banking services and the general financing of trade had been largely provided by the big agency houses – Jardines, Dent, Russell & Co. This did not suit the smaller concerns, for the big ones were to some extent in competition with them, and were therefore not always willing to give them credit. It is true that the hold of the agency houses had been to some degree weakened by the incursion of several major joint-stock banks, but these were without exception based in London or India and had their head offices there. In 1864 a proposal was put forward for the establishment of a new bank to be called the Bank of China. This would indeed have its headquarters in Hong Kong, but to the great indignation of the business community, only 5000 out of its 30,000 200-Rupee shares were allotted to China and Hong Kong, the rest being offered in Bombay and London. The launch of the Hong Kong & Shanghai Bank was a riposte to this. It was to be locally based in the true sense and its shares were also on offer locally, a certain amount being reserved for Jardines and Russell & Co. Dent was in on it from the start.[10]

Jardines refused to take up its allocation. The association with Dent was, no doubt, an element in this decision, but probably the main factor was the threat which a bank based on Hong Kong offered to the highly profitable exchange business of Jardines, which operated on a much bigger scale in this field than anyone else. The Firm did all it could to block the launch, which required a special Ordinance from the Governor, the legislature of Hong Kong, and confirmation by Whitehall. Given the slowness of communication – 50 days even with steam from Southampton to Hong Kong – and the vigorous opposition of Jardines, both in Hong Kong and, via Matheson & Co., in London, it is hardly surprising that the Bank did not finally come into full legal existence until December 1867. It went through some nerve-racking vicissitudes – not least the repercussions of the crisis caused by the collapse of Overend & Gurney and the bankruptcy of Dent, followed by the major slump in the China trade from 1873 to 1876. But it recovered. In 1877 operating perhaps on the principle, 'If you can't beat them, join them', William Keswick allowed himself to be elected as a director of the court, and the feud with Jardines was ended. Since then the Firm and the Bank have been closely allied, and have engaged in numerous joint enterprises. Keswick became chairman in 1880. The proposed Bank of China never got off the ground.

If Jardines had hoped that the collapse of Dent would leave it with a clearer field of competition, it was to be disappointed. On 28 November 1866, John Samuel Swire arrived in Shanghai, established an office there, acquired the Chinese soubriquet of 'Taikoo', meaning 'Great and Ancient' for his firm, and made a press announcement on 4 December that Butterfield & Swire would be doing business as from 1 January 1867.[11] The Swires were a family of small Yorkshire landowners and businessmen. Richard Butterfield was a mill-owner, whose goods among others the firm exported to China, especially cotton during the shortage caused by the American Civil War from 1860 to 1865. The partnership of Butterfield and two Swire brothers, John and William, had not hitherto made much mark. They had exported Guinness to Australia, and John Swire took an interest in shipping, particularly in the Liverpool-based Ocean Steamship Company run by the Holt brothers, in order to find a cheaper way of conveying crates of stout to the Antipodes. John Swire persuaded them to emulate the P&O and venture into the Eastern carrying trade. Although steam was replacing sail, the advantage was not entirely one-sided. A clipper could carry only 1000 tons and took 120 days to reach the China coast. One of Holt's steamers could carry three times as much on a voyage of 77 days.[12] But the cost of fuel made them much more expensive to run, and rates were correspondingly higher. It was vital to have a good agent on the coast of China to secure a cargo for the return voyage.

This was exactly what John Swire was able to do. He was ambitious, tough, shrewd and highly competitive. In the history of the China trade he can only be compared in energy and drive with the original partners of Jardine Matheson. He was brusque and ruthless. He soon got rid of Butterfield – though the name was kept – writing in 1868: 'Mr B retired from our firm at my suggestion – he was grasping and bothered me.' Before long, Jardines found Butterfield & Swire almost as much of a thorn in its flesh as Dent & Co. This was particularly true of shipping, where it did much better than Jardines and made considerably larger profits. It was, however, not true of trading and other activities. The total net profits of Butterfield & Swire, for years in which any comparison can be made, were far less than those of Jardines: for example in 1868–86 its profits were HK $322,865 compared with Jardines' at HK $1,168,000. After Russell & Co. went into liquidation in 1892, Swires may well have been the second-biggest Western hong, but it was always a long way behind the leader.

In 1860, the last Jardines taipan, Robert, the youngest of the four brothers, returned to London. He was succeeded by Alexander Perceval. He was related to the wife of Sir James Matheson whose maiden name was Perceval. He was probably also related to the Earls of Egmont and thus to Spencer Perceval, the only British Prime Minister to have been assassinated. He had been in China since 1846 and amassed a fortune large enough to buy back the paternal Irish estate in County Sligo which had been sold by his father. He returned in 1864 and was followed by the first taipan not to be at all related to the original founders of the Firm. This was James Whittall, who held the post until 1873. But the family ties were soon renewed. Whittall was succeeded by William Keswick, a great nephew of Dr Jardine and one of the most important figures in the history of the Firm in the last quarter of the nineteenth century, indeed well beyond its end. Of the eleven who followed him, only two had no connection by blood or marriage with the founders, and one of them was a nephew of the factor at Castlemilk, which made him almost an honorary member of the family. Out of 32 taipans from 1832 to 1989, at least 20 were direct or collateral descendants of the original partners. As Colin Crisswell puts it:

> The web of kinship binding the partners of Jardine and Matheson throughout the nineteenth century, together with the maintenance of acute business acumen, would make a fruitful study for a geneticist.[13]

He could have extended his chronology well beyond the end of the nineteenth century. More than half the twentieth-century taipans had similar connections. Of the last five, two have been Keswicks, Henry and Simon, great-grandsons of William.

The two decades covered by the reigns of James Whittall and William Keswick were a critical period in the history of the Firm. As already mentioned it was a time when the indigenous Chinese coastal merchants began to compete more and more favourably with the Western and other foreign firms. Within the Western firms competition also became more intense. The collapse of Dent & Co. in 1867 and Augustus Heard in 1875 did not ease the competitive pressure on Jardines. The rise of Sassoons drove the Firm out of opium, and Swires made major inroads on its shipping interests. The repercussions of the failure of Overend & Gurney were a source of difficulty. And, just when these had died away, there came the financial and economic depression of 1873 – a by-product of, among other causes, over-trading consequent upon the opening of the Suez Canal in 1869. Jardines weathered that storm better than some of the firms involved in the China trade. They made a profit of HK $363,000 in 1871–2, HK $179,000 in 1872–3 HK $245,000 in 1873–4, and similar figures in the next three financial years, whereas the Hong Kong & Shanghai Bank had to pass its dividend in 1874 and the first half of 1875; and its reserve fund fell from HK $1,000,000 to HK $100,000.[14] But it, too, pulled through. Many other firms fell by the wayside during this nerve-racking period in international trade.

James Whittall (1827–93) retired from China in 1873. He had been with the Firm since 1856. He was one of its few non-Scottish figures of prominence; his ancestors were Worcestershire yeomen. His grandfather had been a merchant in the Turkey trade and was one of the last surviving members of the old Levant Company. Whittall must have been a man of powerful character and considerable ability, otherwise he could scarcely have broken through the Scottish family barrier and remained taipan for ten years. Along with William Keswick he was an active and prominent member of the Hong Kong Legislative Council. He was by nature cautious and reluctant to take risks. This may have been one reason why the Firm survived the crisis of the 1860s. Precise apportionment of credit can never be possible, but some part of it should surely go to the man at the top. Although the Firm survived, it faced serious financial problems. It had made loans to other firms in difficulties, taken mortgages and given guarantees. It was short of capital. This had not mattered too much when the only major capital commitment was the replacement of clippers by steamers, an enterprise which both Whittall and Keswick regarded at first with suspicion and in which they invested as little as was compatible with preserving the Firm's interests.

By the end of the 1860s it was clear that capital would be needed not only for shipping but for participation in the modernization of China which the Ch'ing bureaucracy now favoured, although with reservations. Whittall and other partners were in debt to the Firm. The situation was saved by an arrangement with Robert Jardine. He had left part of his share in the Firm when he retired in 1860, to remain on credit paying interest to him. He was now reinstated as an inactive but governing partner – in effect the proprietor by which title he is often described. He and his heirs retained a controlling interest until his grandson sold it in 1963.

Robert Jardine's relationship with the taipan and the other partners was like that of the non-executive chairman of a modern public company with the managing director and his executive colleagues. He had a say in broad matters of policy;[15] indeed as proprietor he had a veto. They did the day-to-day business. The new arrangement worked well. The Firm's liquidity problem was largely solved, and fortunately the proprietor and his Keswick cousins got on well with each other. William Keswick knew that he was dealing with someone who had just as much experience of the China trade as he and who could be regarded as a confidant and friend. The same was true of his much younger brother James Johnstone (J.J.) Keswick. From the mid-nineteenth century until 1914 the brothers were, one or other, and often both, key figures in the fortunes of the Firm. As a result of their rapport with Jardine, decisions were made quickly and business despatched without delay.

Robert Jardine had been born in 1825 and educated at Merchiston Castle School. He entered the office of Magniac, Jardine in 1843, proceeded to China six years later and became a partner in Jardines in 1852. He was taipan from 1857 until he left for Britain in 1860. He was the only long-lived son of David Jardine. He was also the only one who was married – to Margaret Buchanan on 4 April 1867. She was the daughter of the last chief of the Buchanans and died on 7 March 1868 leaving an only son, also Robert, who took the name of Buchanan-Jardine. In 1861

Robert Jardine inherited from his brother Joseph the estate of Castlemilk in Dumfriesshire.

He demolished the Georgian house built in 1796 and called on the services of David Bryce, leading exponent of that variety of romantic French Gothic which came to be called 'Scottish Baronial'. Bryce, best known as the architect of Fettes College and the Edinburgh Royal Infirmary, constructed a vast edifice featuring towers, turrets and pinnacles. It was finished in 1870 at the cost of £44,218.[16] On returning to Britain in 1860 Robert Jardine became a partner in Matheson & Co. and was head of the Firm from 1881 when his brother Andrew died, leaving him yet another vast estate, Lanrick Castle in Perthshire.

Jardine sat as Liberal Member for Ashburton, his uncle's old seat, from 1865 to 1868. He was elected by a narrow majority for Dumfries Burghs in 1868 and held the seat until 1874, when he contested Dumfriesshire against a Conservative and lost. It was a bad year for the Liberals. He carried it in 1880, a good year for the Liberals, and in 1885 was made a baronet in Gladstone's resignation honours on 10 July. On 24 June the GOM wrote:

> The Queen has sanctioned a proposal by me to offer you the honour of a Baronetcy, and I trust it will be agreeable to you to accept a distinction so justly due to your position and character and so certain to be marked by general approval.[17]

He held his seat till 1892, when he retired from public life, but sat after 1886 as a Liberal Unionist having broken with his party, like many other Liberals, over Gladstone's Irish Home Rule Bill of that year.

In addition to his activities in the China trade, in politics and in management of great landed estates, Sir Robert Jardine was a notable figure in the world of sport, indeed far better known to the public for this than anything else. He ran horses in China, as did many Western merchants. His colours were first registered in England in 1862, and he was elected to the Jockey Club in 1877. For many years he ran in partnership with his cousin John Johnstone of Halleaths. Their chestnut colt, Pretender, won the 2000 Guineas in 1869 and the Derby in the same year. They had a long series of successes at Ascot. Jardine was even more interested in coursing, winning the Waterloo Cup with

Muriel in 1873. For a time he hunted regularly and was a founder-member of the Dumfriesshire Foxhounds. He is described in the *Dictionary of National Biography* as 'a fine specimen of the country gentleman and sportsman of the old school'.[18] He was a popular character, and his death in February 1905, after a year of illness, was widely regretted.

William Keswick, who took over from Whittall as taipan in 1874 and held the post for eleven years, was in any view one of the most important figures in the history of the Firm. He was a great nephew of Dr William Jardine and first cousin once removed of Robert Jardine. He was born in 1834, eldest son of Thomas Keswick of Beechgrove, Annan, and Margaret Johnstone, daughter of William Jardine's sister Jean, who had married David Johnstone. Like his cousin, Robert Jardine, he was educated at Merchiston and on leaving entered the London office of Matheson & Co., as Magniac, Jardine had now become. He went out to China in 1855, and in 1859 set up the Japanese branch of Jardines at Yokohama. He became a partner in 1862. He married twice, first Amelia Dubeux in 1870, who died in 1883, second, many years later, Alice Barrington of Eden Park, County Dublin. There were children of both marriages, but the only one relevant to the history of the Firm was his son by his first wife, Henry, born in 1870 and briefly taipan in 1910–11.

William Keswick followed the Firm's tradition of serving as an 'unofficial' member of the Hong Kong Legislative Council. It had remained unbroken since 'unofficials' were first admitted in 1850 and David Jardine became a member. Dent & Co. were represented from 1857 until its collapse ten years later, when another house, Gibb Livingston & Co., in effect took over. One can contrast Butterfield & Swire. It fielded only one member and him for only a year in 1900. And that was after the death of the founder, J.S. Swire, whose creed in these matters was clear: that if his employees had time on their hands it should be used in devising new methods 'of improving the business of their employers' and not on public service. William Keswick spent more years on the Legislative Council than anyone else in the history of the Firm or of any other company. He was a member from 1867 to 1872.

He was succeeded by Whittall in 1872–5, and came back again for the whole of his period as taipan from 1875 to 1886.

His entry in *Who's Who* which was, as is customary, written by himself and is remarkably laconic, mentioning neither wives nor offspring, refers to him as 'a Consul and Consul-General'. In an amusing piece on Jardines as 'Merchant Consuls', Alan Reid points out that the habit of taking appointments as Consuls of foreign countries, which had been useful in evading the rules of the East India Company served no real purpose after 1833.[19] However, there was a long tradition of the Firm holding the Danish Consulate. William Keswick became Danish Consul in 1880. Members of the Firm had also, since Joseph Jardine in 1849, represented the King of Hawaii, under the title of Consul-General.

Keswick held the post in 1881 when King Kalakaua II, on a trip round the world, visited Hong Kong. The Governor from 1877 to 1882 was Sir John Pope-Hennessy, whom Keswick, along with the whole Western community, detested. Pope-Hennessy was a Conservative in politics, and the first Roman Catholic to sit on the Tory benches when he entered the House of Commons in 1859. But he was also Irish and had the hereditary conviction that the English are always oppressors. Between 1867 and 1886 he held six colonial governorships in succession, invariably creating the bitterest resentment among the colonists, but enjoying much popularity with the colonized. To that extent the modern historian may feel that he was on the side of the angels, but nothing can gainsay the fact that he was totally devoid of tact, incapable of making a clear statement about anything, and administratively incompetent to a high degree, leaving a train of chaos behind him whenever he departed to another governorship. He was just the sort of person whom hard-headed Lowland Scots like the Keswicks would have disliked even if they did not regard him as far too pro-Chinese.

William Keswick had many clashes with the impetuous governor. As Consul-General he regarded it as his right to be the first to receive and entertain the King of Hawaii. Pope-Hennessy thought otherwise. When Keswick went out to the King's ship to invite him to stay at his house, the Governor's twelve-oared official barge arrived with 'an invitation from the Governor in the name of the Queen to be his guest',

(*Left*) William Jardine. It was said that he allowed only one chair in his office; business was conducted standing to be dealt with as quickly as possible.

(*Right*) James Matheson. More volatile than his partner and a great reader. He founded the first English language news-sheet in China – the *Canton Register*.

Hong Kong Harbour. The view from the site at which Jardines eventually settled at East Point.

The two-mile long peninsula of Portuguese Macao.

(*Left*) Howqua, the most famous of all Canton's Hong merchants,
by George Chinnery c.1835.

(*Right*) Sir Jamsetjee Jejeebhoy, the famous Bombay merchant.

Portraying the selling of English goods in Canton.

Old China Street near the factory area in Canton, 1838.

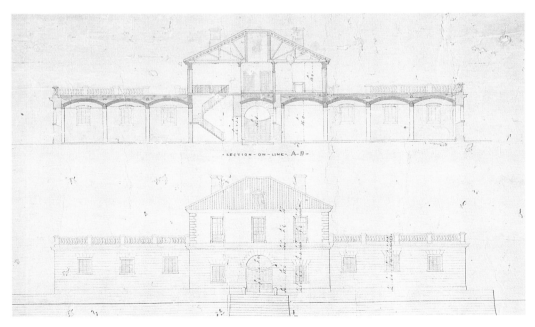

Architects' elevation of East Point Bungalow, Jardines' first proper building in Hong Kong.

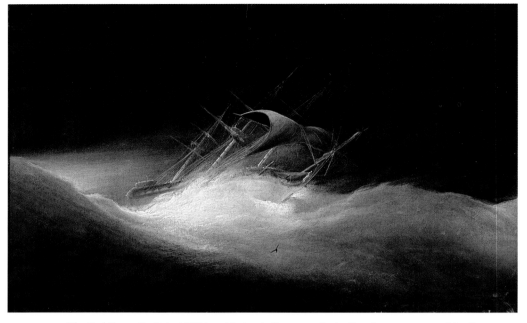

The Red Rover. Built in 1829 to withstand all seasons including the monsoons, this clipper had extraordinary success.

Part of the dinner service ordered by Captain Clifton for *The Red Rover.* Amazingly a large part of the service survived the ship's tumultuous voyages.

(*Left*) The enterprising captain, builder and original owner of *The Red Rover* – Captain William Clifton.

The Jardines' new house at Yokohama in 1868.

(*Below*) Woodcut of a Yokohama street scene of the same period.

(*Right*) William Keswick, great-nephew of William Jardine and moderniser who became *taipan* in 1874.

The Ewo Silk Filature in Shanghai.
(*Top right*) 'China silk flowered satin musters', ordered from Jardines in 1866.

(*Above*) The Hong Kong Cotton
Mills built in 1895.

(*Right*) The interior of a later cotton
mill – No.2 at Shanghai – in the
early twentieth century.

Tiffin – the midday meal – became an institution for unmarried European merchants in China. This winter *tiffin* was at Tientsin in the early 1900s.

(*Right*) Sir Robert Ho Tung by Oswald Birley. He was associated with Jardines for 67 years and bore a striking resemblance to George Bernard Shaw whom he met when they were both revered in their respective professions and countries.

The pontoons of the Indo-China Steam Navigation Company at Hankow, c 1930.

The inauguration of the Jardine-built Shanghai–Nanking railway line in 1908.

The impressive 1922 Shanghai office.

Lombard Street and Cornhill in the 1830s. The present offices of Matheson & Co. are still located here.

while Keswick was still on board. The King, not surprisingly, felt that the Queen's wishes came first and he accepted the Governor's invitation. Keswick, who, as long ago as 1869, had entertained royalty at his house at East Point, in the form of Prince Alfred, Queen Victoria's second son, was furious but he could do nothing about it.

On leaving China finally in 1885, Keswick became a partner in Matheson & Co. In effect he ran the company with responsibility only to Sir Robert Jardine. He was a workaholic who conducted a vast correspondence in his own hand.[20] When Matheson & Co. was converted into a private limited company in 1906, he and his son, and a relation, William Jardine Gresson, were joint managing directors. He was not as Scots-minded as most of the family and bought Eastwick Park in Surrey. He was High Sheriff of the county in 1898, and MP for the Epsom Division from 1899 until his death in 1912, when he was succeeded by his son Henry at the ensuing by-election.

William Keswick had two younger brothers. The elder of them did not go into the Firm but joined Jardine, Skinner. The younger, James Johnstone, born in 1845, was educated at the same school as William and went out to China in 1870 or 1871. He took over the Japan business from Edward Whittall, James's younger brother, in 1875 and became a partner in 1876. He was taipan from 1889 to 1895. In 1884 he married Marion, daughter of Sir Harry Parkes, British Minister in Peking. He was a black-bearded figure of formidable appearance, but the smoothest of manners. He was nicknamed 'James the Bloody-Polite' allegedly because of the courtesy with which after many expressions of flattery and sorrow he dismissed an employee, who said in grateful tones: 'Thank you so much Mr Keswick. Thank you very much indeed.'[21]

ELEVEN

Japan

In January 1852 William Keswick sailed in the ship *Troas* to Japan, putting in at Nagasaki. His instructions were to explore the possibilities of trade. He reported to Whittall that there were potentially profitable openings in the export of silk from Japan, also seaweed and vegetable wax, although it was not clear what the country would take in terms of imports – the same problem as in China half a century earlier. Whittall decided that the matter was worth pursuing. Keswick had been accompanied on the voyage by an independent and energetic trader – a Scot, one need hardly say – Kenneth Mackenzie. In March, Keswick along with Mackenzie was sent again to Nagasaki with orders to 'look after the silk market'.[1] He was jumping the gun, because the treaty with Britain under which Japan ended her long isolation and permitted foreign trade, did not become effective until 3 July. It had been signed on 26 August 1858 when Lord Elgin carried by a naval squadron had extracted concessions by a thinly veiled threat of force. He was merely following in the wake of Commodore Perry of the US Navy, who had begun the process of 'opening up' Japan in 1853.

That remote country, which now felt the impact of the West in a big way for the first time, had been for centuries past a military despotism in a semi-feudal setting. There was an emperor, the Mikado, who had in the distant past presided with ever-diminishing power over a society divided into a number of 'clans' or lineage groups. He traced his ancestry back to the Sun Goddess and he had a quasi-divine status as symbol of the nation and focus of loyalty. But, as long ago as the seventh century, by a process of which little is known, effective power had devolved to successive dynasties of military dictators called by the title of Shogun. The Mikado resided, sacred but unseen, in his palace at Kyoto, performing various religious and ceremonial functions. The Shogun ruled from Yedo (modern Tokyo). His position bore some resemblance to that of the Mayor of the Palace during the declining years of the Frankish Merovingians in the eighth century. But the Merovingians lasted for only 78 years in their shadowy court before they were deposed by the Carolingian Mayors, who assumed formal as well as real rule. Why the Shoguns did not act similarly is one of the puzzles of Japanese history. But, for whatever reason, they did not. The Imperial dynasty survived to get rid of the last Shogun in 1868 and resuscitate its latent power as rulers of Japan. Despite all the wars and revolutions of the next 130 years it is still there.

Japanese culture and religion were largely derived from China, and the cultivated classes for many centuries wrote in Chinese, just as scholars in medieval Europe communicated with one another in Latin rather than the vernacular. But the Japanese have never been slavish copyists of China. Their relationship as an island monarchy with the mainland was like that of Britain with continental Europe – suspicious, uneasy, often hostile but never uninfluenced. Yet from an early stage the Japanese were noted by the few Westerners who penetrated the country as being far more receptive to the technology of Europe than the Chinese; nor did they ever develop a rigid bureaucracy at all comparable to the mandarinate. 'The Japanese are sharp-witted and quickly learn anything they can see,' wrote a sixteenth-century Dutchman. When chiming clocks were introduced by European merchants into the East, the Chinese treated them as amusing toys, but the Japanese copied them to make time-pieces of their own. In the eighteenth century, while the country was still virtually closed to foreigners, there was a rapidly growing money economy which sapped the foundations of military feudalism and made nonsense of the traditional view of merchants as an inferior class, ranking below feudal lords, Samurai, artisans and peasants. Shopkeepers anticipated modern advertising and salesmanship devices. The great house of Mitsui, a name to be conjured with even today, 'gave free umbrellas marked with their trademark to customers caught in their shops by the rain'.[2]

By the mid-nineteenth century Japan had been closed to foreigners for over 250 years. This was a reaction against Christian missionary zeal. The country had been open to foreigners from 1543 for some 70 years after the Portuguese first landed and traded there. In 1549 St Francis Xavier began his task of conversion. By the beginning of the seventeenth century the percentage of the Japanese population who were Christians was higher than it ever has been since. Christianity is a highly subversive religion when introduced into a hierarchical, inegalitarian and deeply traditionalist society. When the Japanese ruling class rather belatedly saw the danger, a ferocious persecution began. Thousands of Christians were put to death. The English departed, the Spanish and Portuguese were expelled. By the middle of the seventeenth century, trade with foreigners had almost ceased. The Chinese were still permitted to do business on a small scale in Nagasaki, but they offered no religious challenge. The only Europeans in Nagasaki were the Dutch, allowed there on condition that they would never proselytize and would, from time to time as an earnest of good faith, trample on the cross and other symbols of Christianity, which they were quite happy to do.

When Commodore Perry's squadron arrived in Yedo (Tokyo) Bay, the Shogunate, occupied by the Tokugawa dynasty since the late sixteenth century, was still the centre of power, though palpably on the decline. Beginning as commanders of the army the Tokugawa Shoguns became hereditary princes exercising vice-regal powers over a centralized and stratified society on behalf of the secluded, unseen Emperor (or Mikado) in Kyoto. The period of Tokugawa rule was known as the 'great peace'. The regime was called the 'bakufu', the government of the camp. The feudal lords or daimyo became the dynasty's vassals. They lived in alternate years at Yedo or on their estates. When they were on their estates their families remained in Yedo as hostages against rebellion. The immense cost of this slow and highly uncomfortable biennial pilgrimage came to be increasingly resented and played its part in the daimyo revolt which eventually brought down the Shogunate. Below them were their retainers, the Samurai. They were a warrior caste, but the 'great peace', however good for the merchant class, had done nothing to prepare the warriors for war. They spent their time in idleness punctuated by antiquated drill in archaic armour. It is true that they were masters of swordsmanship and had weapons sharp enough to cut a piece of fluttering tissue paper in half. But, however useful these were for slicing up commoners (or foreigners) behaving above their station, such weapons were not much good in the event of a clash with European military technology. There can be no doubt that the Shogun and his advisers were well aware from events in Canton and on the Peiho River during the First Opium War that Japan was in no position to resist Western pressure to open the country for foreign trade. A naval bombardment could reduce the largely wooden houses of Yedo to ashes.

The treaties negotiated by the USA, Britain, France, Russia and the Netherlands were much on the same lines as the Treaty of Nanking. There were to be Treaty Ports, commercial privileges and extra-territorial rights for Western residents, foreign consuls in the ports, and diplomatic representation at the capital. Japanese export of opium was restricted to avoid competition with India. This surrender to the West was by no means undisputed in the court of the Mikado or among the members of the Shogun's Council. A series of labyrinthine intrigues and convoluted struggles for power culminated in the abolition of the Shogunate and the so-called Meiji Restoration in 1868. The Emperor became a real ruler and his powers were used in order to 'westernize' Japan. Symbolically he moved from Kyoto to Yedo. Those elements in the governing class who had felt humiliated by Western military and technical superiority were determined to copy it – the Japanese were and are masters of the art of imitation – in order to make Japan a 'great power'. The process took time, but the Sino-Japanese war of 1894–5 and the Russo-Japanese war of 1904–5 attested to its success. In 1899 the Westerners relinquished extra-territorial rights. In 1902 the Anglo-Japanese alliance was signed. In 1910 Korea was annexed. Japan had 'arrived' in no uncertain manner.

Early in July 1859 Keswick sailed from Shanghai in the *Nora* to the new Japanese port of Yokohama with a cargo of cotton piece goods, sugar candy and elastic bands for which there was believed to be a demand in Japan. He also carried 40,000 Mexican dollars. The treaties had specified Nagasaki, Hakodate and Kanagawa as the ports for Western trade. But Kanagawa was on the route from Kyoto to Yedo. Every year there passed along it a regular procession of daimyo accompanied by vast retinues of Samurai, many of whom regarded foreigners with detestation and the treaties as a humiliation to national pride. Trouble was all too likely if they encountered Westerners; and trouble was the last thing that the Shogun and his Council in Yedo wanted. He had signed the treaty without authority from the Mikado, and on a matter of such vital national importance, the imprimatur of the Emperor, however remote he was from normal governance of the country, should have been sought. The Shogun had tried to placate him with a promise that the treaties were temporary accommodations with the Barbarians, to be repudiated as soon as Japan's army and navy could be brought up to suitable strength. Meanwhile it was highly undesirable that there should be 'incidents' giving the foreigners an excuse to intervene and impose further humiliations.

The Shogun substituted Yokohama for Kanagawa. It was at the time a small unimportant fishing village, but it had the advantage of being some miles away from the Tokaido road which linked Kyoto with Yedo. The Japanese authorities decided to lay it out as a little town with port facilities, shops, roads, residences, and even a 'pleasure quarter' – courtesy name for brothels and the subject of much ribaldry by Japanese cartoonists. From the Shogun's point of view the place had another advantage. It was well and truly cut off from the mainland in so far as a town could be, which was not actually on an island. Yokohama stood on a seaward-facing beach with a swamp behind it flanked by two rivers on either side, which were joined by a canal behind the swamp. The only way of getting in or out was via two bridges barricaded at sunset by armed guards. Sir Rutherford Alcock, the first British Consul-General to Japan protested that it looked more like a prison than a free port, and continued to haggle about Kanagawa.

Keswick was not prepared to wait. It was a gross waste of money to have the *Nora* at anchor with her cargo still on board. Not for the first time in the history of trade in the Orient, diplomacy and commerce conflicted, and as usual commerce won. Alcock was very angry, but his protests to the Foreign Office got him nowhere. The Office believed that Jardines had such prestige that trade would go to wherever the Firm settled. Keswick landed his cargo, and other merchants followed suit. Jardines was not alone in seeing the possibilities of trade with Japan. Other firms in on it from the start were Adamson, Bell & Co. and Cornes & Co. and they were also destined to do well. Keswick at once rented a bungalow and proceeded to conduct business, although it was by no means easy to do so. Although the Japanese Government had been obliged by the threat of force to sign the 'unequal treaties', the Shogun intended, without actual repudiation, to make it as difficult as possible for Western merchants to trade successfully. There were complicated currency problems, and their methods of dealing prompted Alcock in a moment of ill temper to describe the foreign traders as 'the scum of the earth'. He was never forgiven for this. When in due course the Westerners formed, as in Hong Kong, Shanghai and elsewhere, a club, one of its rules was that no one from the Diplomatic Service should be eligible.

Relations between Western merchants and diplomats were often as prickly in Japan as in Hong Kong or the Chinese Treaty Ports. Algernon Bertram Mitford, later 1st Lord Redesdale of the second creation, whose memoirs are one of the most vivid accounts of Japan in 1866–70 as seen through Western eyes, varied in his views. He was a member of the British Legation serving under Sir Harry Parkes. He noted of the settlement in Yokohama that it 'is the most curious motley imaginable'. He went on:

English, French, Dutch, Germans, Italians, Americans, Greeks, Chinese, niggers, all live together ... They are rather a rough lot in some cases, but good enough fellows in their way, and men who have travelled so much generally besides knowing how to take care of themselves, are helpful and kind to others in a way quite unknown in Europe.[3]

This was on 24 December 1866. But ten months later, on 29 October 1867, he was writing in a very different tone:

I thoroughly detest Yokohama ... You were never [in your life] brought in touch with such a set of snobs and ruffians as the majority of the Europeans who infest these Eastern trading places, and they give themselves the airs of

Princes of the blood. They look down upon the officials because their salaries are so low.[4]

And on 26 January 1868 in the midst of the civil war which preceded the fall of the Shogunate, he wrote to his father:

All this misery has come on the country simply in order that a few European merchants may be enriched. There is no concealing the fact that the advent of foreigners was the beginning of trouble. The Japanese did not want us; they were rich, at peace and happy in their way. They are now impoverished, hungry, paying increased prices for everything, they have the horrors of a civil war to face; and they have gained absolutely nothing. They have only to show for their money the arms with which they are about to massacre one another. I have seen the so-called march of civilization both in China and Japan, and I have seen it as a curse to both nations.[5]

The process of trading with Japanese merchants was at first anything but simple. Western concepts of free trade were alien and incomprehensible to them. The currency problem alone was enough to drive a foreign exporter to the verge of madness. The Japanese Government wished to protect its local coinage and, accordingly minted a variety of special coins to be used only in foreign trade. The effect was to make Japanese products inordinately expensive. 'I regret,' wrote Keswick to Whittall on 2 July 1859, 'that I am unable to report any progress towards a satisfactory settlement of the difficulties besetting the opening of this port [Yokohama] to trade.'[6] Even such unexciting commodities as mushrooms, seaweed, raw silk and isinglass were so costly, in terms of Mexican dollars, that there was no point in doing business. Keswick thought that soon 'the only way of trading will be by barter because of the currency question'.[7]

Even after the problem of the special new coins had been to some extent solved, there continued to be serious difficulties. The Treasury insisted on limiting the number of coins which could be exchanged for dollars. In the autumn of 1859 the foreign merchants got their own back by the discovery that one could make a killing by purchasing Japanese gold coins with Japanese silver and selling them in China because of the disproportionate ratio of gold to silver in Japan compared with China. The Yokohama Customs authorities riposted by forcing the foreigners to put in a requisition in writing for Japanese silver coins and limiting the supply, to which the Western merchants in their turn riposted by putting in a host of requisitions under bogus names such as Snooks, Bosh and Nonsense. It was this that caused Sir Rutherford Alcock to term them 'the scum of the earth'.[8]

The Japanese Treasury continued its currency restrictions and Keswick, writing again to Whittall, said: 'I don't see how we can ever develop trade here till we are allowed sufficient currency to buy products.' But in November, despite all the difficulties, he contrived to put together a worthwhile cargo for Shanghai, consisting of silk, copper, sea shells, lacquer, porcelain, sharks' fins, sea slugs and gold coins. Whittall was convinced by this success that trade with Japan was worth cultivating and that Keswick should stay on in Yokohama. As a result Keswick, early in 1860, bought Lot No. 1[9] for the Firm. It was on the waterfront and could be expanded behind into Lots 22 and 23 which the Firm also bought. Whittall urged that a good and substantial place should be built. He, like most taipans, before and after, believed that one should never economize about appearances. 'Face' was as important in Japan as in China. An abode of suitable size would show that the Firm was there to stay.

Ei Ichi-ban, as the Japanese called it, was a sign and symbol of its intention. It was probably (no pictures have survived) a long, single-storey building of wood and plaster with the customary open verandah. Near to it there were two allegedly fireproof godowns. Fire was an endemic risk all over the Far East. On 26 November 1866, the Firm's premises including the godowns were totally destroyed, along with many foreign consulates and the buildings of most other firms, by an immense conflagration. It is vividly described by Mitford, who had just landed at Yokohama and taken up residence at the Legation in the Japanese quarter. This was normally in Yedo, but it oscillated between the Shogun's capital and Yokohama, owing to repeated 'incidents' in the former when British subjects had been murdered or wounded.

There was a great gale. The flames leapt from roof to roof, the burning wooden shingles, driven as it seemed, for a couple of hundred yards, finding fresh food for their insatiable greed. There was no crashing noise of falling timber such as one hears in a London fire. The flames passed over the houses and simply devoured like gun cotton passes through a burning candle - a wonderful and appalling sight. In a few minutes of what had been teeming human homes nothing remained but a heap of ashes and a few red-hot tiles ... The European quarter was soon under the curse. Stone houses - warehouses supposed to be fireproof - were of no avail. Had not the wind abated towards the afternoon nothing would have remained. As it was, about one third of the foreign buildings were destroyed.[10]

William Keswick, now based in China, wondered whether an expensive new building would be justified, given the uncertainty hanging over British relations with Japan and the prospect of civil war in the country. But he decided to take the risk and authorized a much more substantial edifice with godowns that really would be fireproof. It was duly opened in 1868.

By then much had changed both in trade and politics since William Keswick had first put in at Nagasaki in January 1859. The mixed cargoes which he had assembled to start the trade had not been a great success, despite their picturesque and colourful composition. The demand for sea slugs and isinglass was limited, and the Japanese Treasury soon vetoed gold coins. Silk, too, proved to be a dubious investment. The quality declined and the price was far too high. The Firm moved out of the trade temporarily and into banking. It could not, however, compete with the commercial banks established in Yokohama from 1863 onwards. Flexibility as ever was the secret of Jardines' success. When many other traders with Japan went bankrupt the Firm flourished by diversifying into new lines. One was tea, grown easily in Japan, and, although English taste stuck to India and China, Jardines did good business in exports to North America. Another was raw cotton of which there was a worldwide shortage during the American Civil War, and which Japan could supply in large quantities.

A third important source of income from Japan was the sale of the Firm's older trading ships. These were kept in good trim and properly looked after. They were entirely seaworthy and the Japanese knew and received exactly what they were buying. Jardines, however, needed the fastest available steamships if only for purposes of communication. In those pre-telecom days, when it could take up to nine months to ship goods from Japan to Europe before learning the results of the sale, speed was vital for a great trading firm, but not so important for a country only on the edge of the world of commerce. It paid the Firm to have the latest vessels and recoup part of the cost by the sale of the older models. The centre of the shipping business was not Yokohama but Nagasaki, which has one of the greatest natural harbours in the world. Jardines was deeply involved in joint enterprises with T.B. Glover & Co., the leading Western company in the port (famous for *Madam Butterfly*).

Yokohama in the 1860s was not a place where any foreigners would have lived for choice. The climate, in contrast with Edo, was sticky and stuffy, and rendered the more disagreeable by the swamp which cut the town off from the mainland. In 1860 there were about 30 foreigners in residence – men of vigour, enterprise and determination. They were mostly bachelors. Several had Japanese mistresses. Others repaired to the 'pleasure quarter' for their needs. Apart from that, amenities were few and much inferior to those available in the Chinese Treaty Ports. But things gradually improved. In 1862 a Municipal Committee was formed with the purpose of doing something about water supply, sewage and street lighting. In the same year P&O inaugurated a regular steamer service between China and Japan. This meant that such matters as insurance claims, salary increases and loans, all of which were handled in Shanghai, could be dealt with more expeditiously. The Firm's business expanded. By 1861 the British share in Japan's foreign trade amounted to £1 million, and Jardines had the lion's share. Two years later the Firm was employing three Britons, ten Chinese and nineteen Japanese. Although there was no love lost between the Chinese and the Japanese, Chinese compradors were valuable assets. They understood the form, and comprehension can be more useful than affection.

The destruction of the Shogunate was welcomed by Western traders. In its latter days the regime had become incompetent, corrupt and hostile to foreigners. Based on an archaic form of what has been called 'centralized feudalism', it was in no position to deal with the now inevitable 'opening up' by the West, which had occurred in China after the First Opium War 25 years earlier. The origins of revolt lay in the south west. The daimyo of the Satsuma and Choshu clans had long been enemies of the Shogunate, although they kept their counsel until the crisis came. In association with T.B. Glover & Co., Jardines supplied them with steam ships. Glover was a personal friend of the Prince of Satsuma. The Shogun's government tried to curb these sales. It actually vetoed the Choshu leaders from employing Jardines' engineers to service a former Jardines ship which the Choshu had bought. Jardines, in association with Glover & Co., did some profitable deals in lending money to the daimyo of Nagasaki and the south west for the purchase of machinery and arms which could be used for only one purpose: the destruction of the Shogunate.

William Keswick in 1863 was personally involved in one important action of support for the clans of the south west. Their leaders were anxious to learn more about European commerce, or at least to encourage some of the younger members of the nobility to do so. That, they believed, was where the future lay. At this time there was a strict veto on any Japanese subject leaving his country – on the pain of death. Five young members of the rebellious clans were determined to flout the ban and discover for themselves what life was like in the mysterious Western world. They made their way to Yokohama and called on the British Consul. He referred them to William Keswick, who arranged in strict secrecy for their passage on a company ship bound for Shanghai. This was safely accomplished and they duly arrived, the plan being to sail onwards on the clipper *Pegasus* bound for England.

The Firm's staff at Shanghai misunderstood the credentials of the young men and the object of the exercise. Two of them were treated as apprentice seamen, working their passage. They had to work very hard. They washed the decks, manned the pumps and spread the sails. Like all apprentice seamen at the time they were expected to subsist on a very thin diet. According to one account, when the two arrived in London they looked 'like hungry crows'. But under the guardianship of Hugh Matheson, who was expecting them, they soon recovered, and spent a profitable time learning and absorbing the culture and usages of Western life. They were destined to be two of the most powerful statesmen after the Meiji Restoration – Prince Ito Hirobumi, who was four times Prime Minister, and Marquis Kaoru Inoue, who became Minister of Foreign Affairs and Finance.

The year 1868 was notable both in the general history of Western intercourse with Japan and in the particular history of Jardines. The most significant episode in the general history was the fall of the Shogunate, the end of civil war and the establishment of the Mikado as a real rather than shadow ruler. British influence had been used to this end for some time past. On that objective British diplomats and merchants, however much they disliked each other, had been united. The disappearance of the Shogun was as welcome to Jardines as to the other companies doing business in Yokohama. The only foreigners to be miffed were the French, whose Legation had supported the Shogunate throughout, in exchange for a host of shadowy grandiose concessions which would in practice probably never have been granted even if the regime had survived. They were furious at backing the wrong horse.

As for Jardines, three important developments occurred. Osaka and Kobe were declared on New Year's Day to be open to foreign trade. Osaka was one of the biggest and most prosperous of Japanese cities, and Jardines' agent, Thomas Glover, was among the first foreigners to establish himself there, being aware of its great trading possibilities. The second was his purchase for HK $60,000 of the Mint in Hong Kong in order to transfer it to Osaka. The Firm shipped machinery and firebricks (which did not stop an early fire) and took a commission of five per cent on the deal. The new Imperial Mint, opened in 1871, was a sign and symbol of the new regime's determination to move into the modern Western commercial world.

The third development was the official opening of the new Ei Ichi-ban (Number One House) in Yokohama, which had by now become the unrivalled foremost Treaty Port. The House was much grander than its predecessor, with a new godown behind it of stone, well-seasoned wood, tiles and copper sheeting described by its designer as being 'as nearly fire-proof as a building partly constructed of wood can be'. The Number One House was more spacious with loftier rooms than the previous building. It had stone foundations, bow-windowed sitting-rooms and chimney-pieces, sent from Shanghai. The general mode of life enjoyed by its inmates was more luxurious than hitherto, with butler, cooks, house-boys, grooms and gardeners to look after their comforts. The House was destroyed by the earthquake of 1922, and Jardines moved to Kobe.

Yokohama as a city was rapidly expanding and life by the end of the 1870s was far more agreeable than it had been when William Keswick first set foot in it in July 1859. There were some 800 foreign residents. There were rail and telegraph communications, banking and postal services. There was even a gasworks. A Chamber of Commerce existed to supervise and co-ordinate trade. A grand hotel and a theatre catered for leisure and amusement. One could walk in well laid-out public gardens and watch the steamers coming and going in the bay. Their number increased every year, and the opening of the Suez Canal in 1869 gave a notable fillip to shipping. Not only the P&O, but, the Pacific Mail and the Messageries Maritimes called regularly, and the flags of many nations flew.

Business flourished after the Meiji Restoration. Currency problems still caused trouble, but less than they had when the Firm first arrived in Yokohama in 1859. It was the great period of Japanese trade expansion, when the new regime consciously decided to imitate the West and bring Japan into the world of the commerical future. In this process Jardines, along with other firms, played its part. It encouraged expansion of Japanese industries and contributed by loans and other financial operations towards the infrastructure; machinery, textile yarns, railways, banks, telegraphs and shipyards helped to bring Japan into the Western world.

The British companies helped to boost the status of the Japanese merchants hitherto regarded by the Samurai as an inferior class. The Japanese hierarchy of the Shogunate was rapidly changing, and Jardines along with other Western firms were contributors to this change. Not, of course, on any grounds of altruism or belief in 'progress', since that was not their business. Their business was to make money for themselves and their heirs. But Adam Smith's 'hidden hand' applied as so often. The money-makers were not only making themselves rich but many other people too. The Firm played its part in one of the most remarkable economic revolutions of the nineteenth century. The world has never been the same since.

TWELVE

Modernization

The social and economic position of the Chinese Empire had been deteriorating since the middle of the eighteenth century. The basic cause was an extraordinary growth in population which led to ever-increasing poverty among the peasant masses who constituted over 80 per cent of the Chinese population. This pressure of numbers upon the means of subsistence had occurred in Europe but had been largely relieved by successful industrialization. Although there was plenty of resistance to that process, Europe had no equivalent of the Confucian ruling class in China – corrupt, rigidly conservative and terrified of change. All its traditions led it to despise traders and, even more dangerous, to be scarcely less contemptuous of soldiers and sailors. The dynamic of Western capitalism was incomprehensible. To the mandarinate, Jardines, Swires and the great Western merchants were lumped together with Christian missionaries and foreign diplomats as irreconcilable threats against the old traditions which sustained its elegant, antiquated and ultimately futile way of life. If a ruling class cannot defend those whom it rules, it ceases to have a raison d'être. By the beginning of the last quarter of the nineteenth century elements of that class were beginning to see that China could not survive without adopting at least some of the techniques of the Barbarians.

In this belated effort by late Ch'ing China to modernize itself, Jardines played an important part. The Firm saw that instability was a major threat to trade and that rebellion and revolution could not be averted unless the Empire moved into the Western economy, as Japan was doing with such speed and success at that very time. The hope was that commerce would not only create prosperity in the Treaty Ports but also spread into the vast interior where most of the population lived. This never occurred. It was the old problem of the two Chinas, the world of coastal commerce and that of the peasant masses whose declining standard of living was the basic cause of the discontent that threatened the Imperial regime.

It is clear now that poverty, low incomes, bad communications and a system of inland taxes as stifling as those of pre-revolutionary France, largely explained Chinese resistance to imported goods. A further cause was the degree of self-sufficiency in the Chinese traditional economy. Other difficulties were the prolonged periods of economic sluggishness and the dominance of a very few products in foreign trade – tea and silk exports, opium and cotton imports. The fiscal reforms which had been achieved on the coast had no analogue inland. What China needed was a Necker or a Robert Peel, but such statesmen were not likely to emerge from the Ch'ing bureaucracy with all its vested interests in 'the system'.

We saw in Chapter Ten that Jardines faced increasing competition after the end of the civil war from Chinese merchants and that the Firm was moving from trade in commodities to deals on commission and the provision of auxiliary services. The hope of the Firm and other Western merchants that they would be able to link the Treaty Ports with the rural hinterland and 'open up' the Chinese interior was not to be realized. The difficulties proved insuperable. Shanghai was the one place 'whose self-generating economic growth constituted a true leading sector which could have initiated fundamental and favourable changes in the traditional economy, if the Ch'ing bureaucracy had co-operated'.[1] But conservatism and timidity prevailed. No doubt, the bureaucracy was already sufficiently disturbed by the effects of Western trade on the coast, which they could not prevent, and were all the keener to avoid its spread into the interior, which they could. Jardines, like the other Western merchants, found its activities largely confined to the Treaty Ports of which Shanghai was by far the biggest and most prosperous. It was also the one where indigenous merchants were least able to compete with the foreigners who were deeply entrenched, possessed more capital and had better communications with the European and American markets.

The obvious, and to Westerners unexpected, growth of Chinese enterprises made co-operation highly desirable. The number of Chinese investors in European firms rapidly rose, and more and more joint operations began to take place. Jardines did not at first abandon the hope that a combination of Chinese capital and its own administrative and technical skills would develop the Chinese interior. The notion that a vast potential market existed there took a long time to die, although doubts had been shrewdly expressed by a Hong Kong official as long ago as 1852 (see Chapter Nine).

Jardines was a highly adaptable business. The partners were fully conscious of the changes which were taking place in the China trade after the Second Opium War and the final defeat of the Taiping Rebellion. There were great opportunities, but there was sharper indigenous competition.

The Firm had always been dependent on Chinese co-operation – or rather the assistance of particular Chinese individuals. The compradors were an essential element in the business from early Cantonese days onwards, and some of them made huge fortunes out of it. The problem in the last quarter of the nineteenth century was how to compete and also collaborate with what were still called 'native' enterprises. The operation, like every transaction in China, was complicated, tortuous and slow. The bureaucracy mistrusted traders whether Chinese or Western. The Chinese merchants longed to be conferred with the button of even the lowest rank of mandarin. They were like the war profiteers to whom Lloyd George sold honours after 1918. But they also had a deep dislike of investing in any sort of joint enterprise with the Government – what was called 'Kuan-tu shang-pan', roughly translated as 'government supervision, merchant operation'.[2] Jardine did not object in principle to participating, with suitable safeguards, in such projects, but it could not, or at any rate would not, do so unless Chinese merchants also invested in them, and this was very difficult to achieve.

Two episodes illustrate the problems faced by Jardines. The first was its plan to establish a cotton mill in Shanghai. One of the partners,

F.B. Johnson, took the iniative in 1877. The idea was to avoid Western ownership and to adopt the principles of Kuan-tu shang-pan. A cotton mill company would be formed under official supervision and local Chinese merchant management. Jardines would come into the affair not as owner but as agent on behalf of the company in Britain – a role which the Firm's close commercial and industrial associations in London would enable it to play successfully and profitably. Johnson suggested to a group of Chinese merchants that they should set up a joint-stock company with the object of building a mill. Hu Kuang-yung, a wealthy Chinese merchant with whom Jardines had done a good deal of business, endeavoured to persuade a group to launch a company to be called the Anglo–Chinese Shanghai Cotton Mill Company with an initial capital of taels 350,000. It was to have 800 looms. James Keswick wrote: 'All I can say at the moment is that if the scheme be carried through at all we shall have the business for I do not anticipate that the Chinese will go to any other firm.'[3] The caveat was relevant. It was far from certain that the mandarins would agree to a scheme initiated by any Western enterprise.

Throughout 1878 negotiations and discussions with, and petitions to, the bureaucracy continued in a leisurely manner. In October, Peng, shortly to become taotai of Shanghai, petitioned Li Hung-chang, Commissioner of Trade for the northern ports, for the establishment of a Chinese-managed cotton mill. It would be an example of the 'self-strengthening' policy which some of the officials had come to believe necessary for the salvation of China. Peng made the point that foreign cloth had become a major import in Chinese foreign trade with the result that millions of taels had to be sent out of the country every year in order to pay for it. A local mill would halt this drain on Chinese resources and put money into Chinese instead of foreign pockets. Li was sympathetic and approved of Peng as manager jointly with Cheng Kuan-ying, a former comprador of Swires, who in 1880 was to become an associate manager of the China Merchants Steam Navigation Company. There were now to be 480 power looms of the latest device. Jardines at once offered to procure these along with British instructors in their use. The officials replied that they would consider the matter. Meanwhile the Firm reflected on the technical problems and the likely market for cotton yarn. It notified Platt & Co. of Oldham that machinery and technical help would soon be needed to start up

> ...a Manufactory by which Native Cotton can be worked into Grey Shirtings...we may be called on at an early date to definitely state the terms upon which we will undertake to supply the plant with machinery... Telegraph to use the total cost in Sterling...(The plant must be capable of turning out 270,000 pieces of Grey Shirtings per annum).

The letter dated 14 November 1878 went on to specify the need for

> ...the following skilled hands viz 1 Chief Superintendent, 1 Engineer, 1 Supt. for carding and spinning machinery, 1 Supt. for the weaving machinery, 1 Mechanic to erect and set up the Plant and Machinery ready for us. All for three years...This letter we forward open through our London friends, Messrs. Matheson & Co.[4]

An ominous pause followed. Peng told the Firm that difficulties in obtaining official agreement meant that their assistance for the project must be 'put on hold', as one might say today. The fact was that 'The Shanghai Cotton Spinning and Weaving Company', as the government-sponsored company had been renamed, did not appeal to the Treaty Port Chinese, precisely because it was government-sponsored. The China Merchants Steam Navigation Company, another example of a government-sponsored enterprise, had been a flop because of ill-informed bureaucratic interference. Today we can see that government intervention in the management of firms is almost invariably disastrous. By an irony of events, modern China is the only big country to stick to state industries. But the Chinese coastal merchants had a choice; they were not obliged to invest in these joint projects which they rightly suspected, and despite 'patriotic' appeals, a promised high rate of dividends, and talk of a government subsidy, they refused to put their money into anything that savoured of government supervision. And if they declined to invest the project would never get off the ground. There was a further difficulty as F.B. Johnson pointed out: 'It is evident that the Mill, if started, will mainly have to compete with Native manufacturing industry and this is just what Li and Shen, its patrons, do not want to do.'[5]

Frustration with the government scheme prompted Jardines, in co-operation with other Western merchants, to organize a new cotton mill company in November 1882. This ran into trouble for other reasons. The officially sponsored Chinese company was still in existence, although financially far from profitable. Did foreigners have the right to set up their own mill in competition? Clearly they could only do so, if at all, in one of the Treaty Ports, Shanghai being the obvious location. But on seeing the prospectus, the taotai of Shanghai protested, and the new Governor-General of the provinces of Kiangsu, Kiangsi and Anhwei backed him. If foreigners were allowed to manufacture cotton in competition with local industry, why not silk and satin? There could be serious unemployment both in town and country. The livelihood of many people was at stake.

The question of the legality of establishing a mill in a Treaty Port was open to argument. The 'consular body' of Shanghai disputed the right of the Chinese provincial government to veto it; they maintained that it could not be settled locally but only in Peking after discussion with the relevant diplomats. One of Jardines' partners, William Paterson, wrote: 'There does not seem any danger of their absurd pretensions being given effect to.' But the legal issue was not clear. Nor was it certain that British diplomats in Peking, never very friendly to British merchants, would be helpful. On 3 January 1883, Paterson wrote:

> Do not calculate too assuredly upon the protection to be given us by the Diplomatic Body at Peking. The rights of foreigners in respect of such enterprises are not in any way clearly set forth in the Treaties ... I do not feel sure that the contention of foreigners to enjoy special privileges in the settlements which are denied to natives, unless expressly granted in the Treaties, would be sustained by our own Government, considering the present drift of its policy.[6]

The last few words remind us that the year 1883 was the heyday of Gladstonian liberalism – a period when anything that savoured of pushing British interests abroad was regarded as rather dubious and slightly immoral. Johnson decided that an appeal to legal rights would be dangerous. They were uncertain, and Chinese xenophobia was already far too much aroused by the missionaries for Western

merchants to risk further trouble. Better to organize joint-stock enterprises with Chinese investors in conjunction with Chinese merchants,
especially rich ones, connected with the mandarinate, who did not
wish to be involved in Kuan-tu shang-pan businesses. 'I would recom-
ment,' he inelegantly wrote, 'that the interests be tacitly allowed to
grow until they become too extensive to be interfered with without
inviting claims for compensation if disturbed.'

As LeFevour points out, Johnson under-estimated the degree of
bureaucratic obstruction which would block proposals of this sort.
There were two powerful reasons for Chinese officialdom to oppose
participation by local merchants in foreign-controlled enterprises, one
creditable, the other less so. The creditable reason was a genuine fear of
the threat to the employment and livelihood of Chinese handloom
weavers. It was not unreasonable for a paternalistic bureaucracy to
regard such competition as a menace to the standard of living of a significant section of the population. The Adam Smith conception that
free trade would in the long run bring greater prosperity to everyone
cut no ice with the mandarinate. How long would the run be? And
what about the stability of the Empire during the period of transition?
The other reason for obstruction was less honourable. 'Industrial projects managed by foreign merchants would be beyond the reach of the
"squeeze" system so vital to many official incomes.'[7] To extort bribes
from Western merchants was more difficult than extracting money
from Chinese subjects vulnerable to a host of threats and pressures
which could not easily be applied to foreigners.

Jardines did not give up the struggle. There was another attempt to
set up a cotton mill at Shanghai in 1889. This time the plan was to act in
co-operation with a Bombay yarn merchant. It would be a purely
Chinese company with Jardines acting as agents. Nothing came of it.
Nor was the Firm any more successful when Li Hung-chang's govern-
ment-supervised company built a cotton mill in Shanghai. Jardines
offered to take on the management if the local Chinese could not cope.
The offer was not accepted. There followed an episode which did
nothing to improve Anglo–Chinese relations. In October 1893, Li
Hung-chang's Shanghai Cotton Cloth Mill was threatened by a fire,
spreading in a high wind from a shop nearby. His Chinese manager

who had foolishly allowed the insurance to lapse put in a frantic plea for help from the Shanghai Municipal Council fire department. The mill was just outside the boundary of the foreign settlements, and the Council, which included in its number a Jardines representative, refused on those grounds to come to the rescue with its fire brigade. They were within their rights, but it was hardly a friendly act, and the result was that the whole mill was burned to the ground. It was incidents like this which fuelled Chinese xenophobia and their sense of grievance against Westerners.

In June 1894 the Firm decided to test the question of the Chinese government's right to veto foreign-owned manufacture in the Treaty Ports. Jardines ordered cotton-spinning machinery from Platt Bros. If the first shipment was not confiscated, Jardines would go ahead. It reckoned that the capital could be raised from Chinese piece goods dealers in Shanghai, making it clear that no government officials would be on the board of directors – a *sine qua non* for enlisting investment from Chinese merchants. The fact was – however unflattering to the Imperial Governments – that the Chinese merchants trusted Jardines but did not trust the Ch'ing bureaucracy. The Firm now realized that Chinese capitalists would never invest a tael in a company in which officialdom had any say. 'The time has come', wrote one of the directors, 'to assert our rights.' Whether they succeeded is unclear. Events overtook the negotiations. The Sino-Japanese war which broke out in 1894 resulted in a crushing defeat for China. The Treaty of Shimonoseki in April 1895 gave manufacturing rights not only to the Japanese but to all foreigners. The Jardine-managed Ewo Cotton Spinning and Weaving Company opened in May 1897. War, as so often, had been the catalyst of change.

The second episode, which illustrates some of the Firm's difficulties in opening up China, was the affair of the Shanghai–Woosung railway. Jardines' partners, like most Western entrepreneurs, were strong believers in the efficacy of railway development. If the great coastal ports could be connected with the interior, trade and industry would follow, new markets would be tapped and a great deal of wealth generated both for foreigners and the Chinese. As early as 1844 a group of Western merchants was considering the idea of a railway from Canton to Calcutta. In the 1860s, M.A. Macleod, one of the Firm's partners, inspired Sir MacDonald Stephenson, who had drawn up a comprehensive scheme for India, to do the same for China. Railways had been a success in India, where conditions were not dissimilar. The snag was the belief among the Ch'ing officials that, in the words of Li Hung-chang, 'Railways would only be beneficial to China if undertaken by the Chinese themselves, and constructed under their own management.'[8] The trouble with this doctrine was that the prospect of anything ever being actually done under indigenous management was virtually nil.

Woosung was the outer port for Shanghai at the entrance to the Whangpoo, twelve miles to the east. If a railway could be built successfully to connect the greatest trading centre in China with the sea, it would be a model for the future. Merchants and officials seeing it in action on the ground would be converted to a belief in the immense potential of railways as a means of 'self-strengthening' – the latest slogan fashionable among the small but influential minority of the less conservative members of the Ch'ing bureaucracy. The key figure in this group was Li Hung-chang. In 1865 the Woosung Road Company was formed. Jardines was the managing agent and shares were taken up by a number of Chinese merchants. The company bought land, plot by plot, between Shanghai and Woosung. Ostensibly, as the name of the company implied, the object was to build a road for horses and carriages, not a railway. Official permission was not sought even for a road, although the taotai of Shanghai may have given some sort of private go-ahead. The costs, however, proved to be so far in excess of estimates that the project was shelved two years later, and the company wound up.

The plan was revived in 1872 by F.B. Johnson who was determined to make Jardines the pioneer of railway development. More land was bought and, although the purpose was still in theory the building of a road, the Firm's railway engineer, James Morrison, was put in charge. A limited liability company was formed in London where further capital was raised. The idea was to lay down a narrow gauge track. For rolling stock the Firm contacted Ransomes & Rapier of Ipswich which was interested in Chinese railway development. The company constructed a small locomotive which could be shipped out to Shanghai in one large packing case. It was tested with four trucks in tow on a private line near Felixstowe and christened the *Pioneer* before being despatched to Shanghai.[9] Two others, the *Celestial Empire* and the *Flowery Land* were to follow.

A section of the line reaching Kiangman, a mile out of Shanghai, was officially opened on 1 July 1876. Alan Reid in his excellent monograph has given an entertaining account of the ceremony and of the celebratory dinner, hosted three weeks later by John Dixon, the contractor, at the Langham Hotel in London.[10] It included the Lord Mayor along with Sir Rutherford Alcock, ex-minister-plenipotentiary at Peking, a number of former Jardine Matheson partners including Alexander Matheson and Robert Jardine. The Ipswich locomotive manufacturers was represented by Richard Ransome and R.J. Rapier.

Meanwhile as a precautionary measure the Imperial Government had been informed about the railway in February. There was no reply. Somewhat over-optimistically the company assumed silence to mean consent and went ahead laying the track to Woosung. The extension was opened on 26 December. Receipts were satisfactory, averaging HK $40 to $60 a day. In its first year the railway carried 187,876 passengers. But it soon became clear that Imperial silence did not necessarily mean Imperial consent. Ominously the taotai of Shanghai ignored an invitation to attend the opening of the extension, and long before that official complaints were being made. While the railway was under construction a Chinese was run down and killed – probably a case of suicide, but the company was prompt to compensate the man's family. The theory advanced at the time that local officials had staged an 'accident' to discredit the whole operation seems to have no substance and was not believed by Jardines, but there is no doubt about the hostility of the Ch'ing civil servants to railways. It was part of an age-old conservatism. Even Li and his sympathisers in the cause of self-strengthening had to work within these constraints.

The episode coincided with the negotiations leading to the Convention of Chefoo, the result of the murder in Yunnan of Augustus Margary of the British Consular Service. He was on a mission to establish a trade route between north-eastern Burma and south-western

China, early in 1875. The Treaty of Tientsin allowed foreigners full rights of travel in the Empire, and Sir Thomas Wade, Ambassador in Peking, at once demanded reparation for the crime and an enquiry on the spot. The Tsungli Yamen (the nearest equivalent in Peking to a Foreign Office) agreed, but inevitably procrastinated. The Ambassador hauled down his flag, left Peking and prepared to break off relations. In the background lay the threat of a punitive expedition, and the Imperial Government, well aware of its impotence in such circumstances, allowed Li to negotiate a settlement.

Among other matters raised at Chefoo between Li and the British Ambassador was the question of the Shanghai–Woosung railway. True to his belief that railways should be controlled in China by the government, Li proposed to purchase it from the Woosung Road Company. Jardines would have liked to refuse, but it was in an awkward legal position. As with cotton factories, the right of a foreign company to build a railway on land it had bought was very doubtful, especially since official permission had not even been asked; the Ambassador could not easily support refusal. Sir Thomas Wade privately indicated to Jardines that it would be better advised to accept on reasonable terms. In England a pro-Chinese pamphleteer asked: 'Are Messrs. Jardine Matheson and Company more powerful than the Chinese Empire, because this railway of theirs has been built in defiance of treaty.'[11]

The Firm took Wade's advice, asking for not less than 300,000 taels. After laborious and time-consuming negotiations, on 25 November 1876 it sold the railway to the Chinese government for 285,000 taels in Shanghai *sycee*. Since this left $10,000 for commission and interest, the bargain was not thought to be too bad. In any case the Firm had always regarded the railway as an expendable loss-leader investment for the sake of future gain. If its demonstration succeeded, might it not lead to railway construction on a far larger scale, in which Jardines could play a major part as agents, procuring and financing the equipment of a great network? And this would be helped, not hindered, by an amicable and generous settlement, about which it had legally little choice.

What followed was, however, scarcely encouraging. Having sold the railway, the Firm had no direct interest in its subsequent management. But the behaviour of the Chinese authorities, the new owners, must have been something of a disappointment. Whether from pique, personal resentments or a new outburst of anti-foreign sentiment, the decision was made to rip up the tracks and fixed equipment and send them to lie rusting away in Formosa (Taiwan). Thus perished the first railway ever to be built in China. Probably the debâcle was due less to dislike of foreign technology than to dislike of foreigners. The Chinese officials responsible were notorious xenophobes, although also supporters of Li's economic reforms.

This somewhat ignominious end to Jardines' original venture in railways did not deter the Firm from having another try. One of the features in its history is not only a remarkable power to adapt to changing circumstances and so often to be one ahead of its rivals, but also a great persistence over long-term projects in which it had confidence. Railway finance is a good example. The attempt began again in the late 1880s. Li, who claimed never to have been against railways, seemed sympathetic. Since the fiasco of the Shanghai–Woosung railway there had been a further minor experiment in 1884. Gaston Galy, who represented the French Decauville Railway Company, which specialized in easily laid light railway systems, signed a ten-year contract with Jardines. The Firm agreed to act as agent for the system in China. The portable track and equipment were demonstrated in Canton and Hong Kong. No one was interested. An effort was then made at Tientsin, two miles of 2ft 6in gauge being laid behind the British settlement. Li's officials seemed to be impressed, and Alexander Michie, special agent and public relations man for Jardines, whose job it was to influence officials in favour of Western enterprises, hoped to obtain an order for an extended line from Tientsin to Kaiping, the great coal-mining centre.

Encouraged by this apparently sympathetic reception, Galy, in 1886, went to Peking. He tried for several months to secure agreement for a demonstration, but the Peking bureaucracy, unlike Li's officials at Tientsin, refused. Then they suddenly suggested that track and equipment should be given as a present to the Empress Dowager, so as to convince the real ruler of China that Western technology was worth having. Michie supported the idea with characteristic optimism and enthusiasm, but James Keswick was sceptical and somewhat annoyed. All that would happen, he believed, would be an experimental line constructed within the precincts of the Imperial Palace at Jardines' expense. What evidence was there that the Government took railways seriously?[12] Protracted negotiations followed, but as Peking would not buy and Jardines would not give, the affair lapsed. The mandarinate seemed just as hostile to railways as it had been ten years before over the Woosung Road Company.

Or, perhaps one should say, hostile to railways built and managed by foreigners. The first steam train, Chinese-owned and built after the Woosung Road Company's fiasco, ran on the tracks of the Kaiping mines in 1882. Li told Morrison that he recognized the importance of the Shanghai–Woosung line in September 1876, and he praised Jardines as a firm of good repute which might well be given business by the government as agents for railway and mining enterprises. The Kaiping line was the first of a number of short lines constructed in north China during the next thirteen years under Chinese auspices. But the hope of a really big development was never abandoned by the Firm. It was clear that anything on that scale would be beyond the capacity of the Imperial Government and only feasible with a large injection of foreign capital in which Jardines could play an important part.

Early in 1887, Li Hung-chang sent a memorandum to the Empress Dowager in favour of linking by rail Kaiping to Tientsin. His case was made mainly on military grounds, but the value of it for trade and the profits of merchants was also mentioned.[13] Permission was given, and the Kaiping Railway Company was transmuted into the China Railway Company. A prospectus was published in April, and it was announced that 10,000 shares would be issued at 100 taels per share. At the same time rumours emanated from the Imperial Court that Prince Ch'un, one of the most influential advisers to the Crown, was contemplating a major trunk railway system based on the Kaiping line. It was said that an initial investment of 14,000 taels would be needed. Jardines was quick to offer its services. They were not at first refused. Months of discussion followed. There were frequent meetings between Imperial officials and Jardines' agents, but no agreement could be reached, and negotiations lapsed early in 1888.

They foundered on the same rock which had so often caused shipwreck. Jardines was willing to provide equipment, skilled labour and capital in the form of loans. But the Firm insisted on also providing the management of the railway construction. This, it believed, was the only safe way of securing its loans, and it was also the only way to induce Chinese merchants to take up shares in a company set up in co-operation with the Imperial Government. As mentioned earlier, they far preferred management by Western firms to management by Ch'ing officials, and with good reason. The Chinese officials were corrupt, dilatory and incompetent. The Western firms were brisk, efficient and, in most cases, honest.

In the summer of 1887 James Morrison drew up an elaborate alternative plan to that of an American syndicate (in effect Russell & Co.) for a major trunk line network in China. He submitted it to an important official, Tseng Chi-tse (sometimes described in the Firm's correspondence as 'the Marquis Tseng'). The plan described detailed routes, an extension of the northern line and estimates of total cost. Like so many proposals about railways, it got nowhere. The rival American syndicate and a German competitor were equally unsuccessful, although prepared to lend at the unprecedently low rate of four per cent. Jardines, after consultation with Matheson, made five and a half per cent their absolute minimum, and this was low by Chinese standards. The normal form was eight per cent or more, even when secured as a charge on the Chinese Customs' Revenue which, being managed by a highly competent Englishman, Sir Robert Hart, on behalf of the Imperial Government, was regular and reliable. In 1875, on this security, Jardines had made a loan of 1 million taels to the Peking government at a rate as high as ten and a half per cent.

In fact, rates of interest were not the main consideration of the Ch'ing bureaucracy. The truth was that enlightened and seemingly 'progressive' officials like Li and Tseng regarded projects such as railways in the light of 'self-strengthening' against foreigners, steps in increasing their independence from the Barbarians; not at all as Jardines and their colleagues believed, steps towards industrialization and assimilation with the Western world. The difference from Japan, which was assumed by Westerners to be the model for China, could scarcely have been greater. Foreign managers were regarded as a potential threat. No doubt they were not as bad as missionaries, but their presence would be a contradiction of the whole purpose of the sort of modernization supported by the progressive element in the Ch'ing bureaucracy.

There was another difficulty for the 'progressives'. They were a minority in an intensely conservative officialdom which adhered to its traditional beliefs, despite military defeat by Britain in 1840–41, by Britain and France in 1859–60, and by France in 1884–5, and despite all the evidence that China was no longer the Middle Kingdom and could not isolate itself from the modern world. The traditional Confucian examination system with its emphasis on such archaisms as the 'eight-legged essay' and elegant calligraphy remained in the ascendant. Only very slowly and gradually did the learning of foreign languages, the teaching of Western mathematics, science, astronomy, engineering and technology creep into the educational system, thanks to the efforts of Li and others. But they had to proceed with care and to walk warily and cautiously along the thin line between tradition and modernity.

The conservatives, after all, had some arguments on their side. Even in England there had been bitter opposition to railways on the part of most landowners. They had to be bought out at enormous expense by a series of private Acts of Parliament which made fortunes for the lawyers and landowners. As a result the cost of railways per mile was higher in England than anywhere else in the world. But England was the richest country in the world and could afford it. China was one of the poorest and, although its area was almost infinitely larger, that did not alter the impact of railway construction on particular peasant plots in particular places. The livelihood – and perhaps more important, the way of life – of a large number of people would be affected. And in a country where superstition and rumour thrived, who could say what sort of knock-on effects might result in regions which were nowhere near to the line of rail? The memory of the Taiping Rebellion was all too vivid.

Matters were made no easier for Jardines and other Western firms by the extreme difficulty of discovering which officials in Peking were responsible for decisions. In theory none was; only the Crown, in the form of the Empress Dowager, could have the final say in these matters, but everyone knew that some officials carried greater weight than others. In many ways the Imperial regime was like a Tudor Court, without the potential opposition of Parliament. The problem was to find out who were the Walsinghams or Burleighs. As James Keswick wrote in connection with a possible Sterling loan of £1,000,000 in 1887, to be arranged by Matheson & Co. in the event of the American Syndicate losing out, he would 'try to get some comprehensive proposal laid before the proper officials in Peking (but who are they?) to provide money, railways and everything connected with it'.[15] The question 'Who are they?' was a perpetual problem. It still is. The way in which decisions are made in Peking remains as mysterious and enigmatic in the last days of the twentieth century as it was in the days of the Empress Dowager.

THIRTEEN

Railways and Governments

The refusal by the 'Marquis Tseng' to accept Morrison's railway memorial of 1887 seemed to imply that the Imperial Court had taken a policy decision against railway construction. But the Firm learned two years later, or thought it had learned, that Prince Ch'un and Li Hung-chang, who now appeared to be the key figures in this matter, were contemplating a major development of their own. Morrison's document was duly extracted from the dusty files where it had lain dormant, the accuracy of its Chinese translation was checked and corrected, and a fresh copy was despatched to Li. The two ministers were believed to have in mind a major trunk line from Canton to Hankow. Li was to be in charge of the northern sector and his brother would deal with the southern.

Yet at the same time there was persistent gossip that the Imperial Court had decided to postpone any substantial railway construction for five years.[1] This was because the Conservative Party had got the ear of the Empress Dowager, or so it was alleged, and the traditional doubts about railways were now in the ascendant. There was not only the argument about unemployment and peasant plots of land, there was also the fear that foreign-built railways might constitute a military threat to Peking. The logic of this argument is hard to understand; railways, however built and financed, would be, prima facie, an advantage for the defenders and make the movement of their troops easier in the event of a hostile invasion, but the Manchu Court was not at its best when considering military logistics.

In October 1889 Robert Inglis, an employee of the Firm's Shanghai staff, went to Peking. His object was to negotiate loans for railway projects. There was much talk about a loan of 30 million taels. This was an offer by the Chinese Board of Revenue. Formally it was for general purposes, but Li Hung-chang was believed to control its allocation which would be largely for railway construction. Inglis spent many months in the capital trying to bring matters to some sort of conclusion in 1890–91. He telegraphed to Shanghai that an American-German syndicate was prepared to lend at four and a half per cent and two and a half per cent commission for floating the loan. Payment of interest and repayment of capital would be in silver. John Macgregor, one of the Firm's partners, found this incredible. Chinese currency was on the silver standard, but silver was constantly going down against gold. Such a loan would need a number of collateral advantages and guarantees, none of which was mentioned in the offer by the Hupu of Peking.[2]

The whole matter was so obscure, and the conflicting rumours emanating from the Imperial Court and its officials so diverse and numerous, that the Firm engaged in a combination of intelligence operations and 'douceurs' for officials who might provide reliable information. Jardines was especially anxious to discover which mandarins stood where in the mysterious pecking order of power, precedency and influence in the Court. It was vital to deal with those who were 'in' or 'coming in' and not waste time and money on those who were 'out' or 'going out'. This was Robert Inglis's job, and Macgregor congratulated him on his work, noting with satisfaction 'the connection for information in high quarters which you have been able to establish'. He expressed the hope 'that something tangible will come of this long period of waiting and negotiation'.[3]

Nothing did. Matheson & Co., whose support was vital, was not prepared to lend on a silver basis, and Inglis was informed of this decision in July 1890, at the same time as he learnt that the Chinese Government would not borrow on any other basis. Gold was 'out', as far as the Imperial Court was concerned. Russell & Co., the Deutsche-Asiatische Bank and a French consortium were prepared to make a silver-based loan on the same conditions as the American-German Syndicate. Jardines had a friendly arrangement with the Hong Kong & Shanghai Bank under which the two companies would operate respectively in

Peking (JM) and Tientsin (HKSB), where Li was based. Each would help the other and, if the loan was in the exclusive gift of Li or other officials, two-thirds would be settled at the place of negotiation, the rest at the other city. Jardines departed from the spirit, if not the letter, of this agreement by secretly offering Li Han-chang (Li's brother) a loan of 30 million taels on a gold basis at six and a half per cent, with repayment over 50 years. It was refused on 21 July within a week, on the grounds that any amount of money on a gold basis could be got at four and a half per cent.[4] Perhaps the rejection was just as well for future relations between the Firm and the Bank.

Inglis continued to do what he could in Peking, but his story was one of great expectations and hopes deferred. On behalf of the Firm he made the occasional small loan to grease the palms of officials alleged to be able to help (but were they really?). He was faced with the difficulty that the Jardines loan of 1884 was alleged by the Hupu of Peking to have been exorbitant in terms of the exchange rate. On behalf of the Firm, Inglis denied this accusation and cited the change since 1884 in the gold-silver ratio.[5] He battled on with indefatigable energy. When Prince Ch'un died early in 1891, Inglis busily lobbied possible successors about an Ewo offer of a 30 million taels loan. Prince Ch'ing seemed the best bet. Inglis used his intelligence system in Peking to get copies of the Prince's letters, note who called on him and discover his attitude toward the Firm's activities over loans and railways.

There were three loans under discussion: 'the Big Loan' of 30 million taels, a 5–7 million Admiralty loan and a loan of uncertain amount to the Hupu of Peking. The second became merged with the first, the Hupu undertaking to defray naval costs from his own borrowed funds. Inglis was told that the Firm would offer for both. The terms for the Hupu Loan would be 5 million taels at six and a half per cent (with no repayment of principal), interest in Sterling and Imperial guarantee. The Hupu officials were doubtful. As for the Big Loan, the relevant mandarin demanded a commission of ten per cent, 3 million taels. Macgregor regarded this as an 'exorbitant squeeze'. He authorized a 'cumshaw' of three per cent – 90,000 taels – a maximum to be kept lower if possible, and pressed Inglis to make the most of the collapse of Russell & Co., the firm most likely to underbid Jardines in this highly competitive and uncertain business. In October 1891 the Chinese authorities decided that loan negotiations would be held over until the new year and possibly later.

This was a setback. The early months of 1892 saw a serious slump in the China trade, and the economic outlook suddenly became bleak. A major casualty was Russell & Co. The company had a long history behind it, almost as long as that of Jardines. It departed in 1839 from the line taken by Jardines and Dent in Canton and gave up the opium trade. The company moved to Macao and then to Hong Kong. It had strong connections with that greatest of merchant bankers, Baring Bros. in London, and established itself in the Treaty Ports as the resident exchange broker by reason of the acceptability of its Sterling bills in India. Its main office after 1846 was in Shanghai, but eventually the Oriental Bank put it out of the exchange business. From 1850 it was for over 40 years the mirror image of Jardines, competing in shipping, insurance, banking, import/export trade and railways. Russell & Co. successfully undercut Jardines' offer of a railway loan in 1887 to the Chinese government. Undercutting does not always pay off, and it may have been one reason for the company's demise, but the principal cause was just what Jardines had now avoided for some years: overspeculation in a particular commodity – in this case sugar.

The collapse of Russell & Co. was followed by that of the Oriental Bank, and by the bankruptcy of the comprador of the Hong Kong & Shanghai Bank, who had been a key figure in the affairs of the Treaty Ports. The alarming crisis caused Jardines to circulate a confidential report about the Firm's financial situation. William Keswick, writing to his New York agents in June 1892, admitted 'how disastrous Eastern trade has been for some time' and sought to relieve anxiety by clarifying the situation of the Firm. He stated that US $8.6 million was represented as capital on the Firm's 1891 balance sheet. Of that $7.5 million was almost immediately liquid – 'a very ample amount which provides the utmost security for all contingencies'. He went on to say that the rating given to the Firm by the New York Bankers' Association was quite safe. The Firm's working capital was over $1 million and was all in gold, 'absolutely intact', which was well above the minimum requirement. He did not mention the large resources of the

London-based Matheson & Co. , which would also presumably have been available in the event of a real emergency. His assurances related simply to the China Firm, and seem to have carried conviction.[6] But the economic recession which affected all businesses involved in the China trade put a stop to loan negotiations for the next three years. They were revived only on the eve of the Sino-Japanese War of 1894 which was to transform the whole situation.

Jardines, like all Western trading enterprises, had to deal, however remotely, with what in European eyes was a bizarre and barely comprehensible system of government. Since 1862 China had been ruled by the Empress Dowager or, rather, by two Empress Dowagers, Tzu-An and Tzu-Hsi. Tzu-An, aged 25 in 1862, had been the wife of the previous Emperor. Tzu-Hsi (1835–1908) was the 'Imperial Concubine': they were Regents on behalf of the late Emperor's son until he came of age, and they held their position as the result of a quasi *coup d'état*.[7] The future Emperor was the son of the Imperial Concubine, and it was this which, under the rules of the Manchu dynasty, gave Tzu-Hsi a claim to be a co-Regent with the childless wife of the late Emperor. Tsu-An was an amiable nonentity, unlike Tzu-Hsi. The Imperial Concubine was a woman of formidable ability and determination, comparable to Elizabeth I of England, or Catherine the Great of Russia. She was to be the real ruler of China for 47 years. Her son, who came of age in 1873, died or, as many believed, was murdered two years later. Tzu-An died in 1881. Again there were stories that her death was hastened by her co-Regent. There is no proof of homicide in either case. People die natural deaths, even when it is convenient for relatives that they should, but the suspicion remains strong.

Tzu-Hsi inherited the enormous prestige and authority of the Manchu Emperors. Like them she was a complete autocrat. Like them she had total and arbitrary control over the mandarins who from time immemorial had administered the vast empire. Although she ruled from 'behind the screen' – as a woman she could not actually sit on the throne – she had all the *de facto* authority of an Emperor. She could appoint, promote, dismiss officials at will. She could degrade them, exile them to the frozen northern province of Ili, confiscate their property, condemn them to death. Inevitably she had to delegate authority in such a huge country. The provincial viceroys exercised immense power, but only on behalf of the Crown. If there was no trouble in their areas and if they remitted enough money to the Court to keep up the Empress Dowager's standard of living, which was high, they could rule undisturbed and live in great luxury themselves. If there was disorder, riot or rebellion, they were accountable and could be punished by confiscation, exile or death.

The objective of the surviving Empress Dowager was to preserve herself in power. Her regime had no other purpose. She believed that she could remain in authority only by adhering to the principles of a rigid conservatism. This entailed resistance to every initiative by the Western Barbarians that could be resisted. The notions of economic growth, improved standard of living, industrial expansion, better communications – all that the West meant by 'progress' counted for nothing at the fossilized Manchu Court in Peking. Survival might require some concessions to Western pressure, but these should be as few as possible. Western merchants found it hard to understand an attitude which lay so far outside their own mental terms of reference – all the harder since Chinese capitalists in the Treaty Ports seemed to share the Western outlook. It was a case of coming to terms with what Lord Aberdeen, a generation back, had called 'this strange Empire'. It was also a matter of the profound difference mentioned earlier between the coastal Chinese world of commerce, shipping and enterprise, compared with that of the interior – vast, overpopulated, xenophobic, illiterate and enigmatic; and far more important in the eyes of the Imperial Court than jumped-up compradors from Shanghai, let alone pushy merchants on the make from Europe and America.

The sheer power of resistance to change displayed by the Ch'ing dynasty is one of the most remarkable features of Chinese history. The Taiping and Nien rebellions shook the regime to its core. If its survival was partly due to the help of Barbarian troops, when the foreign devils decided that victory for the rebellion would be worse for trade than preservation of the status quo, there still remained the threat of the Barbarians themselves. Living in a complacent atmosphere of isolated grandeur, the dynasty managed nevertheless to achieve survival and a restoration of its essential features. This was helped by Western arms, but it could not have been achieved without the solidarity and determination of the Confucian governing élite which had identified itself with the continuance of Imperial rule, and produced some very able ministers – Tseng Kuo-fan and Li Hung-chang among them – who, though 'creatures of China's past, did succeed in putting down the rebellions, restoring the dynasty's position, and even reviving the spirit of its statecraft'.[8]

The survival of the Ch'ing empire is all the more surprising when one considers its long series of military defeats and total inability to learn any lessons from them. The Imperial army and navy were crushed by the British, with huge casualties for the losers and scarcely any for the winners, in the First Opium War of 1839–42. Anglo-French forces achieved much the same result in the Second Opium (or 'Arrow') War of 1856–60. A desultory but unsuccessful campaign resulted in the French annexation of Annam in 1885, a step in the creation of its Indo-China empire. These setbacks culminated in the major disaster of the Sino-Japanese War of 1894. Once again the hopeless inferiority of Ch'ing armed forces in the face of the modern military technology was displayed to the world. The issue at stake was which country would have Korea as its sphere of influence. The Japanese won every battle, which was not surprising as the Chinese army was equipped with wooden cannonballs painted to look real and the navy's big guns had no shells because the Empress Dowager had diverted the relevant funds to the reconstruction of the Summer Palace burnt down in 1860. It was hardly a good example of 'self-strengthening'.

The Imperial Court and its ambivalent ministers were not the only authorities whom the Western merchants had to deal with and hopefully understand. The policies of their own Governments, particularly, as far as Jardines was concerned that of Britain, were highly relevant to the advance of commerce in China. In other areas of British 'imperialist expansion' there were mixed motives, political and strategic as well as commercial. In the case of China, trade was the only purpose. The two so-called 'opium wars' were fought primarily to open up the markets of China to world trade – a purpose generally approved in Britain even by advanced liberal anti-imperialists like Cobden. It was part of the free trade ideology of the mid-Victorian years. 'What British interests are at the present day,' wrote Sir Rutherford Alcock, 'and what the sole object of our policy [is] needs no explanation. Both should be, if they are not, patent to the world. Commerce is with us in Siam, China and Japan ... the one sole object.'[9]

It was not a matter of pressing for a British monopoly. On the contrary, Lord Elgin, when negotiating the Treaty of Tientsin, was instructed to bear in mind that 'Her Majesty's Government have no desire to obtain any exclusive advantages for British trade in China, but are only desirous to share with all other nations any benefits which they may acquire in the first instance specifically for British commerce.'[10] This was one aspect of the nineteenth-century Western view of free trade and the 'Open Door' as panaceas of peace and progress, which would not only benefit the West but also China and Japan themselves. It followed that British diplomats and Consuls should not press for exclusive privileges in China. It was legitimate in the general interests of British commerce to urge the Chinese Government for its own long-term advantage to remove its trade barriers and reform its fiscal system. It was also legitimate to press for navigation facilities on the inland waterways and railway construction to open up the interior. These were measures which would benefit the whole of the China trade. No doubt they would benefit British traders above all, because by 1880 they had some four-fifths of it – but this was thanks to efficiency and competitiveness in a free and unrestricted market, not to monopoly, tariffs or concessions.

The British Government's belief in the Open Door and *laissez-faire* meant that any support for projects by individual British firms must be emphatically avoided. It was one thing to try to persuade the Imperial officials to create conditions of a general nature conducive to the advancement of British trade along with that of other countries, quite another to become, however indirectly, involved in the affairs of a particular business. Until the mid-1880s Foreign Office instructions forbade any action of this sort by its representatives in China. The British Legation at Peking gave no support at all to Jardines in its project for the Shanghai–Woosung railway in 1875–6, nor to the proposed Shanghai cotton mill in 1883.[11] Admittedly, the Firm was on shaky legal ground in both cases, but it would have got little help even if this had not been the case. In other parts of China, where no legal problems arose, the Foreign Office was equally discouraging, especially towards railway concessions. It was not that the British Government was against railways, merely that it was determined to avoid official involvement.

What successive Foreign Secretaries wanted was the preservation of the Manchu empire, freedom of trade and a 'level playing field', as modern jargon puts it, for commercial competitors irrespective of nationality. What they did not want was the collapse of the regime and political partition. Scarcely less unwelcome was what actually happened – not political but economic partition into 'spheres of influence'; Britain, the largest trading nation with commercial interests throughout China, was bound to be the loser. But if the other Western powers refused to play the game according to the rules of the Open Door, the British Government would have to follow suit, or lose even more trade.

The first sign of trouble came, as one would expect, from the French who, after the war in Annam, imposed in June 1885 the Treaty of Tientsin on the Chinese Government. This included 'the differential duties, the preferential treatment, and the national railway concessions which gave a death-blow to international equality.'[12] The Eastern trade was far too important for any British Government to remain passive in the face of this threat, which affected Japan as well as China. There were already signs that diplomatic representatives were beginning to use their governmental muscle to extract concessions from Tokyo. Lord Salisbury, who doubled as Prime Minister and Foreign Secretary, decided to abandon the neutrality which had hitherto been the hallmark of British commercial diplomacy. He told the Minister in Tokyo on 2 August 1885: 'In cases where foreign Representatives interfere to the detriment of British commercial interests you are at liberty to give the latter your support.'[13] The threat in Tokyo came from Germany, whose representatives also soon became active in Peking. The French and German actions at opposite ends of the Celestial Empire set in train a process of economic partition which Britain could not resist; but, if free trade was to be replaced by spheres of influence, the Foreign Office was going to take good care that Britain got the lion's 'sphere'.

In a history of Jardines there is no need to go into the highly complicated story of what followed. Many observers thought that political partition on the lines of the contemporaneous 'grab for Africa' would be inevitable, but China was a very different proposition with its ancient civilization and its vast population. None of the great powers wished to embark on a process which could easily disturb the balance of Europe and involve unforeseeable consequences for the future. The colonization of China was not practicable; division into areas of economic interest was feasible.

The process began after the Sino-Japanese war of 1894. The Treaty of Shimonoseki next year revealed the full measure of the weakness and decay of the Manchu regime, and the emergence of Japan as a formidable competitor in the China stakes. Japan annexed Formosa (Taiwan) and the Liao-tung peninsula, and imposed an enormous indemnity. A joint démarche by Russia, Germany and France persuaded the Japanese Government to forego the cession of the peninsula in return for an even larger indemnity, but this European intervention was bitterly resented and had lasting consequences.

The effect of the Treaty was to open China to all the trading nations of the world. The rush for spheres of influence began almost at once. In 1897, Germany acquired a 99-year lease of the coaling station at Kiao-chan, and Russia did a similar deal over Port Arthur. Next year the French negotiated a 99-year lease of the southern port, Kwangchow-wan. Britain riposted by securing a lease of the northern port of Weihaiwei, and – far more important for the future – of some 200 square miles north of Kowloon known as the Hong Kong 'New Territories'.[14]

By 1900 the spheres of European influence had been demarcated. Russia had Mongolia and Manchuria, Japan, Korea and Fukien, Germany Shantung, Britain the Yangtse Valley – far the richest area of all – and France claimed the provinces south of Canton. What mattered in every case was the coast. Contemporary maps show the spheres going back far into the interior, reaching to the frontier with Russia. In practice Western officials and merchants seldom penetrated into those teeming but remote areas. The vast majority of Chinese had never seen a foreigner – which in no way diminished their instinctive hatred of these unknown interlopers of whom they had heard on the grapevine.

The year 1898 saw not only the division of China into European spheres of interest; it was also the year of the reassertion of power in Peking by the Empress Dowager. In 1889 her nephew and heir had come of age. After mutual expressions of admiration and esteem, he accepted the resignation of his aunt as Regent and assumed the role of Emperor. He was a weak and ineffective figure, but after the fiasco of the Sino-Japanese war, he had the sense to realize – or his advisers had – that the Imperial administration must be reformed. A short-lived 100 days' flurry of change ensued. The party of reaction soon put a stop to it and brought back the Empress Dowager. Her feeble nephew was retired into virtual house-arrest, his decrees were reversed and his advisers executed, apart from their leader who escaped. His aunt ruled for another ten years until they both died in 1908. Meanwhile the Court issued high-flown, empty edicts and memorials, devoid of any contact with reality – in Peter Fleming's words: 'The pompous futility of turkeys gobbling at the rumble of distant thunder.'[15]

The carving up of China into Western spheres of influence had no immediate impact on Jardines as far as trade was concerned. The Firm's activities had for many years been mainly concentrated on the large and rich area now claimed by Britain – Shanghai, the Yangtse Valley and the provinces extending southward to Kwangtung which included Canton, still an important Treaty Port and trading entrepôt. In any case, trade could cross the boundaries of the spheres of interest, and the rights of the 'suzerain' powers were shadowy and ultimately unenforceable. Nor were loans affected. These were accepted or rejected in Peking on considerations which were frequently puzzling, but had nothing to do with the sphere of influence from which those who tendered the loans emanated.

What mattered in the contest of this economic partition was railway concessions. These had a geographical relevance which could not be ignored. They also had major financial implications. The Chinese Governments's resistance to railways collapsed after the Sino-Japanese war. The regime was now too feeble to hold out any longer. There were signs soon after the Chinese defeat that some of the mandarins were working for a modernized China. The Viceroy Chang Chih-tung, one of the important officials, had asked the Firm, even before the war had ended, for a gold loan of $1 million at six per cent secured on the Chinese Maritime Customs. Jardines was inclined to agree, but Matheson & Co., understandably, insisted on waiting to see who won the war.[16]

The same Chinese official was believed by rumour – nothing seemed ever to be certain in the mandarinate – to favour contracts and a concession in respect of the frequently discussed Peking–Hankow railway. This might be the forerunner of a large-scale attempt at economic and military progress. Timothy Richard, a missionary of some celebrity, was engaged by James Keswick to negotiate with Chang Chih-tung, even while the Chinese Government stood in a most unfavourable position over the Treaty of Shimonoseki. Richard informed Keswick that a railway would be built, the first section to run from Nanking to Ching Kiang, a city on the Grand Canal. This seemed an encouraging sign that Imperial resistance to railways was on the wane. Morrison prepared a survey, and the *taotai* of Ching Kiang told Jardines that work would be under way as soon as possible and that it had Imperial authorization. He also invited a loan of 5 million taels.

The question now arose whether the Firm should deal with central or provincial authorities. This raised the important issue of the Open Door against spheres of exclusive influence. Was it better to support free trade for all, maintained by a moderately reformed central government or to acknowledge that this was no longer practicable and do one's best in spheres of economic interest supported by provincial autonomy? The former was still the policy favoured by Sir Robert Hart with all his great authority. It was also that of the Hong Kong & Shanghai Bank, probably encouraged by the British Government. The Japanese had demanded a large indemnity which could be paid only by the Imperial Government raising a loan. Keswick was told that the Bank wished 'to discourage all loans except at Peking where they hope to get an opportunity in the shape of an Indemnity Loan of thirty to fifty million Sterling'. He had doubts. The big Indemnity Loan might well be 'a very mythical matter'. He thought that 'it would be far more

Chinese-like for the Central Government to permit or even order provincial Viceroys... to raise money as urgently required in sums of one or ten or more millions.' And he informed Matheson & Co. that it would be better to deal with a provincial Viceroy, Chang Chih-tung, than go along with the Bank's 'central' policy. China had, he said, no national pride and the delay involved in a central loan might give the government a chance to wriggle out of its obligations if, as seemed likely, a conflict soon took place between Japan and Russia.[17]

The belief held by the Firm that the Emperor and his court would retire from Peking and that a provincial party led by Chang Chi-tung and his brother would constitute a new government proved to be wrong. James Keswick thought that Chang and his supporters were so strong that the Hart policy of a big consolidated loan floated in Peking would be certain to founder. In the months following the Treaty of Shimonoseki, the balance of power swung back to Li Hung-chang. It was perfectly reasonable for Keswick to have assumed that the Imperial Court and Li himself, as one of its principal advisers, would have been so discredited by the fiasco of the Sino-Japanese war that neither he nor the Government could survive. Nevertheless they did. There was no move to replace them, and the negotiations for a large Indemnity Loan went ahead in Peking, and not in Nanking as the Firm had expected.

This renewed evidence of the tenacious conservatism of the Imperial regime resulted in an important development in the history of the Firm. Ever since 1877 when William Keswick was elected as a director of the Hong Kong & Shanghai Bank, relations between it and Jardine Matheson had been friendly, although the leading figures in the two institutions did not always agree about everything and the businesses were entirely independent. Thomas Jackson, who occupies something of the same position in the history of the Bank as William Keswick in the history of the Firm, came to the view in 1895 that closer co-operation was desirable in the interests of both. This appreciation coincided with a decision by the Firm that, since its efforts in Nanking had run into the sand, it should try to stake out its own share in a central loan to Peking in co-operation with the Bank. It was suggested to James Keswick that the Firm 'could be connected with the Hong Kong & Shanghai Bank as joint agents... and we will try to work on these lines through Sir Robert Hart'. The particular project of a HK $16 million loan did not come off as far as the Firm was concerned. It became a joint French-Russian loan, sponsored and backed by the two governments. James Keswick was soon convinced that private firms could not compete in financial transactions involving complicated diplomatic dealings with foreign governments unless the British Foreign Office was prepared to intervene, which was not the case quite yet.

However, the affair led to a decision by the partners in Jardines and the directors of the Bank to put their relations on a more formal basis. They had been co-operating under *ad hoc* arrangements for a good many years, but it was now clearly desirable that their respective areas of activity should be defined. In the autumn of 1895 an agreement was drawn up. It was not contractually binding, rather a series of general guidelines for their respective roles in the newly developing national competition for the China trade. Three years later the British & Chinese Corporation was founded and legal form was given to a new institution jointly owned by the Bank and the Firm with the principal object of obtaining and exploiting railway concessions. The leading figures were William Keswick for Jardines and Ewen Cameron, the Bank's London manager. The Jardines' part was that of a contracting firm, ready to build railways, supply rolling stock, recruit staff, engineers, and to oversee the actual working of the lines. The part of the Bank was to supply the necessary finance. The two complemented each other. They had a happy relationship for over half a century, and in the period of the battle for concessions which began in 1898 the British & Chinese Corporation was described by the *China Mail* as 'the chosen instrument of the British Government'.

FOURTEEN

The Turn of the Century

The exact position of the Firm in terms of profit and loss when it entered the twentieth century cannot be determined. This is because, as stated earlier, the ledgers, account books and journals for the period 1888–1907 are missing. One can only assume that Jardines fared reasonably well, otherwise it could not have survived the trade crisis of 1891–2 which killed its rival, Russell & Co. When that was over, the Firm coasted comfortably enough through the rest of the decade. Land values in which it had an important stake were rising in both Shanghai and Hong Kong. Railway concessions were no longer vetoed, and after the fiasco of the Sino-Japanese war even the Chinese Government belatedly saw the need for modern weapons. Jardines had been involved in the great expansion of European armament manufacture for some time, being agents for Armstrong which, along with Krupp, was one of the biggest companies operating in that field. By and large the 1890s was a satisfactory and presumably prosperous period under the capable management of the two Keswick brothers.

In Shanghai life for the Firm's employees was by no means uncomfortable. This had been true ever since the 1860s and it applied also to staff in the lesser Treaty Ports. Salaries were adequate, though not lavish, and there were numerous benefits in kind, although there was no pension scheme. The cost of living was low. The climate, it is true, was not agreeable; but greatly improved sanitation, together with medical advances, made conditions much healthier than they had been earlier in the century, when the death toll from disease was very high.

Tours of service were for five years and marriage was not allowed until after a junior's first home leave. This could be for as much as a year if the employee could afford it, for his salary was paid for only six months while he was on leave. Thereafter he had to fend for himself. The Firm paid for the return ticket. The journey was either by a P&O ship, or, after 1900, via the Trans-Siberian Railway which was in those days a comfortable, even luxurious, mode of transport. Whichever route he took, he enjoyed a valuable perquisite, unlike officials in the Chinese Consular Service, who, owing to the long-established and still continuing tradition of Treasury stinginess, had to pay for themselves and were obliged to meet bills of up to £700 if they had a wife and dependants.[1]

The marriage ban was imposed because junior staff were expected to do a good deal of travelling and to be ready to move from one posting to another at short notice and for short periods. It does not seem to have been resented; young men accepted their jobs with their eyes open and knew where they stood. As for sex, the facilities, especially in Shanghai, were famous. In 1877 there were 30 European, and a much larger number of indigenous, prostitutes. No one looked askance at Chinese mistresses. Marriage was another matter and occurred seldom. Once the five-year novitiate had ended, a man could bring his European wife out to the China coast, but a couple often had to spend long periods apart because of placing children at schools and other reasons. As time went on, this became less of a problem. A second or third generation of Britons constituted a community with its own high-quality schools and its own style of life. Many school-leavers joined Jardines or other British firms. Thus the system perpetuated itself.

Life in the Treaty Ports for the younger men was rather like the bachelor life of an army mess in contemporary India – the same sort of all-male and slightly boisterous existence. There were plenty of opportunities for sport: riding, hunting, polo, horse-racing and shooting. The neighbourhood of Shanghai was particularly well stocked with pheasant, partridge, woodcock and quail. These activities were enjoyed by young men who, as in the Indian army, could not, in most cases, have had a chance of affording them at home.

'Tiffin', the midday meal, was a lavish affair. The food was of high quality. Wine and spirits flowed freely, along with a variety of excellent iced drinks. There was much hospitality. According to the *Times* special correspondent, Wingrove Cooke:

> Where the junior partner, with his employees of silk inspector and tea taster and bookkeeper and clerks, holds a separate mess, the allowance from the house to that mess is never less than 50 dollars per month per head, or something more than £200 a year to each employee for the table alone... There is no chance of finding people making shift with small commons in China... Everyone is able, and is indeed obliged to have a lordly indifference to expense. They cannot control it and they must let it go. There is no struggling or contriving to keep up appearances. The profits are large and the expenditure – *laissez-aller*.[2]

He ends somewhat austerely: 'Tiffin, however, is a bad habit; if we can, keep out of it.' They certainly did themselves well. £200 was a lot of money in Victorian times – the equivalent today of £8,000 if one measures by the change in the general retail price index, and a good deal more if one compares like with like. For example, a three-course dinner without wine at the Savoy in 1900 cost the equivalent of 38 modern pence, and in 1990 £28.75.[3] Tiffin and dinner in Shanghai normally comprised soup, fish, entrée, joint, sweets, curry, salad, cheese and dessert. Overeating was accompanied too often by overdrinking. A doctor who deplored this nevertheless advocated wine 'in moderation' – half a dozen glasses of sherry or port daily.[4] There is no doubt that alcoholism was a serious menace, whether in the commercial or the consular world. Some believed that it was a greater danger to the Europeans than opium was to the Chinese. The expatriates did not indulge in opium. It was regarded as *infra dig*, although there was nothing in contemporary British law to prevent it, and a few people made the occasional experiment.

It tended to be very much a young man's world. In 1851 there were about 350 British residing in Shanghai. Fewer than 30 were more than 40 years old. There were under 50 adult women.[5] Much of the social life in the ports revolved round clubs. These were very characteristic and widespread institutions, not only in the colonies and dependencies but in the informal commercial enclaves, which British trade had established in many foreign countries. Every port of any size had one for the élite - 'The Club' for which consular officials, customs commissioners and merchants were eligible along with their juniors in the same profession or trade. There was another called the 'Customs Club' for inferior persons such as constables, tide-waiters (a customs official who boarded ships on arrival to enforce customs regulations) and the like. The line of demarcation was crystallized by a decision in 1870 that all British subjects in China should be annually registered with the relevant consul at a fee of $5, reduced to $1 for 'artisans'. Then came the delicate question of who was an artisan. Clearly a $1 payer would not be eligible for 'The Club', but what would happen if a socially ambitious tide-waiter insisted on paying $5? Conversely, what would be the social position of a missionary whom a pious and benevolent consul let off with $1? It had been known even for a bishop to be thus treated. The complications of Victorian society transplanted into China were subtle, elaborate and multifarious. All one can safely say about the Firm is that its employees would all have been $5 men and members of 'The Club'. Eventually the social problem was alleviated by the introduction of a uniform registration fee for all British subjects.[6]

Although even quite young merchants liked to think of themselves at any rate after their first tour of duty as 'Old China Hands', in fact the commercial world lived almost entirely on its own and had very little direct contact with the Chinese apart from servants and labourers. They depended for business affairs entirely upon their compradors, and communication was in English or Pidgin. The original object of the treaties had been to oblige China to open up its cities and allow extra-territorial settlements within them. In practice, apart from Canton, nearly all the settlements were outside the port's city walls – suburbs which escaped the noise, filth, stench and airless summer heat within. Life outside if not agreeable was much less disagreeable. But a result was that the Old China Hands knew very little about China or the Chinese. Hardly any of them attempted to learn the language. One can compare the British port-shippers dwelling on the Douro who never bothered to learn Portuguese until the nationalist sentiments fuelled by the revolution of 1974 made it a reluctant necessity. Chinese is a far more difficult language to learn – 4000 characters – and to pronounce since different inflections of accent can give totally different meanings to the same written words.

Sir (as he later became) John Keswick who went out to Shanghai in 1929 was the first member of the Firm to learn the language. He wrote:

> I went into the office on the Bund for the first time. I asked if I might learn Chinese. B. D. F. Beith [the Taipan] said, 'Good idea – none of us do – but a good idea,' and the comprador, Pan Ching Poo, was asked to find me a teacher – an old scholar from Peking, accustomed to teaching Mandarin to Shanghai ladies. He spoke not a word of English, but despite my pathetic lack of progress I did acquire a Peking accent.[7]

But one can see why most employees felt that there were better things to do than spend hours a day on tedious repetition by rote. Even the consular officials, who were constantly pressed by their Foreign Office masters to learn the language and had far more time to do so, had only limited success. A few natural linguists became fluent but they were a tiny minority. The Europeans and Americans who had closest contact with Chinese of the humbler classes were the missionaries. One or two of them, like the famous or notorious Gutzlaff of an earlier generation, mastered the language. Most did not, and even those who did were unpopular because of their cavalier treatment of Chinese traditions, which caused constant rows and disputes. As a result they were scarcely less popular with the European laity who could happily for the most part have done without their presence.

It was partly because of missionary zeal that the last great crisis in the history of the Ch'ing dynasty occurred. This was the Boxer Rising of 1900. It was a northern affair and only marginally affected the interests of Jardines, but its branch in Peking had a nerve-racking ordeal, and no history of the Firm can ignore an outbreak which had a lasting effect on the regime of the country in which it operated. China was never to be the same after 1900.

The rebellion stemmed from the same causes which had produced that of the Taipings and many comparable outbursts over the previous two centuries. Basically, the reason was poverty, produced by overpopulation pressing on the means of subsistence. The demographic factor was aggravated by famine in Kiangsu and Shantung and by widespread unemployment caused by the breakdown of the Grand Canal and the demobilization of the traditional forces in the Imperial army, which was being reorganized after the humiliations of the Sino-Japanese war. The impoverished illiterate northern peasantry could not be expected to comprehend the underlying socio-economic causes of their plight; but famine and loss of livelihood were obvious enough. The Taiping Rebellion, which was on a far greater scale than the Boxer Rising and stemmed from some of the same causes, had not been aimed at foreigners, but at that time foreigners had not made the inroads into Chinese life that they had by the 1890s. There were few missionaries and no railways. The situation was different 30 years later. Although European commercial business in the Treaty Ports made no particular impact on the life of northern Chinese peasants, other foreign activities did.

Foremost were those of the missionaries. Their zeal and insensitivity came right up against the superstitions and religious practices of the peasantry. In 1860 the French Government, self-constituted protector of Roman Catholicism, secured a Charter of Rights for all missionaries, which exceeded even those of foreign merchants. They could travel and live anywhere, unlike merchants who could indeed travel but had to be domiciled in the Treaty Ports. They had scant sympathy with the peasants' fear of disturbance of the spirits of earth, air and water, who featured in the pre-Buddhist and vaguely geomantic creed to which the peasants still adhered. The tall spires of Christian churches were particularly inimical to these mysterious beings. It was easy to attribute any natural disaster to missionary enthusiasm.

Then there was the question of ancestor-worship. This was an even more important strand in the mixture of Buddhism, Taoism and Confucianism which formed the complex tapestry of Chinese religious beliefs in every rank of society, not just the poor. Missionaries were of course bitterly opposed to it and made renunciation a *sine qua non* for conversion to Christianity. Converts therefore boycotted the village temple, ceased to pay for its upkeep and thus adversely affected the financing of the traditional festivals, plays and ceremonies which brought some colour to the drab, narrow lives of the millions. Converts were to be, along with missionaries, the first victims of the rebellion –

especially Roman Catholic converts, since the French-supported claims of the Vatican were particularly resented.

Another major grievance, part-economic, part-religious, concerned railway construction. Although in 1900 only three short railways had actually been built in China, the routes for many more were being surveyed, especially in the north. Jardines was itself deeply involved in the process. It was obvious that, unless it was checked, a network comparable to that of Europe would in the course of time cover the Celestial Empire. This constituted both a social and a spiritual threat. Socially it meant unemployment for thousands of people in the short term, whatever its long-term implications for economic expansion. The same was true of the steamships on the Yangtse – another source of hostility to foreign commerce. Spiritually it was a threat to ancestor-worship. It was almost impossible to build a railway on any feasible route, which did not disturb one or other of the inconspicuous Chinese burial places. A further Barbarian invention which caused alarm was the telegraph. Surely, the mysterious moaning noise made by the wind in the wires must disturb the spirits.

The history of China is full of the manifestations of secret societies about whose origins, personalities and organization very little is known. The Boxers until 1899 was a relatively obscure sect confined to northern China. Its Chinese name, Yi Ho Quan, is literally translated as 'the righteous and harmonious fists'. The English name was bestowed on the sect by the *China Daily News* of Shanghai, the principal English language newspaper in the Chinese Empire. It stemmed from the ritual exercises, punching into the air, which, they believed, conferred, if correctly performed, invulnerability against their enemies. It was a variant form of the callisthenics practised in China from time immemorial. One can see people doing it still in the early morning, although not for the same reasons as the Boxers. The English name for the sect has stuck ever since.

The Boxers did not start the revolt. It began with the violent reaction by another secret society, the Big Swords, against German retaliation for their murder of two German missionaries in 1897. German troops burnt down a number of villages in the Shantung province with indiscriminate ruthlessness. For the Big Swords, credulous and super-stitious like most of the secret societies, the Boxer claim to invulnerability was highly persuasive. A revolt against superior foreign and Imperial arms might go a long way if the rebels could not be killed.

One sceptical magistrate put the matter to the test and arranged for a Boxer to receive the death penalty which he did not survive, but the death of that Boxer, or any others, could always be attributed by the faithful to astrological inauspiciousness, or incorrect performance of the ritual exercises. The Boxers and the Big Swords were allied in deter-mination to bring down the dynasty and exterminate all foreigners. The two objectives might at first sight seem inconsistent. The Manchu Court could hardly be regarded as friendly to the Barbarians. But the missionaries enjoyed to some extent the reluctant patronage of the offi-cial class if only because the Government wished to avoid incidents which might provoke, as in the case of the German missionaries, foreign intervention. If this happened often enough, the regime, which had tottered on for so long against all the odds, might collapse beyond hope of restoration.

It soon, however, became apparent that the Empress Dowager and her advisers were sitting on the fence. Officials received decrees which, if read between the lines, as was so often prudent, indicated that exces-sive zeal in suppressing what was undoubtedly an illegal movement might be unwise. Many officials themselves detested foreigners, espe-cially missionaries. And so the Boxers in their colourful garments, poorly armed, hungry, but actuated by fanatical enthusiasm, rose in rebellion in Shantung, where the Governor Yuan Shi-kai, the man who had double-crossed the 'reforming Emperor' in 1898, at first dealt with them firmly, but soon trimmed his sails to the wind blowing from the Forbidden City. The revolt then spread to the province in which the capital was situated. In the course of the Boxer Rebellion some 30,000 Chinese converts, mostly Roman Catholics, were massacred. Two hundred European missionaries were killed, usually by decapitation and often after torture. The wives and children of Protestant missionaries were also beheaded, adding another 50 to the grim total.

Early in 1900 it became clear to those who understood the subtle, enigmatic nuances of Court language that the Empress Dowager was going to enlist the support of the Boxers, divert them from their original slogan – 'destroy the Ch'ing, restore the Ming' – and give them the support of the Imperial army. The dynasty and the rebels would combine to exterminate every foreigner. It was only late in the day that diplomats in the Peking legations realized what was afoot, for the Court played its cards with masterly duplicity. But the Boxers with their flaming red trappings were allowed to enter Peking, and on 20 June the German envoy, Baron von Ketteler, was assassinated on his way to the Tsungli Yamen, significantly not by a Boxer, but by a Manchu soldier.

The deliberate purpose of the Court in conjunction with the Boxers – to slaughter all foreigners, including those with diplomatic immunity – was atrocious even by Chinese standards. The attack on the legations was, in the famous phrase, not only a crime but a blunder. It might well have resulted in a successful massacre, but the repercussions were bound to be as disastrous as those of failure. Eleven powers were represented in Peking. It was certain that there would be devastating reprisals which the Manchu Court could not hope to resist. In the centre and south of China, where the Boxers never had any hold, the viceroys and governors were horrified at what was happening. Their response to an appeal from Peking for troops was as negative as was compatible with continuance in office. Promises were made but very few men were sent.

In Peking, as in many oriental cities, special areas were set aside as the location for particular trades and professions – silversmiths in one, saddlers in another, etc. The same principle was applied by the Manchu rulers to the Diplomatic Corps. The eleven legations occupied an area of about three-quarters of a square mile bounded on the south by the high wall of the Tartar City, on the north and west by that of the Forbidden City, and on the east by a wide road to which a gate through the Tartar Wall gave access. A shallow canal running north and south bisected the enclave. The events of 1900 determined the diplomats subsequently to convert an enclave into a semi-citadel guarded by their own troops, self-contained and self-administered. But this was a later development. In the summer of 1900 the legations were close to each other but not protected by a fortified perimeter.

It was natural that other foreign institutions and businesses should congregate in what later came to be known as the Legation Quarter. Jardines had its offices in the south-east corner, just north of the usual club, south of the Peking Hotel and east of the German Legation. The Hong Kong & Shanghai Bank abutted upon that legation from the other side, to its immediate west. The British Legation was sited diagonally opposite Jardines in the north-west corner of the area, about a quarter of a mile away as the crow flies. It was easily the largest of the legations.

The siege 'at Peking', as Peter Fleming describes it, began later on the day of the murder of von Ketteler, when the Diplomatic Corps refused an Imperial ultimatum to depart en masse to Tientsin under safe guard. It would have been fatal to accept. The Boxers would have massacred the lot while the Imperial forces stood complacently by. That afternoon it was abundantly clear that the Boxers were in alliance with the Imperial forces. On the expiry of the ultimatum at 4pm heavy firing began.

The history of the siege cannot be given here. There is a multitude of accounts; the best and most illuminating of all is by Peter Fleming, already cited. It is enough to say that the Empress in a fit of megalomaniac xenophobia declared war on all the countries with legations in Peking, that the siege lasted 55 days in blazing heat occasionally diversified by torrential rain, and that it was eventually relieved on 14–15 August by a joint expeditionary force launched by all the great powers, the Japanese playing the major part. Jardines' office lay within the improvised perimeter defence line of 20 June, but on the very edge. After the later strategic withdrawal it was just outside. Those not involved in defending the perimeter were accommodated in conditions of extreme discomfort in the British Legation – some 900 people in an area whose normal quota was 60. Food and water supplies were just about adequate and there were large stocks of champagne and other alcoholic refreshments. But the stench of putrifying corpses and undisposable sewage was appalling. Ladies who would never have dreamed of smoking puffed away at cigars and cigarettes – luckily in plentiful supply – to counteract these horrible odours. Temperatures of over 100°F, swarms of flies and mosquitoes, the constant danger of stray bullets or shell splinters, fear of explosive underground mines, fear of never being rescued – these were the features of a very disagreeable two months for the foreign community.

On the face of things the combination of the Imperial forces and the Boxers ought to have crushed the improvised inadequate defences of the legations with ease. But it has been surmised and may well be true that Jung Lu, the commander of the Imperial forces, although trusted by the Empress, did not have his heart in her foolhardy enterprise. He had to go along with it outwardly, but he may well have used his position to see that it did not succeed. There is no clear evidence of this, but his distaste for the whole business is well documented. Sir Robert Hart, without naming a name, believed that there was only one explanation for the failure of the besiegers. 'That somebody intervened for our semi-protection seems, however, probable... Somebody, probably a wise man who knew that the destruction of the legations would cost the Empire and Dynasty dear, intervened between the issue of the order for our destruction and the execution of it.'[8]

And the Empire did survive. One of the bizarre features of the whole affair was that the Empress retained her throne. When the siege was relieved she fled the capital in haste with few attendants, little baggage and even had to borrow chopsticks; she was disguised as a peasant woman and brought her nephew, the nominal Emperor, along with her. After two months with a gathering train of acolytes she reached Sian, 700 miles south-west of the capital, and spent the winter there with her attenuated court.

Meanwhile in Peking confusion prevailed. There was looting on an heroic scale, and the top people were as guilty as those below. Lady MacDonald, wife of Sir Claude, who commanded the legations' defence forces, 'devoted herself most assiduously to looting', wrote a British officer.[9] More serious than looting, which was inevitable in the circumstances, was how to negotiate a settlement and with whom. The flight of the Empress Dowager and the Emperor had left a vacuum. There was no legitimate authority in Peking. However, shortly before she fled the Empress Dowager had appointed Li Hung-chang with plenipotentiary powers. This was a shrewd move. He was the ablest statesman produced by nineteenth-century China. Now Viceroy at

Canton he was as far away from Peking as any major Chinese official could be and had been in no way involved in the events that led to the siege.

He was strongly pressed by the other southern viceroys. He slowly and cautiously felt his way to Peking. To deal with him was in effect to recognize the continuing legitimacy of the Emperor whom he formally represented – in reality of course the continuing authority of the Empress Dowager. The Allies had no choice. After seemingly interminable wrangles, a peace treaty was signed. The details are of no concern to this book. In a procession of immense grandeur Tzu-Hsi returned in 1901 after a two-month journey to the capital, arriving in bitter December cold at the exact day and hour fixed by the astrologers and, in the presence of a vast crowd which included foreigners for the first time, she entered the appropriate temple for the appropriate rites and prayers. Astonishingly she was to reign for another seven years.

The first fruits of the co-operation between Jardines and the Hong Kong & Shanghai Bank were gathered in 1899 when their jointly owned subsidiary, the British & Chinese Corporation, applied for a contract to finish the railway network in northern China, planned by Li Hung-chang in the early 1890s.[10] He had foreseen the threat of a Japanese attack well before it occurred and had tried to take steps against it, despite the apathy of the Imperial Court. One of these was to modernize the army. Another was to build a nationwide railway system. He had no realistic chance of achieving that but he could make a beginning in the metropolitan province of Chihli of which he was governor at that time and in which the capital was situated. The Japanese struck before he made much progress with either of these policies – certainly not enough to affect the course of the disastrous war. But one result of defeat was to convince even the Imperial Court that railways were essential.

Under Li Hung-chang's leadership a body called 'The Imperial Railway Administration' was set up to construct and manage the new lines. A line of 83 miles was built from Peking to Tientsin and another 30 miles to Taku at the mouth of the Peiho River. From Taku it continued north-west via the coal-mining and steel-mill complex of Kaiping for another 146 miles to Shanhai Kwan on the Manchurian border where the Great Wall begins. The plan was to extend it to Mukden, the capital of Manchuria and then bend back southwards to the port of Newchwang. By 1899 the money to complete this programme had run out. The Chinese Government wanted to keep railway construction in its own hands. Foreign concessions could lead to foreign territorial infiltration. But the enormous indemnity imposed by Japan under the Treaty of Shimonoseki and the perpetual difficulty of raising money by higher taxes or internal credit meant that the Government would either have to abandon self-financed railways altogether, or obtain money by foreign loans with all the risks involved.

There was no practical alternative. Railways were vital for national defence and economic development. The Government accepted an offer by the British & Chinese Corporation to lend £2.3 million in return for a contract for the completion of the line to Mukden and Newchwang. The security for the loan was that section of Li's line which had already been built – Peking to Shanhai Kwan. In the event of default, the British & Chinese Corporation would have the right to manage the line and the adjacent property in its own financial interest until the terms of the loan had been fulfilled. The bank received a commission of £46,000 for floating the loan. Jardines received its profit from the sale as contractors of rails, rolling stock, equipment, etc. Arrangements were not finalized until after the Boxers had been crushed. They were then confirmed by Li, who died soon afterwards.

The concession was resented by the Russians, who regarded northern China, and Manchuria especially, as part of their sphere of interest. There was at the turn of the century a major conflict boiling up about the whole future of China – a dispute which inevitably had its implications for the principal British firm operating in the country, however much Jardines would have preferred to keep out of politics. Tsarist Russia was an aggressive expansionist power which, during the last century, had acquired a vast Asiatic overland colonial empire. In Europe, Russian ambitions were to some degree blocked by Imperial Germany and the Hapsburg monarchy. But in Asia the Russians had for many years been eroding Chinese sovereignty. British statesmen attributed similar intentions towards India. The reality of these may have been exaggerated; the threat to China was not. Along with fears about India, memories of the Crimea and the more recent Near East crisis of 1878, when Russia and Britain nearly went to war over Constantinople, anxiety about Russian aims in China was a major element in the background of British diplomacy. After construction of the Trans-Siberian Railway, Russia could bring an army to the gates of Peking sooner than any other foreign power except one. That was Japan, whose military strength, despite the defeat of China in 1894–5, was too often under-estimated. Not by Britain, however, whose Foreign Secretary signed on 30 January 1902 a defensive treaty of alliance under which the two countries became joint guarantors of peace in the Far East. This was a major departure from Britain's traditional policy of 'splendid isolation' and a clear signal of the importance attached by Whitehall to the China trade, potentially threatened by Russian expansionism.

Jardines was not involved in further railway operations until 1903. By then the key minister at the Imperial Court was Yuan Shi-kai. He was a slippery conservative opportunist who, after the final collapse of the Ch'ing regime, became the first President of the Chinese Republic. At this time he was the Court favourite of the Empress and in view of her changed attitude to railways was ready to be co-operative over requests for concessions. The proposal this time was for a railway linking Shanghai with Nanking in the very heart of the British sphere of interest. The British & Chinese Corporation was now involved in high politics, albeit reluctantly. The Russians were anxious to secure the concession for themselves. They were at this time very much in an expansionist mood. They had recently secured a lease of the Liao-tung peninsula, which included the much prized ice-free harbour of Port Arthur – the very area which, along with France and Germany, they had forced Japan to retrocede to China after the Treaty of Shimonoseki on the grounds that it involved occupation by a foreign power of a place too close to Peking. The Japanese were understandably furious. If a Russian syndicate got the contract for a line from Shanghai to Nanking, Russia might have an opportunity to push Britain out of the best region for trade in China and one informally, if not legally, agreed during the carve-up of 1898 to be in the British sphere. Fortunately for the British & Chinese Corporation, the Chinese Government, already menaced by Russia in Manchuria, had no desire whatever to see an extension of this danger in the Yangtse Valley, and the concession was granted in 1903 to the British & Chinese Corporation, which, as before, operated with the Bank as its financial agents and Jardines as its contractors.

The Bank raised a loan of £3,250,000 in London, in July 1904, in the form of Sterling five per cent bonds, issued at £97 10s. The conditions were authorized by an Imperial Edict, which was communicated to the British minister in Peking. The Chinese Government guaranteed principal and interest and as security made repayment a first charge on the earnings and assets of the railway, which would be exempted from tax. Each subscriber of a £100 bond was offered a certificate which gave him a claim on the relevant share of the railway's net profits for 50 years, the period of the length of the loan. The prospectus quoted the Commercial Attaché at the Peking Legation as saying that 'The Shanghai–Nanking Railway should prove a first-rate investment'. It would go through the centre of the tea, cotton and silk industries. 'The length of time occupied by passengers will be reduced from about thirty hours (the time now occupied by fast passenger steamers) to eight hours, and goods which at present take a week would arrive in twenty-four hours.'[11] No rival railways would be allowed by the Imperial Government, so the rates would not be subject to competition. The Bank and Jardines possessed a potentially very profitable monopoly and the British & Chinese Corporation had three out of the five directors who would manage the railway, the other two being Chinese nominees of the Imperial Railway Administration.

The circumstances of the negotiation of this second loan symbolize a significant change in the traditional relationship between British officialdom and British business in China. It was a clear sign that official neutrality about particular firms had been abandoned. 'Hands off' no longer prevailed. The British minister in Peking received the Imperial Edict with its very specific guarantees and duly passed it on to the Foreign Office. The British Commercial Attaché was allowed to give his public support in the prospectus for the loan in London. This would have been inconceivable ten years earlier. The truth was that the British

Government, taking as a precedent Lord Salisbury's decision about German pressure in Tokyo in 1885, had resolved that the threat by other foreign powers to British trade in China had to be countered by the same methods that they were using. One could no longer sit back and let 'natural' economic forces take their course. China was by no means the most important area in the world for British trade, but it was quite important enough not to be abandoned to the designs of Russia, or any other exponent of economic imperialism.

Already in 1898 Salisbury had strongly opposed a suggested railway concession for a line from Hankow to Peking, backed by a Belgian syndicate in conjunction with the Russo-Chinese Bank. 'A concession of this nature is no longer a commercial or industrial enterprise, and becomes a political movement against British interests in the region of the Yangtse,' he wrote to the British minister in Peking on 9 June 1898, and on 23 June, in a letter to the same minister, he urged him to press for the British & Chinese Corporation's Nanking–Shanghai railway as first priority, mining concessions for the Peking Syndicate (another British company) second, and the Newchwang extension, also sponsored by the British & Chinese Corporation, third. These moves effectively excluded other foreign powers from the Yangtse Valley.[12]

Among many other railway loans in which Jardines was involved through the British & Chinese Corporation, two are worth mentioning. Both took place after the end of the Russo-Japanese War of 1904–5, which Japan won to the general satisfaction of the British everywhere; they could hardly be expected to foresee that Russia would be soon replaced in the Far East by an even more menacing expansionist power. In 1907 the British & Chinese Corporation obtained a concession from the Imperial Court for a line from Canton to the recently leased New Territories at Hong Kong. The arrangements were very similar to those for the Shanghai–Nanking railway. The loan was £1.5 million Sterling at £95. The Viceroy would acquire the land and it was an instruction that his wishes should be courteously considered, and obeyed unless they impaired efficient construction. In 1908 a loan of £5 million was raised by the Bank for a line from Tientsin to Pukow. On this occasion the British & Chinese Corporation was not involved; part of the line ran through the German sphere of interest, and the British & Chinese

Corporation was not considered suitable in view of the involvement of the Deutsche-Asiatische Bank. But the Corporation was the contractor for the last railway built before the death of the Empress Dowager in 1908. This ran from Shanghai south to Ningpo, and the loan was for £1.5 million.

There is a good deal of Marxist-Leninist nonsense talked and written about economic imperialism. Jardine Matheson is singled out from time to time as the archetypal firm to be engaged in this activity. In January 1993 it came in for particular attack from the Chinese Government in connection with its alleged support of increased democracy in Hong Kong, which was said to be a back-door method of overthrowing communism and re-establishing capitalism in China. Inevitably the opium trade and the 'unequal' treaties of 1842 and 1860 were resuscitated, as was the battle for concessions in 1898.

The theory of economic imperialism was that, as capitalism became more and more 'advanced' in the leading industrial powers, capitalists were bound to accumulate more funds than they could invest at home. They therefore had to seek foreign fields in which to place these surpluses of capital. The nation states which the capitalists controlled sought to limit international competition by political domination in the particular areas of the 'underdeveloped' world, where they could achieve investment monopolies through protected markets, protected sources of raw material, differential railway and shipping rates, and all the paraphernalia of mercantilism. This political domination, driven by financial pressure in 'the City' and other comparable centres in Europe and America, did not necessarily mean political sovereignty, though it might easily do so and often did. There could be an informal as well as a formal empire. Latin America was an example. But in either case it meant a breakdown of the existing social and economic structure and *de facto* if not *de jure* control by the metropolitan power with consequences which, according to Lenin, were almost always deleterious. In China, if this theory was correct, Britain, America and Germany should have been the great powers most likely either to annex territory or establish puppet regimes and protectorates. They were in any definition of the word the most 'advanced' capitalist countries. In fact, the two most expansionist states were the least 'advanced' – Russia and

Japan. Both had only recently emerged from semi-feudalism and both were very far from having a surplus of capital to invest. Yet along with France, which had been relatively late in adapting itself to the industrial revolution, they were foremost in staking territorial claims and demanding special privileges and advantages. As has already been said, Britain and the USA were consistently in favour of free trade and the Open Door.

The battle of the concessions in 1898 forced the British Government to join in the fray. But Lord Salisbury was determined, even if he could not prevent economic partition, to block a territorial carve-up. The German attitude was at first ambivalent. There was a vociferous 'colonial' party in Berlin: hence the German claim to a sphere of interest in Shantung. On the other hand, German industry was highly competitive and its leaders tended to favour equal commercial opportunities for foreign countries throughout China. That view prevailed. In 1901, Britain and Germany signed an agreement by which each undertook to eschew any territorial claims on China. A leading historian of China surmises that this may have been one reason why the long-expected political partition of the country never in the event occurred.[13]

The truth is that Britain was not involved in a policy of economic imperialism in the Leninist sense, nor can Jardines or any of their British competitors in China be tarred with this particular brush. Salisbury and his successors did encourage the British & Chinese Corporation's bids for concessions and loans, but essentially as a political counter-measure to the economic imperialism of other nations, not as a boost for an individual firm under pressure from the City or any other source. The British political position in the Yangtse, as Platt puts it, could only be consolidated, if at all, by the introduction of private capital:

> The interests of the individual British concession hunter had very little if anything to do with [Anglo-Chinese diplomacy]; indeed concessions were obtained by MacDonald [the British minister in Peking] in rather greater numbers than British capitalists or concessionaires could cope with. This was no case of British capitalists pressing for Government assistance in obtaining concessions for their private enrichment; the British

Government was pressing concessions on an often reluctant City in the political interest of the Empire and the general interest of British trade.[14]

This verdict by a distinguished economic historian cannot easily be challenged, except by the more fossilized exponents of the doctrines of Marx and Lenin.

FIFTEEN

Jardines in the Twentieth Century

On 22 November 1906 an important change was made in the Firm's legal position. Instead of being a partnership it became a limited liability company – Jardine Matheson & Co. Ltd – and the partners became Directors. But in many respects the old structure continued as in the past. In 1905 Sir Robert Jardine, last of the nephews of the founder, died at the age of 80. William Keswick, who was 71 thus lost a governing director and proprietor with whom he was on terms of close friendship and who knew the China scene almost as well as he did. The proprietorship and majority holding in the Firm now passed to Sir Robert's son, also Robert, who was 37; he knew little about China and took no personal interest in the business. Although he had, like his father, the ultimate power of decision on major issues of policy and senior appointments, his control was more nominal than real.

In 1908 Matheson & Co. in London followed Jardine Matheson and also became incorporated as a limited liability company. From the mid-nineteenth century onwards Matheson & Co. had been more and more closely involved with Jardines. Acting as agent for the export to China of coal, metal, machinery and drinks from Britain and the import into Britain of tea, silk and much else from China, Matheson & Co. contributed largely to the growth of the parent firm. It played an important part in floating Chinese Government and railway loans in London to the advantage of Jardines; and Matheson & Co. was also vital in the matter of recruiting staff for China. But, although the two firms co-operated cordially and there were numerous overlapping partnerships, they did not always see eye to eye, and they remained legally independent. There was clearly a case for unified ownership. By 1900, there were no longer any Matheson partners in the London firm, although the family were major shareholders. In 1912, Jardines bought them out and acquired a controlling interest. The remainder of the shares went to the Keswick family. William Keswick died on 9 March. Just before his death it was announced at the Jardine annual general meeting by David Landale, the taipan, that the managing directors would in future reside in Shanghai and that their office in this city would henceforth be regarded as the headquarters of the company, instead of Hong Kong. He added that the move had the approval of the new proprietor, Sir Robert Buchanan-Jardine.

David Landale, who became taipan in 1912, was a shrewd operator on his own behalf as well as the Firm's. In 1909–10 the booming demand for motor-cars produced a global and equally booming demand for rubber for their tyres, especially in the USA. Along with other Shanghai merchants he played the market in Shanghai, speculating heavily on rubber shares. He was at the time president of the Foreign Chamber of Commerce and created a firm called Anglo-Java Estates Limited. Some of his activities seem to have attracted censure, but, given the get-rich-quick atmosphere of the time, it is difficult to assess the ethics of speculation then, or to distinguish between critics who had a genuine grievance and those who had simply been out-smarted. The boom lasted for six months. The crash came in July 1910. At least eight Chinese banks failed. Clearly the Firm (and, one can safely guess, David Landale himself) got out at the right moment, if one can go by the profits in 1911 and 1912 (see below).

From 1907–8 onwards, the gap in the documentation of Jardines' accounts comes to an end, perhaps because of the Firm's new status as a limited liability company. Profits in 1907–8 were HK $800,000, the following year HK $1.7 million. In 1910–11 there was neither profit nor loss. Between 1911 and 1914 profits varied between HK $800,000 and HK $1.2 million. The war, however, brought about striking gains. The figures, again in HK Dollars, were 5.3 million for 1915–16, 4.5 million for 1916–17 and averaged 3.1 million for the next three years. The reasons for this are discussed below. It is enough to say that the boom did not last. Many years were to pass before such figures were to be seen again – in fact, not till after the Second World War.

There were big changes in the political situation in China during the run-up to 1914. The Russo-Japanese war of 1904–5 changed the whole balance of power in the Far East. As the first occasion when an Asiatic state defeated a major European country, it had significant implications for the future. White military and naval supremacy was no longer unchallengeable. The world watched with astonishment the undeclared Japanese attack upon and destruction of the Russian Far Eastern fleet – a portent of Pearl Harbor; then the capture of Port Arthur followed by the destruction of Russia's Baltic fleet which had steamed halfway round the world to meet its fate under the guns of Admiral Togo in the Straits of Tsushima. There were no immediate consequences for Jardines, although it became increasingly difficult for the Firm's shipping to compete with its heavily subsidized Japanese rivals. It was only much later, in the inter-war years, that Japanese economic imperialism seriously affected the interests of all the Western firms trading in China, including Jardines and Swires. Even before 1912, however, 50 per cent of Japanese foreign trade was carried in Japanese ships.

The deaths in 1908 of the Empress Dowager and the nominal Emperor soon brought the Celestial Empire to an end. The victory by the Asian and apparently constitutionalist monarchy of Japan over the autocratic, European, polyglot, monarchy of Russia made the Manchu Empire impossible to sustain. Demands for a constitution and a parliament could not be resisted, and the minority rule of the Manchus over the Chinese rapidly lost its legitimacy. The puppet boy Emperor Pu Yi, last of the Ch'ing dynasty, was persuaded to abdicate on 12 February 1912. A republic was proclaimed under the temporary presidency of Dr Sun Yat-sen, a Chinese expatriate brought up in Hawaii and educated in Hong Kong where he gained a degree in medicine. He had no pretension to permanency. The man whom both the Manchu Court and the provincial revolutionary assemblies wanted – unwisely – was Yuan Shi-kai, creator of the Chinese 'North Seas' Army. He became president in October 1913 before the constitution under which he should have been elected had even been drafted. He remained for two years in this dubious position, regarded with ever-diminishing respect by the political classes who had put him there.

In a moment of autocratic *folie de grandeur* Yuan decided at the end of 1915 to convert himself into an emperor. His authority had already been shattered by Japan's 'twenty-one demands' which fell little short of insistence upon a virtual protectorate. He felt obliged to accept. Perhaps he had no alternative. Britain, France and Russia were preoccupied with the war and Japan, their ally against the Central Powers, had in effect a free hand in China. Yuan, however, attracted all the odium excited by patriotic sentiment. He felt compelled to abdicate a few months after assuming the throne. Seldom can there have been such a loss of 'face'. He did not outlive it for long, dying on 6 June 1916 at the age of 56. For at least the next decade China was in a state of military feudal anarchy. There was for practical purposes no central government. The period of the warlords had begun, and although the Peking Government in 1918 made the gesture of declaring war on the Central Powers, no one took it seriously. It was rather like Piedmont declaring war on Russia at the end of the Crimean War in order to be in on the peace conference.

These chaotic conditions did not at first have much effect on Jardines and its competitors. For the Firm, Shanghai was the only place that really mattered in China. Jardines remained the largest concern among foreign traders. Its offices in the Ewo Building at 27 The Bund overlooked the harbour which it had helped to build. Its nearest rival was Butterfield & Swire which had offices on the French Bund. The peculiar arrangements of the International Settlement and the French Concession operated to distance the trading community as effectively as possible from the government in Peking and from the civil war in the interior. Jardines controlled the Shanghai & Hongkew Wharf Company, three cotton mills, a silk filature, a brewery, an insurance company and an important shipping line.

The outbreak of the First World War in 1914 was alarming at first, especially at the Matheson & Co. end in London whence C.H. Ross, director 1906–20, wrote that the banks were closed for four days and the Stock Exchange indefinitely. 'Trade has come to a dead stop ... and all commercial paper is practically worthless.' Henry Keswick, who had taken over the management since the buy-out of the Matheson interest, joined up with the Third Battalion of the King's Own Scottish Borderers. Ross took his place during the war years. The Firm was helped by the disappearance of German and Austrian competition, and the fact that since 1906 it had diversified into various commodities which by sheer luck came to have an important strategic value in 1914–18, such as silk for parachutes, Very lights and packing explosives. Moreover the celebrated 'British Warm' was a product of north China camel hair. There was a negative side too. The Firm was obliged to release part of its staff to serve in the Chinese Labour Battalions in Europe – the 'Bamboo Rifles', as they were called. More serious, one of its ships, the *Kutsang* was torpedoed in 1918 with severe loss of life. Financially, however, the Firm did very well indeed, as is shown by the figures quoted previously. Its profits had never been higher, and the war casualties among its employees were by no means heavy. Out of some 100,000, most of whom would not have been liable to war service, Jardines suffered nine deaths, and its affiliate, the Indo-China Steam Navigation Company, suffered the loss of twelve.

The end of the war produced a strong, if fleeting, sense of euphoria among those who supported the winning side. Everyone's lives had in some measure been disturbed and distressed. There were losses to mourn, wounds to heal, careers to resume; but at least 'the war to end all wars' was over, however little that phrase was to be justified by events. With the Armistice came a rush of the Firm's employees of military age to be demobilized, return and be married. It was not always easy to bring back into the ways of commerce young men whose business experience had been brief before 1914 and who had had a responsibility for life and death on land, sea and air for four years of bloody combat at an age when they would have been 'juniors' in the Firm. It required tact and diplomacy among the directors to ease them back and recruit new members. A suitable war bonus was not forgotten.

A more light-hearted piece of post-war euphoria was Henry Keswick's decision to buy an unfinished naval destroyer, convert her into a steam yacht and name her the *Cutty Sark* after the most famous of all tea-clippers. He steamed round the world from Stranraer, called in at Hong Kong, Shanghai and ports in north China and Japan where the Firm operated. He decided that the business needed 'gingering up'. He returned via the Panama Canal after a voyage of nine months.[1] It is difficult to assess his opinion about what he evidently saw as a somewhat torpid, or at best unenterprising, attitude in the Firm's offices. Its great wartime profits may have resulted in an element of *dolce far niente.* If so, it was a fairly general attitude in the business world of the post-Armistice victors everywhere. There was soon to be a disagreeable shock. The Firm's profits, HK $3.4 million in 1919–20, were followed by a loss in 1920–1 of HK $1.4 million. This was the first recorded loss since the Firm had become a limited liability company. It was not catastrophic; although Jardines made only HK $100,000 in 1921–2, the figure shot up the following year to HK $4.3 million. In 1923–4 and 1924–5 it was down but still satisfactory at HK $2.4 million and HK $1.8 million respectively. Nevertheless these fluctuations were enough to banish any undue complacency. The price of profitability, like the price of liberty, is 'eternal vigilance'.

David Landale, who as taipan had presided over some of the most financially successful years in the history of the Firm, retired in 1918 after six years in office. He was succeeded by John Johnstone who was descended from a sister of Dr William Jardine. In London the senior managing director was Henry Keswick, back from his trip round the world. The Firm faced a new situation in China. Although it had in 1920 more branch offices than ever before, the trading and economic circumstances of the country were very far from stable and the position of Western traders was uncertain and controversial, especially in Shanghai.

There were three clouds on the horizon: there was Japan whose ambitions were becoming ever more threatening towards China and towards the foreign merchants resident in the country; there was the chaotic instability of Chinese governance; and there was the growth of Chinese nationalism, which ultimately threatened the International Settlement and the French Concession. The peculiar extra-territorial arrangements in the Treaty Ports were sure to be attacked sooner or later. They had come into being only because of the extreme weakness of the Manchu Court and survived after its disappearance because the regime of the warlords was even weaker. They were an obvious affront to nationalist sentiment.

Most Westerners realized that the system could not last. In the preface to his admirable study of Shanghai in the 1920s, *Spoilt Children of Empire* (1991) Nicholas Clifford points out the parallel between Shanghai then and Hong Kong in the 1990s. Shanghai, of course, was not actually a colony, but it was very largely under foreign control and this control was largely responsible for its prosperity. Hong Kong would never have developed commercially as it has but for colonial rule, nor would Shanghai if there had been no concessions and no international settlement. But both are essentially Chinese cities. Hong Kong reverted to China in 1997. There was no similar fixed date for the ending of the concessions, but any Westerner who thought at all must have realized in the 1920s that the system could not last indefinitely. The question in Shanghai was what would replace it, just as people asked the same question of Hong Kong prior to 1997. It is not that foreigners in either place have been the sole or even principal architects of commercial success, which stems largely from Chinese acumen, energy and enterprise. Some foreigners have, of course, made a great deal of money, but the real effect of foreign rule or quasi-rule has been to protect the natural entrepreneurial talent of the Chinese themselves from the corrupt and stifling bureaucracy of Peking which, until recently, has been as oppressive under the People's Republic as it was under the Celestial Empire.

Yet, although the Treaty Port system gave some Chinese a degree of affluence which they would never otherwise have attained, the well-to-do were numerically a tiny minority in the country as a whole and even in the ports themselves. Most of the inhabitants of Shanghai lived in ramshackle decaying slums, intersected by narrow filthy streets. Whether they were worse off than the rural peasants is an arguable point. Plenty of people poured in from the countryside, but there were reasons for this other than hope for a pot of gold at the end of the rainbow – famine, flood, the ravages of the warlords and the general instability of rural life. The Chinese were well accustomed to the huge gap between the rich and the poor. There were Chinese bankers,

merchants, and shipowners every bit as wealthy as their European ana-
logues. This was a part of life and the contrast always had been a feature
of the Chinese Empire. Few people seriously expected the republic to
make any difference in that respect.

What was changing in the consciousness of Chinese intellectuals was
rising resentment not only at the wealth but at the privileges of the
Europeans in Shanghai. Rich Chinese tended to be cautious about displaying their affluence too publicly. It had always been dangerous to do
this under the Empire, and the tradition lingered on. No such reticence
was shown by the European merchants and their employees. They were
essentially birds of passage, much more so than the white administra-
tors and businessmen who dominated the Indian Raj; although most of
these did intend to return to Britain, they spent far longer in India than
all but a few Europeans ever spent in China. No doubt there were
exceptions in the Consular Service and the Customs, but in general the
British and other Europeans in Shanghai were there to make their fortunes as quickly as they could, and return with the proceeds to their
home country. A prominent but anonymous Briton is said to have
summed up in 1929 his own position thus:

> It is my business to make a fortune with the least possible loss of time by
> letting my land to the Chinese, and building for them at thirty or forty per
> cent interest, if that is the best thing I can do with my money. In two or
> three years at farthest, I hope to realise a fortune and get away; and what
> can it matter to me if all Shanghai disappears afterwards in fire or flood?[2]

This was quoted by a Chinese author Ching-lin Hsia, as a 'candid
opinion' by 'one of the most influential residents of Shanghai' in his
The Status of Shanghai (1929). The candour may have been unusual.
The opinion was not.

All the same it should not be thought that every foreign merchant
and trader in Shanghai or in the other Treaty Ports was devoid of
public spirit or totally selfish. As in Hong Kong, members of Jardines
took part in local and municipal government. Sir John Keswick, who
first became active in the Firm's affairs in China in 1929, wrote:
'Jardines were in the forefront of commercial activity. Jardine men also
played a leading part in public life. My grandfather, and his brother,

my father and elder brother were all Chairmen of the Municipal Council of Shanghai in their day. In Hong Kong Jardines were almost always asked for one of their senior men to serve on the Executive and Legislative Councils.'³ In Hong Kong, which was, after all, a British crown colony this was not so surprising. It was a less obvious role for British businessmen in a foreign city.

The Shanghai Municipal Council, however, was not like any other local government institution in the world. Until the 1920s its electorate, based on a complicated system of plural voting among landowners was confined to foreigners and excluded the Chinese. It consisted originally of six British, two Americans and one German. The German was pushed out after the war and replaced by a Japanese. In such circumstances, unless they quarrelled among themselves, the British had complete control. After the troubles in Shanghai in 1925–6, a belated effort was made to enlarge both the electorate and the Council in order to include some of the indigenous population. The first Chinese were elected in 1928, but British control remained. It is true that the Council in the 1920s chose a genial American lawyer, one Stirling Fessenden, as its chairman, known colloquially as 'Lord Mayor of Shanghai'. But this did not satisfy American opinion, for he was widely regarded as a puppet – more British than the British. An American grumbled that the International Settlement was 'about as international as the Tower of London, or Westminster Abbey'.⁴

The importance of Jardines in the public as well as the commercial life of Shanghai was probably enhanced by the appointment in 1922 of Sidney (later Sir Sidney) Barton as Consul-General in the city. He had married in 1904 a daughter of one of the partners in Jardines, Alexander Palmer MacEwen.⁵ He had been Chinese secretary to the British Legation in Peking from 1911, and was described then by G.E. Morrison, the famous *Times* correspondent, as 'a narrow-minded man who has had no experience outside of the consular service in China, and who is much dominated by his wife'.⁶ Whether or not this was true, Lady Barton was evidently a vigorous character who received the OBE in 1928. This was followed by the CBE in 1937 for her welfare work in Addis Ababa where her husband was ambassador from 1926 to 1936. G.E. Morrison probably underestimated Barton's ability. In the words of the *Dictionary of National Biography*: 'He was able to render most valuable services to British interests which he defended to the limits of his great vitality and nervous energy. This naturally made him very popular with the British community, but cordially disliked by the Chinese officials with whom he had to deal.'[7]

The situation in Shanghai was politically anything but comfortable from 1924 onwards. That summer a war for the control of the post broke out between the warlords of the Kiangsu and Chekiang provinces. It died away for the moment in the autumn but not before there had been great disruption of communications near the city and an alarming influx of refugees into the International Settlement. The Settlement itself was not seriously threatened, but there was looting and disorder on a massive scale in the suburbs of the Chinese city. War was resumed in the winter followed in February 1925 by another uneasy peace. The Shanghai branch of the China Association, the group representing the principal British firms in the country, pressed for military intervention to ensure their security and Shanghai's neutrality. This obviously raised tricky points of international law. Western consuls in Shanghai did not agree with it, though they pressed the Diplomatic Corps in Peking to authorize the sending of troops to keep Chinese forces out of rifle-shot of the settlement. The Peking legations were not convinced, and, although the American minister, J.G. Schurman, while going along with non-intervention, warned the State Department that the problem of defending Shanghai could not be put on ice indefinitely, the powers let matters drift.[8] Shanghai, with its arsenal on the border of the Concession and its huge revenues enjoyed by the Chinese bureaucracy, remained a mouth-watering prize for the contending factions in mainland China.

The war had been bad for trade. Large areas within a 30-mile area of the city were laid waste. The damage done to the infrastructure was substantial. Many foreign and indigenous concerns were on the verge of bankruptcy. British textiles accumulated in the godowns of Shanghai. Dealers in the interior lacked money and means to take delivery. Jardines had to put up with two loss-making years in succession – to the tune of HK $1.2 million in 1925–6 and HK $700,000 in 1926–7, but by 1927–8 it was back in the black.

*

Much had happened in Shanghai during those years, and not only there but also in Hong Kong and Canton, the two other major centres of the Firm's activities. On 30 May there occurred an episode long to be remembered as the symbol of foreign oppression in the annals of nationalist and communist China. It altered the course of history. It has been compared with the Bastille and the Massacre of Amritsar. On that Saturday afternoon a police detachment of Sikhs commanded by a British officer fired on a crowd of demonstrators in the Nanking Road only ten seconds after an announcement, barely audible, that they must immediately disperse. Casualties – eleven killed and twenty wounded – were insignificant compared with Amritsar, let alone with the slaughter perpetrated month after month by the warlords. But that was a matter of Chinese killing each other. For foreigners in a foreign enclave to shoot down even a small number of Chinese citizens was an outrage felt all over China. Bitterness was increased because the demonstrators were protesting against the trial of some radical students that day before the Mixed Court for breach of the peace.

The Court was a curious institution which could have existed only in Shanghai. It was founded in 1864 to deal with civil and criminal cases in the International Settlement involving both Chinese and foreigners. Chinese magistrates sat on it with foreign assessors. After the revolution of 1911 it had acquired, with dubious legal validity, jurisdiction even where no foreigners were involved. It was widely regarded as an appendage of the Municipal Council and equally offensive to Chinese national pride. A demand for its abolition was a common cause since indignation was felt not only among the Chinese nationalist followers of Sun Yat-sen, their communist rivals and various groups of radical students, but also among the Chinese merchants and property owners. The result of this unusual and short-lived alliance was a general strike in Shanghai and widespread disruption in many parts of China. In Canton an incident occurred far worse than that on 30 May. On 23 June a Nationalist procession, including cadets from the Whampoa Military Academy, paraded before the British and French concessions on the island of Shameen which were protected by British and French sailors. Firing broke out. Fifty-three Chinese and one foreigner were killed. The Chinese swore that it was started by the sailors; the foreigners said that the cadets were guilty. Whatever the truth, the episode caused further damage to commerce. The Nationalist authorities in Canton called a general strike against the British. It spread to Hong Kong and lasted for sixteen months, contributing substantially to the Firm's losses in those years.

By now the period of warlordism, except in the north, was drawing to an end. The result was to enhance the demand for the abolition of the concessions. The warlords did not greatly care one way or the other, but the two forces which were replacing them – the Kuomintang, or Nationalist Party, and the Communists – however much they distrusted each other, were united in their hostility to the whole notion of 'extra-territoriality'. On 12 March 1925 Sun Yat-sen died and was succeeded as leader of the Nationalists by Chiang Kai-shek, his Chief of Staff and head of the Military Academy of Whampoa. At this stage he tended to be favoured by Moscow. Indeed, Stalin did not finally come down on the side of the Communists and against the Kuomintang until after the Second World War.

Chiang established a Nationalist-dominated regime in Canton, and, with a combined Kuomintang and Communist army of 100,000 moved north, defeating various warlords during 1926 and setting up his government in Hankow. It was his declared aim to abolish foreign concessions. He did this early in 1927 in Hankow with the assent of the British Government which could do little about it, and was in any case anxious to pursue a policy of propitiation towards Chinese nationalist aspirations. This 'surrender' provoked apoplectic symptoms in foreign Shanghai. But the Foreign Office view that most of the concessions should be handed back to Chinese rule admitted one important exception. The author of the relevant memorandum, John Pratt, who favoured this policy, wrote on 15 January 1927:

> The above remarks do not apply to Shanghai. The International Settlement at the port is a huge city with a population of 30,000 foreigners and one and a half million Chinese. It has completely dwarfed the adjacent native city of Shanghai, and it is altogether too big a concern to hand over to a Chinese administration. The annual budget of the Shanghai Municipality is greater than that of most provinces.[9]

There was increasing alarm in London and even more in the International Settlement during the autumn of 1926 when the southern armies moved closer to Shanghai. There was a double danger, both that Chinese troops might move into the concessions, as they had come near to doing in 1924, and that Communist-inspired strikes might disrupt the labour force as they had in 1925.

On 15 January Sidney Barton and the other relevant consul-generals met and agreed that an international force of 4–5000 was needed to suppress possible local risings. Admiral Sir Reginald Tyrwhitt, who commanded the China Station, considered this quite inadequate if there was also a threat of attack from Chiang's forces. At least 20,000 would be required. The alternative was evacuation of all foreigners. Barton considered it impossible practically, even if one set aside the deplorable loss of face. On 17 January 1927 the British Cabinet decided that the International Settlement must be defended, come what may. Britain would if necessary act alone even if America and Japan had cold feet. Not only were there huge commercial investments involved – far greater than those in Hankow, though these were considerable – but the whole question of British prestige in the East was at stake. What would be the repercussions in India? Shanghai was not part of the Empire and the Settlement was not exclusively British, but surrender would have a knock-on effect far beyond the China coast.

These sentiments were of course heartily echoed by the British mercantile community which had long regarded the Foreign Office as far too feeble in the defence of British rights and welcomed a change, as they saw it, from appeasement to resistance. A substantial contingent of foreign troops, largely British and known as the Shanghai Defence Force, arrived in February 1927. Chiang's troops early in April captured the Chinese city. Shanghai was now under the rule of the Nationalist government which had moved its capital yet again, from Hankow to Nanking. But there was no attempt to occupy the International or the French Concessions. The presence of the Defence Force and numerous foreign warships was a sufficient deterrent. Although Chiang's policy was to bring an end to the extra-territorial privileges of foreigners, he was not anxious, now that he had effective control of Shanghai's revenues, to kill the goose with the golden eggs. He would, he said, seek to remove the concessions by peaceful means. 'General Chiang will never use force to achieve these ends.' The upshot was that extra-territorial privileges were abandoned peacefully by some nine countries in the course of the next few years. The British, the Americans and the French were on the verge of a similar diplomatic agreement when, in 1931, the Japanese invasion of Manchuria threw everything into confusion. In the end the last foreign concessions were not abandoned until 1943.

The victory of the Kuomintang over the warlords was advantageous to the foreign community, despite the substantial changes brought about in the governance of Shanghai. The threat of Communism, far more serious than that of the Kuomintang, largely disappeared for the time being when Chiang definitively broke with his former allies. On 12 April 1927 a major 'purge' took place in Shanghai, hundreds were executed and the Communists were effectively crippled for the next 20 years as an urban movement. The Kuomintang was not anti-capitalism, only anxious to get a share of its profits.

The fortunes of the Firm began to look up. A loss of HK $700,000 in 1926–7 was replaced by a profit of the same figure the following year and of HK $1 million in 1928–9. It was only a brief revival before the great slump of 1929–31 adversely affected the fortunes of business all over the world and before Japan began a policy of conquest which was to have even more damaging effects on European commerce in China. For the moment, however, Jardines was flourishing and had more branches and outposts than ever before. In China those were Hankow, Tientsin, Foochow, Tsingtao, Suratow, Ichang, Changsa, Chung-King, Nanking, Newchwang, Harbin and Wuhei. There were branches in Japan at Kobe, Yokohama and Taipei (Formosa was then a Japanese province). There was also a branch in New York.

Sir John Keswick, as a young entrant into the Firm's business, was sent out from Britain via New York on 1 January 1929 and spent two or three months there and elsewhere in the USA. In New York the office dealt in tea, furs, skins and silk. It ran a special train from San Francisco to New York carrying Tung oil from China, which was then much prized in the manufacture of fine varnish.[10] Tea, however, was the main commodity. He then went to Pennsylvania where the Firm was owed a lot of money by a Polish-controlled silk mill. Thence he travelled via Vancouver to Shanghai where he was met by his elder brother W.J. ('Tony') Keswick, later Sir William, who at once took him to his house-boat for a weekend's snipe-shooting. Getting down to work he entered the Book Office 'since business is money, and money is accounts, and the Book Office staff developed a good sense of the shape of the whole business'.[11]

The Firm was what would now be called a 'conglomerate'. It exported a wide variety of goods from China all over the world. The export of tea from Fukien was still a major activity. Besides the commodities mentioned above in connection with the New York office there were seeds, vegetable oil and eggs. There was a silk factory in Shanghai, a press/packing plant for hides and skins, two cold-storage plants to freeze egg yolk, and several cotton, jute and woollen mills. The Firm, also by accident rather than design, diversified into brewing. It had sold tea in Germany to a company which owned a brewery. The company could not pay in cash but agreed to pay in kind with its brewing equipment which was shipped to Shanghai. The result was Ewo Beer – a very popular Pilsener-type brew.[12]

Another important aspect of Jardines' business continued to be shipping. The Indo-China Steam Navigation Company (ICSN) formed by William Keswick in 1881 was an independent public company in theory, but in practice it was so closely identified with Jardines that most people regarded it as part of the Firm. Its activities were not confined to coastal routes. Its ships penetrated deeply into the inland waterways of China. By 1920 it had steamed up the Yangtse as far as Chung-King, 1400 miles from the sea. Sir John Keswick described shipping as 'the key to much of our activity'. This remained true until the Japanese invasion of 1937 changed the whole situation.

In 1928 a portent of Japanese imperialist ambition was seen when the train of Chang Tso-lin, one of the warlords in the north, was blown up by a Japanese bomb and everyone on board was killed. The situation in Peking and Manchuria was highly unstable, and, although Chiang's forces had penetrated as far as the capital, he did not feel strong enough to base himself on it, but instead announced the official transfer of the capital to Nanking. The murder of Chang Tso-lin, 'the Old Marshal', faced Jardines with a problem. The Company had been engaged in a substantial trade in agricultural and other machinery in Manchuria, which was his fief and which was one of the richest areas of China in terms of raw materials. Chang's son, 'the Young Marshal' Chang Hseuh-liang, had set up his own regime at Peking. The question was whether he would pay the money owed to the Firm. In 1931 John Keswick as a junior member was given the unpromising task of going to Peking to recover the debt, perhaps because he had a smattering of the language. He was, in characteristic Chinese style, kept waiting for several weeks before an interview. His patience was, however, rewarded. To the surprise of the Firm and most of foreign Shanghai the Young Marshal paid up.[13]

That same year saw one of the greatest natural disasters in Chinese history. Some of the worst floods of all time occurred. John Keswick was sent back temporarily to Shanghai while he was waiting in Peking and was flown there in Chang Hseuh-lin's plane. He flew for 250 miles without seeing dry land. It is said that six million people perished in this tragic episode. Jardines played its part in the widespread international relief effort. John Keswick himself was seconded to help to organize the transport of food up the Yangtse River on British, Japanese and Chinese ships. The floods were so bad that a notice was posted in Hankow: 'Junks must not moor to Jardines' chimneys'.[14]

The political and economic situation in China in the early 1930s was anything but easy, and the two aspects were closely connected. Without political stability economic prosperity was hard to achieve; and without economic prosperity politics could easily deteriorate into faction fighting. China was in effect divided into at least three hostile regions. There was the Kuomintang regime which held the principal cities and controlled sea and land communications in the coastal areas of the centre and south. There were warlords competing in the north with each other and increasingly with Japan, which was infiltrating into Manchuria. Finally, there was the self-declared Communist republic far inland in the west. This was in the end to be the winner, but few people could have predicted its victory at the time of the Shanghai coup of 12 April 1927.

The situation in Shanghai was sufficiently worrying for the Firm to move its headquarters back to Hong Kong in 1930, although Shanghai still remained the most important centre for business. The obvious threat now was Japan, which was beginning to embark on a voyage of imperialist and commercial conquest that reached its high point at Pearl Harbor in December 1941, and blew Jardines, Swires and the rest of foreign Shanghai out of China for many years to come. The 1930s were not an easy time for trade in China or anywhere else. Superimposed on the local Japanese threat was the world-wide economic recession which began in 1929; there were few signs of recovery before 1935 at the earliest. In 1930–1 Jardines recorded a loss of HK $1.2 million. In the next financial year things improved and there was a profit of HK $ 1.1 million. But in the three years that followed there were losses in HK $ of 300,000, 700,000 and 500,000. In 1935–6, however, the Firm was back in profit and has remained so from then onwards.

The Japanese believed that they suffered from overpopulation. This was the key to their aggressive policy in the 1930s. Their home islands did not produce enough food for a country whose numbers were growing by a million a year. Food imports had to be paid for by industrial exports, but these required imported raw materials. They also required fuel in a country which had no indigenous sources of coal or oil. Japan's only exportable primary product was silk, demand for which collapsed in the great slump. In the 1920s Japanese governments had pursued an internationally orthodox policy of free trade, adherence to the gold standard, deflation and cuts in public expenditure. But by the end of the decade they became convinced that this had been wrong.

A complete reversal followed. The gold standard was abandoned, the yen devalued and public expenditure, principally on armaments, greatly increased. The army and navy came to dominate a policy which looked to the creation of a Japanese-controlled economic sphere of influence, at a time when living space for emigrants was restricted by the quota policy of the USA and the 'White Australia' policy of Canberra. The first step was taken in 1931 when, on a dubious pretext, the Japanese army in Manchuria seized the administration of its three provinces, still in theory a part of China, and set up a client state named

Manchukuo, subsequently installing as its head the puppet Emperor Pu Yi, who had resigned as a boy in 1912.

These developments, together with the general unrest in China, made the position of the Western merchants in Shanghai and elsewhere increasingly insecure. It also made the British traders more unwilling than ever to abandon their special position. The International Settlement guaranteed by treaty seemed to be the key to the continuation of the China trade. Foreign residents responded to the potential military threat by enrolling in the Shanghai Volunteers or its subordinate unit, the Shanghai Light Horse, though one may doubt whether they would have been very effective against the Japanese army.

The currency ran into trouble as the situation became more and more unstable. The advice of a prominent British economist, Sir Arthur Salter, who had been seconded from the League of Nations secretariat early in 1931, was to go off the British silver standard and adopt a paper currency. The advice was not taken then, but five years later the Chinese Government accepted similar counsel from Sir Frederick Leith-Ross of the British Treasury. This was a period when distinguished foreigners were often pulled in to advise. Jean Monnet, later a founding father of the EEC (European Union, as it later became), was asked to reorganize Chinese railway finances and the justice system. Richard Feetham of South Africa was invited by the US State Department in 1929 to suggest reforms in the International Settlement. These advisers and many others interviewed, and were entertained by, the top people in Jardines. The Firm was an obvious and important source of experienced information, and its directors were often asked for advice, which was not always taken.

The trouble was that no amount of advice was going to make much difference at this stage in the tottering fortunes of Shanghai and of a China riven by Nationalist and Communist dissension and threatened by the predatory ambitions of Japan. It was all very well for Justice Feetham, inspired by Lionel Curtis and a gaggle of high-minded do-gooders based on All Souls College, to produce three heavy fact-laden volumes on the constitution of the International Settlement. But his evidence was taken principally from foreigners, and his conclusions postulated a process towards ultimate Chinese control so leisurely as to be quite unacceptable to any shade of Chinese opinion. It was the less acceptable by being laced with frequent criticisms of Chinese administrative shortcomings.[15] 'Foreign' or 'Western' Shanghai naturally welcomed the report which, if adopted seemed to give a new lease of life to the status quo. Jardines and other firms had no reason to complain at recommendations which supported, at least for the time being, the regime under which they lived and flourished.

The early 1930s were not, however, a good period for Jardines or Western Shanghai. The worldwide recession hit everyone. It seemed essential to cut down administrative costs and reduce the numbers employed. There was a moratorium on the recruitment of European staff, and those who remained had to take a reduction of five per cent in pay. This sort of thing was happening all over the Western world. In Britain public servants had to put up with a ten per cent cut, and in the private sector of the economy the situation was even worse – greater cuts and massive redundancies. The situation became rather better after 1935–6 when the Firm's profitability improved – a by-product of the general economic revival in trade. And one has to remember that salary reductions were not as damaging as they might seem today, given the worldwide fall in prices and in the cost of living.

The Japanese occupation of Manchuria and establishment of the illicit state of 'Manchukuo' resulted in an appeal by the Chinese Government to the League of Nations and an undeclared war between Japan and the Kuomintang regime. In 1931–2 fierce fighting broke out between them in Shanghai itself and a large part of Zhabei (the Chinese city) was burned to the ground. A truce of sorts was mediated in March 1932 by the British naval commander-in-chief Admiral Kelly on the cruiser *Kent* moored near Shanghai, and the International Settlement was not itself threatened by the Japanese who as foreigners, like the British, could make use of it for their own purposes. The abortive talks between the League of Nations and the American and British governments about sanctions against Japan for its flagrant breach of international law in setting up Manchukuo lie outside the scope of this history. It is enough to say that they were totally futile, and their failure sounded the death knell of the League, moribund already but perhaps not yet quite beyond hope of a kiss of life.

What is still puzzling about the history of Japanese relations both with the British Government and the British merchants in Shanghai – bodies which by no means always saw alike – is the failure of the British to recognize where their real danger lay. They were more worried about Chiang and Chinese nationalism than about Japanese ambitions.

The British Government had been advised by the Chiefs of Staff that it could not engage in war with Germany, Italy and Japan simultaneously. It had also been advised that without American help it could not take on Japan with any hope of success, even if Japan had no allies. The Americans were loud in denouncing the illegal status of Manchukuo, and the iniquity of Japanese aggression. But the British Government, well aware that these denunciations were mere froth and wind, preferred to appease Japan. In any case Chiang and the Kuomintang seemed a far more immediate threat than Japan to Britain's great commercial investments in China, above all in Shanghai. The British ambassador in Tokyo, Sir Francis Lindley, strongly supported this view. He implored the Foreign Secretary not to quarrel with 'the most powerful nation in the Far East ... whose power to injure us is almost unbounded'. Japanese good-will should be weighed against 'that of a handful of Chinese politicians who are here today and gone tomorrow'.[16] The head of the Far East desk in the Foreign Office, Sir Victor Wellesley, agreed: British 'interest in the territorial status of Manchuria is infinitely less than their interest in maintaining cordial relations with Japan.'[17] These feelings were shared by the Western community in Shanghai, to whom the two factions contending for supremacy inside China were equally odious. The Communists would sweep capitalism out entirely. The Nationalists would not do that, but they would certainly give short shrift to the foreign capitalist. 'The only difference being that in the one case he would probably be killed; in the other he would doubtless be given the opportunity to buy a ticket home.'[18]

Nor did it seem self-evident that a Japanese 'co-prosperity sphere' covering China would be more damaging to Western Shanghai than an unqualified victory by the forces of either Chiang or Mao. This attitude may have been a piece of complacent wishful thinking but it was not entirely implausible. Even after the fighting of 1931–2 leading British and American businessmen saw it as an exercise in law and order which might pave the way for their old ambition, a 'Greater Shanghai', an enlarged International Settlement which would be for practical purposes independent of Nanking. Delusions about Japan as a policeman dealing with a fractious nationalist China vanished when overt war broke out in 1937. Japanese forces invaded the country on a major scale, and the International Settlement practically, if not legally, came under Japanese control.

Even so, much remained normal. People dined, drank and danced at night, played tennis and polo by day. The clubs were as much frequented as ever. Silent servants glided between the tables, and assiduous barmen provided members with the traditional variety of cocktails. It was, wrote Sir John Keswick, 'an exciting rather unreal life'.[19] The port remained open for trade. There was, however, trouble over the Firm's shipping services to Hankow and onwards to Chung-King when the Chinese sank a number of block-ships to keep the Japanese troops from penetrating upriver. The route was an important artery for trade to central China. Ships were kept above and below the blockade while an ex-RN submarine officer was employed to explore the various creeks and find a way past the boom. Cargoes began to move and the Firm was even able to convey members of the British diplomatic staff by motor boat through the creeks to Hankow from Shanghai.

The Sino-Japanese war was inconvenient but not disastrous for trade. Profits in 1935–6 were HK $400,000. In 1936–7 they went up to HK $1.5 million. The figures for the next year were HK $1.7 million, and rose to HK $2.9 million in 1938–9. The war had as a by-product a ban on radio communication imposed by both the Japanese and Chinese authorities. Communication from dealers in central China was an important aspect of business and its absence very damaging. Resourceful as ever, the Firm took up collective membership of the Shanghai Racing Pigeon Club. The birds conveyed valuable commercial details attached to their legs. Competitors were bewildered by their rival's advance knowledge until 'an inexperienced young pigeon came down for a drink in a Chinese tea house'. As Sir John Keswick wrote, 'He was caught and so were we.'[20]

War as always gave opportunities for those with business acumen. The Japanese army had an almost insatiable appetite for beer. As it advanced through rural China, leaving a trail of ruin and destruction behind, it also left gigantic quantities of empty beer bottles – some 2 million. This was just what the Ewo Brewery needed. It offered the impoverished peasants 2 US cents for every bottle they could pick up and deliver. Its rivals, reimporting their own stock, had to pay 10 cents a bottle.[21] The Ewo Brewery flourished accordingly.

Jardines' profits in the late 1930s were made despite an increasingly gloomy international background. The European war did not immediately involve Japan, which had already occupied most of the strategic and commercial centres of China. It was clear that the foreign community in the International Settlement and the French Concession existed only on sufferance and that the Japanese could sweep both away whenever this suited them. People live on hope, however, and there was clearly a difference between the capabilities and the intentions of the Japanese. Many members of Jardines and other British businesses in Shanghai returned to Europe to serve in Whitehall or the armed services. Some of the older ones stayed on to do what they could on the spot to ease the tense situation. Among them was Sir W.J. Keswick ('Tony'), Sir John's elder brother. He was Chairman of the Shanghai Municipal Council. It had become clear that taxes would have to be increased in 1941 despite Japanese objections.

A meeting of all ratepayers was convened on the Shanghai racecourse. Tony Keswick had the uncomfortable task of announcing the rise in rates when the head of the Japanese community, a Mr Haiyashi, took out a revolver from his pocket and fired two shots at him on the dais. It was a bitterly cold day and Keswick was wearing the thickest possible clothes including a fur-lined overcoat. The bullet that hit him went through, grazing a rib. The meeting broke up in tumult. Keswick was conveyed away in an ambulance and soon recovered. Years later at a party he was able to say 'last time I made a speech I was shot'.[22] At an adjourned ratepayers' meeting the tax rise went through. The Japanese, who were still in diplomatic relations with Britain were too embarrassed to object, but the assassin manqué, Haiyashi, was hailed in Japan as a hero.[23]

On 8 December 1941 the aircraft from Japanese carriers attacked Pearl Harbor. The world was never to be the same again.

SIXTEEN

War and its Aftermath

The Japanese war had an instant and temporarily devastating effect on the fortunes of the Firm and of all foreign businesses in China. Ever since 1937 Japan had *de facto* control of Shanghai and the other Treaty Ports, but there was an element of the velvet glove while the Japanese Government still had diplomatic relations with the major Western powers, and this remained true even after war had broken out in Europe in 1939. The formalities continued to be observed, and the privileges of the International Settlement remained – at least on paper. Pearl Harbor brought this pretence to an end.

All foreign enterprises, along with most Chinese businesses, were taken over and commandeered for the purposes of a wartime economy. The foreign residents of nations not at war found their movements and activities rigidly controlled. 'Enemy aliens' – the category to which the Firm's employees belonged – came under even closer surveillance and ever increasing restrictions. They had to wear distinguishing red arm bands marked with 'A' for Americans, 'B' for Britons, 'N' for Dutch and 'X' for everyone else. The French, because of the ambivalent position of Vichy, did not count for this purpose, and the French Concession was treated less severely than the International Settlement. Restaurants and other places of entertainment in the Concession soon displayed signs saying 'No Americans or Britons allowed'.

Another curious anomaly was the treatment of Jews. Those of Russian origin, thanks to a treaty of neutrality between Moscow and

Tokyo, were regarded as 'non-enemy aliens'. Stateless Jews who had escaped from Germany were even luckier. They were counted as Germans – presumably Hitler was not consulted – and enjoyed the special advantages, within the category of non-enemy aliens, accorded to German and Italian nationals. This was an accidental stroke of good fortune for some of Jardines' employees who, like other enemy aliens, had been interred from the beginning of 1943 in concentration camps. The German firm of Orenstein & Koppel which had had dealings before the war with Jardines in the manufacture of locomotives and rolling stock had been forced to dismiss its manager in China, a Jew named Hans Bernstein. Jardines protested, declaring with truth the Firm's own impeccable Aryan ancestry. Bernstein, though Jardines did not draw attention to the fact, was at once re-employed by the Firm. During the Japanese occupation, Bernstein used his privileged position as a German to spend all his available money to provide food and comforts for his friends in the camps in Shanghai. It was a risky, honourable and generous act never forgotten by its beneficiaries.[1]

The only commercial 'presence' of Jardines was in unoccupied China at Chung-King where Chiang Kai-shek had his capital. It was a one-man office looked after by H.H. Lennox who kept up a desultory illicit link by word of mouth down the river to the Firm's remaining friends in Shanghai, some of whom managed to escape back to Chung-King. Another Jardines employee, H.H. Tod, opened a small shipping agency at Bombay to deal with what little remained of the Firm's fleet. The most important member of Jardines in Chung-King was (Sir) John Keswick who was now serving the British Government in charge of SOE (Special Operations Executive) in China. He later became political adviser on Chinese affairs and liaison officer at South East Asia Command on Lord Mountbatten's staff. It was not an appointment entirely to the liking of the Foreign Office. Mountbatten paid more attention to Keswick than to his Foreign Office adviser. To quote the foremost historian of Anglo-American relations with war-time China, Christopher Thorne:

> Numerous interviews with those concerned together with documentary evidence have made it clear that Mountbatten relied far more on Keswick's advice than he did on that of his chief political adviser (Sir Esler) Dening. It

is equally apparent, however, that Keswick's approach to questions involving China was a 'harder' one than that of the Foreign Office itself, that the office was not entirely comfortable over Keswick's position in the light of his Jardine Matheson connections, and that its Senior Far Eastern officials had a high regard for the abilities and reporting of Dening.[2]

'Harder' in this context meant a firmer line against any move to propitiate Chiang Kai-shek by the promise of post-war concessions which might prove embarrassing. That did not apply to the abandonment of extra-territoriality. It was generally agreed that this had to be given up. The American administration was keen to do so and the British Government was in favour too. Even the China Association with which Keswick had close links could not seriously resist a step which was on the verge of being taken as long ago as 1931. Early in 1943 extra-territoriality was abandoned.

It was another matter when the Americans, who had absurdly idealistic notions about Chiang Kai-shek and his corrupt, incompetent regime, pressed Britain to cede Kowloon, or even Hong Kong. The Chinese Government at the time of the signature of the agreement to end extra-territoriality had reserved the right at a later date to raise the question of the New Territories north of Kowloon leased to Britain for 99 years in 1898; this would clearly be a first step towards recovering Hong Kong itself. Roosevelt more than once indicated that he thought it would be an admirable gesture for Britain to give up Hong Kong and make it an international free port. There were voices in the Foreign Office which favoured this course. The China Association was bitterly opposed. There was no likelihood of any concession by Churchill who firmly told Roosevelt and Stalin at Tehran in 1943 that 'nothing would be taken away from Britain without a war'.[3] British ministers resented American preaching on this subject. Thorne quotes a conversation in January 1945:

PRESIDENT ROOSEVELT: 'I do not wish to be unkind to the British, but in 1841 when you acquired Hong Kong, you did not acquire it by purchase.

OLIVER STANLEY (Colonial Secretary): 'Let me see, Mr President, that was about the time of the Mexican War, wasn't it?'[4]

CHURCHILL on another occasion declared: 'I have not become the King's First Minister in order to preside over the liquidation of the British Empire.'[5]

But in the months that followed Pearl Harbor much of the eastern portion of the Empire seemed already in a state of liquidation. The first colony to fall was Hong Kong. The effect on the Firm and all British trading interests was even more drastic than the occupation of Shanghai. Whitehall had long havered over the defence of the colony. In 1937 the chiefs of staff debated whether to add more troops at once to the four battalions normally stationed there, or send reinforcements if and when war broke out. It was agreed that the existing establishment was not enough. Major-General Bartholomew, GOC Hong Kong until 1938, argued that at least a division was needed. Otherwise there was no point in fighting at all.

His successor, Major-General A.R. Grassett, was more optimistic. Disregarding the precedent of the Russo-Japanese War, when Japan not only destroyed the Russian navy but the ground forces too, he believed, like many British servicemen, that the Japanese were an inferior race. They might do well enough against third-rate Chinese troops but they would soon get their come-uppance from his battalions. But in the spring of 1941 Churchill, at the time more realistic than some of his advisers, thought it better to reduce the garrison to a 'symbolic scale', certainly not reinforce it. 'We must avoid frittering away our resources on untenable positions.'[6] However, General Grassett, now posted back to England, was a persistent lobbyist. He persuaded the Chiefs of Staff and through them Churchill that two more battalions would make all the difference. In mid-November two courageous but almost untrained Canadian battalions disembarked at Kowloon. 'When do we get to grips with the goddamned little yellow bastards?' one soldier asked.[7]

By this time the collapse of France and the Netherlands, along with the isolation of their eastern colonies, had altered all naval calculations about Hong Kong, Malaya and Singapore. There was little hope of any help from the British or any other navy.

Hong Kong was expendable and the Canadians should never have been sent. Its only value was as a source of potential delay in the way of an all-out Japanese attempt to achieve their new empire on the Pacific rim. Until the last moment it was not certain that this reckless, ruthless and ultimately fatal step would be taken by the Japanese Government. Meanwhile life for the Europeans and the wealthier Chinese proceeded agreeably enough – in separate compartments of course. The employees of such concerns as Jardines, Swires, the Hong Kong & Shanghai Bank, even at the lower grades, could count on a car and at least two servants. On Victoria Peak, where the rich lived, one would have as a minimum a cook, an amah, a gardener (or two), a coolie and a house boy. Hotels and restaurants (white dinner jacket *de rigueur*) flourished. Bands played and guests danced by night. Office hours were not extensive. Weekends could be devoted to racing, polo, golf, tennis, or to swimming in beautiful blue bays. When darkness fell there was always bridge to kill the time. Cuisine was excellent, alcohol abundant. It was somehow symbolic that the ill-fortified chain of pill-boxes and outposts intended to halt the invaders in the New Territories should have been called the 'Gin Drinkers Line'.

It may seem in retrospect that the Hong Kong British were living in a dream world, but what difference could it have made to events if they had opted for puritanism and eschewed self-indulgence? Surely very little. And one should not forget that at least some effort was made among the civilian population to prepare for war. Conscription for British residents up to the age of 55 had been introduced early in 1941. Most of the conscripts joined the Hong Kong Volunteer Defence Force ('The Volunteers'). They came from all social levels from artisan to taipan. They included Chinese, Free French, Russians, Scandinavians and Americans 'who can even more truly have been considered Volunteers since their nation was at this time neutral'.[8]

A group of the over-55s, determined not to be left out, formed their own special Company. The founder was Colonel A.W. Hughes, Chairman of the Union Insurance Company of Canton. They were called the 'Hughesiliers'. Colonel Hughes was in England on business when the Japanese attacked. In his absence his second-in-command, Major J.J. Paterson, the Jardines taipan, took over. He was also the senior member of the Legislative Council, and he had had a distinguished record in the First World War with six mentions in despatches.[9] The Hughesiliers were destined, despite their age, to play a distinguished role in the battle.

This began on the morning of 8 December simultaneously with the attack on Pearl Harbor, which put paid to whatever slim hope there was of naval aid for Hong Kong. The Japanese had complete control of the sea and overwhelming air superiority which they quickly used to eliminate the few antediluvian RAF planes parked on the Kai Tak runway. Numerically the infantry of the Japanese 38th Division which made the attack amounted to about the same as that of the defence – some 12,000. But they were tougher, hardier, better equipped and more highly motivated. To die in battle was an honour, to be taken prisoner a disgrace. The Japanese were adept at getting across country. The British stuck rigidly to the roads. The Japanese mortars, handled with great skill, were far superior to the defenders' equivalent. The regular garrison was enervated by an overlong sojourn in sybaritic Hong Kong. The newly arrived Canadian battalions were courageous but quite untrained. It is doubtful whether higher grade or even 'crack' troops could have done more than postpone by a week or so the inevitable end. Hong Kong, its back-streets packed with fifth columnists and spies, was a plum ripe for the picking.

The Japanese forces soon overran the Gin Drinkers Line, and on 11 December General Maltby, GOC Hong Kong, decided to withdraw his forces from the mainland. On the evening of 18 December, after a week of devastating aerial and artillery bombardment, the first Japanese landings began on Hong Kong Island. This is not the place to describe the campaign which was fought with great courage by the defenders but culminated in formal surrender on Christmas Day when it was clear that further resistance would merely mean butchery of the civilian population.

Among many acts of gallantry was that of the Hughesiliers. Too elderly for any very active service, they were assigned the task of safeguarding the North Point power-station, along with a platoon of 44 volunteers from the Electric Company and 30 from the China Light & Power Company, who had made their way to the island after Kowloon was occupied. When the Japanese assault boats landed they found themselves in the very front line but cut off from any support. The nearest help was 2,000 yards away. Efforts were made to reinforce them but none succeeded. The Hughesiliers fought with great tenacity under Paterson's leadership but by 4pm on 19 December they were overrun, their ammunition exhausted. It is worth quoting the authoritative account by Oliver Lindsay:

> The Hughesiliers battle was remarkable not only because of the age of the veterans who sought action rather than safety but also because they won time for fresh defences to be established in their rear. Their courage was typical of most who fought on in isolated positions long after there was no hope of relief or reinforcement. Bullet-scarred, impersonal pill-boxes hidden by overgrown vegetation in long forgotten gulleys are today a mute reminder in Hong Kong of other less celebrated actions. The long list of 'missing in action' is indicative of their courage. All too often there were no survivors, and so there is no possibility of recording their no less gallant deeds.[10]

In his Despatches written later General Maltby commented: 'The delay the force caused was very valuable to me.' The value of a delaying action against an ultimately victorious enemy is difficult to assess, but at least one can say that more of the enemy were killed than if there had been early surrender. War is a grim balance sheet. Those who fight to the end cannot know what difference, if any, their courage will make. The defence of Hong Kong contrasts vividly in the annals of British military history with the surrender of Singapore a few weeks later.

The prisoners of war and the civilian internees now faced an indeterminate period of squalid misery. Despite sporadic gleams of hope, it was to last for three and a half years in ever deteriorating conditions. Alan Reid in his chapter in *The Thistle and the Jade* says that 'Neither prisoners of war nor internees had been well treated in Hong Kong.'[11] This is one of the understatements of all time. In fact they were treated atrociously. The Japanese were brutal captors. Nations can change. Modern Germany is very different from that of Hitler's time and modern Japan from that of General Tojo, but the cruel and detestable nature of both the earlier regimes is a matter of historical record. It should neither be forgotten nor forgiven. The survivors of the Jardines' staff who were interned on the Stanley peninsula were unlikely to forget. They were a small group out of 1,300 who lived in miserable conditions until August 1945 when the atomic bomb brought Japanese resistance to an end. Their condition would have been even worse but for the undercover help given by Jardines' comprador Henry Lo who was supported by other members of Jardines' Chinese staff. Those whom the Japanese for one reason or another spared from internment ran great risks. The Chinese in Hong Kong were even worse treated than the Europeans, and anyone who helped the internees would have been executed either at once or, more likely, after torture. Luckily no army anywhere uses its crème de la crème to guard prison camps. The Japanese were not always on the alert.

The camp at Stanley was at first in a state of anarchic confusion. The Japanese kept external guard and complete control over diminishing supplies, but otherwise left the internees to organize their own arrangements, and did not care whether there was order or chaos. An important Jardines' director, D.L. Newbigging, played a major part in restoring order. After a period of almost subversive anger against the Hong Kong Government the internees accepted as their leader (Sir) F.C. Gimson who had arrived as 'Colonial Secretary' the day before the Japanese attack. Since the Governor, Sir Mark Young, had been, along with General Maltby, removed to an unknown destination, Gimson was the representative of Britain. He kept an unpublished diary, 'Personal Impressions as Recorded in a Diary' which is one of the most useful sources for Oliver Lindsay's second book on the Hong Kong tragedy – *At the Going Down of the Sun* (1982). Newbigging came in for special praise. He accepted the task of ensuring a fair distribution of the deplorably inadequate food supplies. 'He showed patience, imagination and understanding. The internees owe him and his assistants a great debt. All displayed an outstanding record of devoted service.'[12]

In the Hong Kong campaign twelve of the Firm's staff were killed or died soon afterwards and six were wounded. Of these, five killed and six wounded were in the Dockyard Defence Company – members of Jardines' affiliate, the Indo-China Steam Navigation Company (ICSN) when a launch received a direct hit from a bomb. Four of the company's ships were scuttled to prevent capture and two were sunk by enemy action. In the whole of the war, nineteen employees of Jardine Matheson were killed and 35 of the staff of ICSN.

On 14 February 1942 the ICSN ship *Liwo*, an armed merchant cruiser, was sunk in a sea battle off Singapore by Japanese warships after ramming a Japanese transport which later also sank. Of the crew, Lieut. Thomas Wilkinson was awarded a posthumous VC, Lieut. Stanton received the DSO and there were two DSMs, one Conspicuous Gallantry Medal and six mentions in despatches awarded to members of the crew. In 1951 Tony Keswick presented Wilkinson's Victoria Cross to the Imperial War Museum. Admiral of the Fleet Viscount Cunningham of Hyndhope received it on behalf of the Museum. He said in reply to Keswick: 'We can share your pride that the ship was commanded and largely manned by officers and men of your company ... an exploit worthy to rank with the most outstanding exploits of the Merchant Navy of the two World Wars, to be compared with the *Jervis Bay* and the *Rawalpindi*.'[13]

On 6 August 1945 the first atomic bomb was dropped by an American plane on Hiroshima, and a second three days later on Nagasaki. On 15 August Japan accepted the Allies' ultimatum. The British Government was determined that the surrender of Hong Kong must be received by a British officer. Rear Admiral Harcourt, in charge of a Naval force detached for this purpose from the US/British Pacific Fleet, landed at the Naval Dockyard on 30 August. He did not receive the formal surrender until 16 September. The delay was caused by Chinese claims which the British Government rejected. Chinese, American and Canadian representatives could be present at the ceremony but only Harcourt was authorized to receive the Instrument of Surrender signed by two high-ranking Japanese officers. One of the brush pens used for this purpose reposes in the Jardines archive in Hong Kong.

Long before this the POWs and internees had liberated themselves and walked out of their dismal camps. They were ragged, emaciated, weak, dirty and unkempt. Many suffered from illness. Dysentery, TB, beriberi and malnutrition were rife. But they were free, and members of the Jardines' staff, prominent among them Paterson and

Newbigging, despite poor health, were keen to get the Firm going again. As soon as they could leave their camp a group of Jardine internees reopened the Firm's office. Someone bribed a professional lock-picker to force the door of the strong-room. There to their surprise – and pleasure – they found two cases of whisky which a member of the staff had had the foresight to set aside when the Japanese invasion began. As the authors of *Jardine Matheson & Company: a Historical Sketch* put it: 'What presence of mind some people have in adversity! It turned out to be "only Bourbon", but one cannot be too fussy when under fire.'[14] 'Scotch' would obviously have been better, given the history of the Firm, but it was lucky that the cases had never been discovered by the Japanese who were and are great whisky devotees. They would have swigged the lot with relish.

John Keswick was sent by Lord Mountbatten to Hong Kong to liaise between his headquarters and Admiral Harcourt and General Carton de Wiart, the Prime Minister's representative in Chung-King. This involved a non-stop journey of 24 hours by a Catalina flying boat from Madras. He was accompanied by David MacDougall of the Colonial Office who had the task of assisting the civil administration under Admiral Harcourt. This was quickly established, but Hong Kong remained for many months in a state of sordid squalor. Food supplies were still scarce, the streets were piled with garbage, houses and offices were looted, the Triad Societies and various gambling gangs threatened stability, policing was incompetent, transport was deplorable, international telephones non-existent, and the famous harbour was full of sunken ships. Keswick was able to take the first steps in reviving the Firm's fortunes before reporting back to London to be discharged from his Foreign Office duties. Meanwhile Alan Reid came out to organize the official shipping services which he did with characteristic efficiency – a vital task in view of the shortage of food imports. Hong Kong soon revived and with it the fortunes of the Firm. Its headquarters, which had been in London since 1941, were reinstated in Victoria. Profitable trading began. In 1947–8 the figure was HK $4.29 million. Firing of the Noon Day Gun was revived on 30 August 1947.

The big question was what would happen in China? The Firm had long relied upon its operations there, mainly based on Shanghai. China at the end of the war was divided between the forces of Chiang Kai-shek and the Communists, led by Mao Tse-tung. Both had quite separately opposed the Japanese invaders; there was little liaison between them. They had only refrained from mutual hostilities because of shared hatred of Japan. After Hiroshima and Nagasaki this truce had no rationale. Japan's forces had vanished, not thanks to either of the Chinese factions, but to American bombardment. The rivals could now fight it out. In retrospect one can see which was bound to win. The hardened, puritanical fanatics of the Long March were likely to prevail over the lazy, corrupt forces of the Kuomintang, despite their heavy American backing and numerical majority. But this did not seem clearly predictable at the time. Jardines resumed its activities in Shanghai without any great alarm for the future. After all, civil wars of one sort or another had been sporadically waged in the hinterland for generations without much effect on the Europeans of coastal China.

In 1945 John Keswick flew back from England to Shanghai via America and Honolulu. His wartime bride, Clare, came out by troop-ship through the Panama Canal to Manila. The passage took 82 days. Keswick found the ex-internees in remarkably good heart. J.L. Koo, the third generation of a family who had worked for the Firm, had done much to help them. The Mayor of Shanghai, Dr K.C. Wu, was an old friend and one of the few Kuomintang figures not tainted by corruption. He was very helpful in dealing with the problems of re-establishing business in the city where, headed by Jardines at 27, The Bund, the famous European firms – the Hong Kong & Shanghai Bank, Butterfield & Swire, Shell, Sassoons – were soon back in business. They could not have guessed how soon they would be out of it.

John Keswick records the misery of the winter of 1945 in Shanghai which was exceptionally cold. In the closing stages of the war the Japanese authorities had commandeered all the central-heating pipes in the city for scrap iron. He was sitting unhappily in his office wearing a long Chinese silk padded gown with his hands up the sleeves to keep them as warm as he could. An American sailor walked in and, with a deplorable lack of 'political correctness', called, 'Hey Chink, where's this guy Kes-wick?'[15]

It soon became clear that the People's Liberation Army (PLA), as

Mao had christened his forces, was a formidable force. Members of the Firm saw that it might well overthrow the Kuomintang but did not believe that it could unite the country. They also thought that Marxism was an alien creed unlikely to be acceptable to the allegedly traditionalist Chinese. 'How wrong we were!' wrote Sir John Keswick. A lot of others were wrong too.

In April 1947 the PLA launched a major offensive. The Nationalist forces melted away like snow in summer. At the end of January 1949 the PLA had captured Peking. In May they occupied Shanghai. On 1 October the People's Republic of China (PRC) was proclaimed. On 10 December Chiang Kai-shek fled to Taiwan. During those years the Shanghai branch did what trading it could but laboured under increasing difficulties. The Firm as a whole was making good profits but this, though there is no geographical breakdown, must have come largely from business in Hong Kong. In Shanghai, apart from the general difficulties posed by the advance of the PLA, there was the further problem of a complete breakdown of the Nationalist Government's control over the currency. The Gold Yuan which had replaced the old Chinese dollar was officially worth four to the US Dollar. On the black market at the beginning of April 1949 it stood at 80,000 to the dollar, a fortnight later at 600,000 and early in May at 9 million. Interest rates were 30 per cent per day. In these circumstances trading was almost impossible. During the summer of 1948 the European firms in Shanghai became increasingly apprehensive. It seemed wise to have a common front: the various Chambers of Commerce joined together in an international body of which John Keswick became Chairman. Mao issued a statement that all who remained would be fairly treated. Keswick and his colleagues, feeling that almost anything would be better than the rule of the Kuomintang, decided against complete withdrawal, but Jardines, like most of the other firms evacuated all their non-essential staff. The residue was there to protect the interests of their Chinese employees, some 10,000 (it had been much higher), and to do what they could about property worth between £8 and £10 million. There was also the matter of people and property on a smaller scale in Canton, Tientsin, Hankow and many other places.

The 'liberation' – as it was euphemistically called – of Shanghai took place at the end of May. On the 27th, Communist forces entered the city. There was no serious resistance to speak of, although a certain amount of shooting took place. David Middleditch, a young man who had only joined the Firm in Shanghai on 23 April, gave a vivid account in some letters written to his grandfather.[16] On 22 May he wrote:

> The 13th of this month was the night I first heard gunfire and there was a strong rumour that Mao Tse-tung would take over the next day. The weather was perfect during the weekend and the Country Club solemnized this phase of the war by opening its grass tennis courts and serving strawberries. I played ten sets on Sunday and by the end of the day was finding the war most fatiguing... There's a good deal of artillery fire at night, though none of it has landed in the main part of Shanghai. The Nationalist gunboats have shelled the Communists from the river.
>
> As far as the life of the foreigners is concerned, there hasn't been much change. We still have our clubs and our homes; we go to the office, play games - I've been out riding on the race course twice this week...
> 28th May
> By Tuesday morning it was pretty clear that the fight was on and the fact that the Nationalists were beating it down the road from Hungjao provided some indication of the way things were going. Everyone except myself and Michael Keyes was sent home from the office after lunch. We stayed on as fire guards, but before settling down to a pleasant afternoon of squirting each other with hoses I went round with the cashier to collect the trifling sum of 50,000 million Gold Yuan in five large packing cases...

He and his colleague returned to the office later to find themselves with 'one of the taipans, Hector Tod, and John Keswick and his wife, who have a flat in the compound. As it turned out we were cut off there for the next three days, so we saw a good deal of one another.' He was struck by one phenomenon –the total silence and absence of movement on the Bund and the river, 'which is so sensational in this part of Shanghai that no one has ever seen the like before ... All appeared to be over bar the shouting.'

It was not quite all over, however, for firing broke out in the area of the Garden Bridge.

By midday it had got very loud indeed and lunch in the Keswicks' flat was like a Pont cartoon on the English character: we sat in a beautifully furnished room, complete with bowls of flowers and a dog asleep on the carpet while three imperturbable Chinese in long white gowns served cocktails followed by roast beef and Yorkshire pudding and rhubarb pie. Not more than a hundred yards away a full orchestra of rifles, machine-guns and mortars was making so much noise that speech was frequently impossible.

After a stray bullet narrowly missed Keswick meals were taken in the Correspondence Office. John Keswick shook some good cocktails and Mrs Keswick presided gracefully over excellent meals on a stenographer's desk. Actually of course we were in no real danger as neither side were in the least interested in us.

Well, we are now in Communist hands and very good they have been so far. Their troops are extremely well disciplined and polite and they have gone out of their way to the most extraordinary extent to conciliate not only the local population but the foreigners. None of our houses, offices, factories have been so much as entered and even the curfew has been lifted. This all seems too good to last but one assumes that they feel they are going to need us, for the time being at any rate.

The assumption was correct. The new regime had no intention of allowing foreign firms to trade in China other than on sufferance and very short notice to quit. But it was convenient not to expel them at once. Keswick, who spoke the Shanghai version of Mandarin, may have gained the Communists' confidence by taking over from the incompetent and departing UNRRA the task of distributing that body's 500,000 tons of rice at a cost of 25 per cent below the current price extorted by predatory dealers.

A new currency along with price and wage controls was introduced with speed and efficiency, and foreign trade came under strict regulations – all carried out by 'Workers Unions' which had no analogy with Western trade unions but were instruments of government. A union was soon set up in Jardines. There followed some two to three years of hard negotiation. It was the period of what is sometimes called 'Hostage Capitalism'. That is, say, the handing over of the assets and ownership of a firm in exchange for the release of all foreign staff who wished to return to their own country. Presumably the new government could have simply expropriated the firms and expelled the foreigners. But that would have been flagrantly contrary to international law. If the same objective could be achieved under the forms of legality, so much the better. Then there was the benefit from retaining foreign firms during the reorganization of the economy. They could be forced to trade for the benefit of China, not their own shareholders, and the transition to a Communist command economy could be made with the minimum of disruption.

The effect on Jardines and other foreign firms in Shanghai was highly frustrating. Life there in 1950 was not uncomfortable, except that one had no freedom of movement. Food, drink and servants were plentiful. But a firm could neither close down nor trade profitably nor send back its foreign staff, and it had to remit in hard currency funds to pay the ever-increasing wages and benefits demanded by the Union (the Chinese Government). Various measures in retaliation were considered, one being to stop foreign remittances. But there was no solidarity among the various firms, and the Keswicks themselves were divided about the desirability of, or use, of such a combine. A Socialist British Government was unlikely to give any help even if it had the power to do anything. Another possibility was to sell off the Firm's shares so as to be free of management liability, or to negotiate a sale of its Chinese assets. The Chinese Government's reply was that there were no buyers, and so the assets were worthless. All that the Firm could do was to try to minimize losses, reduce overheads, refuse any new business, trade in such few lines as were profitable and prepare to pull out.

The Chinese Government, inheriting an empty treasury and totally lacking in foreign exchange, was ready to be quite ruthless in extracting by taxation or 'voluntary' (in reality compulsory) subscription to 'Victory Bonds' the very last dollar they could get from any foreign firms surviving in China. By June 1950 there was a flicker of economic improvement. A few ships came into Shanghai harbour. The first was a Jardines ship, the *Mausang*. The Government relaxed its tight money policy. Keswick and his wife were allowed to travel by train to Peking and occupy for a few days an old Chinese courtyard house which he had bought. Meanwhile the Korean War had broken out and the economic sky darkened. In 1951 the Keswicks received an exit visa. Negotiations for signing away the Firm's assets in exchange for its liabilities continued, and were not finally completed until the late summer of 1954. After more than 120 years Jardines was out of China.

Epilogue

The story of Jardine Matheson was far from over in 1950, but the end of its major role in China does mark the end of an epoch. It is therefore convenient to look back from mid-century and consider where it stood and what it had done.

Jardine Matheson in the perspective of history was simply one, though a very important one, of the firms involved in the vast expansion of English and then British trade all over the world. This was a European phenomenon too, embracing Portugal and Spain in the fifteenth and sixteenth centuries, the Netherlands in the seventeenth and France in the eighteenth. But Britain, especially after the industrial revolution, out-gunned the lot.

Of the various regions of the globe where the British traded, the Far East was by no means at the top in terms of volume. North and South America counted for much more. So did India. But the peculiar three-cornered trade between Britain, India and China in terms of tea, opium and bullion gave the Far East an importance to British Government finances which outweighed the trade statistics. It was enough to pull Britain into two wars, the morality of which has been disputed ever since. The first led to the annexation of Hong Kong, the second to that of Kowloon. In the first Jardines was deeply and directly involved. This alone gives the Firm a unique place in history, and one which has never been forgotten. The triangular relationship ceased to be significant after the 1860s when the firm of Sassoons cornered the Indian opium market and India began to grow its own tea. By then Jardines was diversifying into a host of other activities: shipping, insurance, silk, cotton and, rather later, armaments, railways and railway loans.

Inevitably and rightly, the early history of the Firm has always been regarded as the most interesting part of the story. It, or its background, has been the subject of two fascinating historical novels: the late James Clavell's bestseller *Tai-pan* (1966) and Timothy Mo's *An Insular Possession* (1986). The stories are of course fiction, but fiction can illuminate history and set a scene, as Tolstoy did in *War and Peace*, Walter Scott in *Quentin Durward* and Dickens in *The Tale of Two Cities*. The events which led to the acquisition of Hong Kong and the establishment of the Treaty Ports are an extraordinary compound of idealism and greed, piety and contraband, cut-throat competition and political intrigue.

Moreover, to a degree unparalleled elsewhere, British firms, and in the end the British Government, were encountering in China a culture and civilization so remote from Western ideas and so entrenched, self-sufficient and convinced of its own superiority as to make mutual comprehension virtually impossible. It still is. Even eighteenth-century India, the nearest analogy, was easier to understand and 'open up' than Imperial China. But in India this was achieved by annexation which caused endless burdens and complications. No British Government was going to repeat that process in China. Hong Kong was quite enough. When from time to time Jardines and the other British firms complained that Whitehall was dragging its feet and was insufficiently supportive, that is the explanation. The tension between the worlds of business and officialdom was endemic throughout. It has not vanished even today.

The successive partners in Jardines did have the same objective as those in rival firms. They were all there to make money and we have Dr Johnson's authority that 'there are few ways in which a man can be more innocently employed'. They all regarded the Ch'ing Empire as hopelessly effete and long past redemption, and, although it was certainly not their motive, they genuinely believed the impact of Western commerce on China to be for the good of the Chinese as well as themselves; it would bring prosperity and Christianity. True, it also brought opium. But 'the drug' was perfectly legal in Britain, and British governments were not going to interfere with a trade, however illicit in China, which was indirectly so important for the Exchequer.

As for prosperity and Christianity, it is fair to say that missionaries did make considerable advances even if they provoked temporary reaction, such as the Boxer Rising. It is undoubtedly true that Western trade brought great wealth to individual Chinese merchants. They made at least as much as the foreigners out of opium and other trading activities.

The Jardines compradors gained huge fortunes, not only from the drug but from general business. The impact of foreign commerce raised the standard of living in the Treaty Ports, and most of coastal China benefited too. There was no comparable effect on the vast peasant population of the hinterland. Perhaps this was an element in the Communist triumph of 1949.

The attitude, outlook and practice of Jardines were not different from those of the other Western firms operating in Canton, Hong Kong, Shanghai and the Treaty Ports. They worked under the same constraints and enjoyed the same opportunities, but they easily outlasted their two earliest rivals – Dent, which collapsed in 1867 and Russell & Co., which went down in 1891. Swires and Sassoons, however, entering later, are still there. If Jardines remains 'Number One' it is as *primus inter pares* and it owes its position to a combination of commercial enterprise and prudence, which other Far Eastern firms may have equalled but never surpassed. It is difficult to single out any particular features of the Firm's transactions which account for its long run of success. But perhaps two deserve mention, though there may have been many more. One was positive. Jardines was quicker than most to see the importance both in Hong Kong and Shanghai of buying land, and did very well out of its purchases. The other was negative. After the opium period, Jardines operated almost entirely on commission and avoided speculation in commodities. It thus rode out the two great nineteenth-century financial crises – that of Overend & Gurney in the 1860s, which ruined Dent which had speculated heavily in tea, and the Baring crisis of the 1890s which wrecked Russell & Co. because of a similar speculation in sugar.

The Jardine/Keswick 'connection' had three great assets, family tradition, genetic commercial acumen and geographical propinquity. For the first two one can compare the Barings and the Rothschilds. The Jardines and Keswicks never figured to the same extent in public life, although they certainly could have done so had they wished. What distinguishes them from other commercial dynasties is the extent to which they were geographically as well as family based. The Lowlands of Scotland do not have clans, but there is such a thing as 'clanishness'. The Jardine homeland was one where everyone knew everyone. Recruitment was by selective family and local patronage. The history of the Firm is a remarkable testimony to how successful and enduring this unfashionable tradition can be.

Notes

CHAPTER 1

1 Maggie Keswick (ed.), *The Thistle and the Jade* (1982), p. 14.
2 J.M. Roberts, *History of the World* (1976), p. 442.
3 Keswick (ed.), op. cit., p. 244.
4 Ibid., p. 244.
5 Ibid., pp. 246–7.

CHAPTER 2

1 The reason was that Chinese junks could convey goods to and from the Philippines much more cheaply than Spanish vessels.
2 Originally a Supercargo or Supracargo (from Portuguese *sobre cargo*) was an officer on board a merchant ship who superintended the cargo and managed the commercial transactions of the voyage. But the word came to have the wider meaning of agents who managed a merchant's affairs in a foreign country. From 1770 the East India Company no longer ordered its Supercargoes to come home with their ships but required them to remain in Canton as a joint body in charge of trade from year to year. There were normally twelve, of whom some four, ironically called 'the Select' by the Country Merchants, managed the Company's affairs.

3 Michael Greenberg, *British Trade and the Opening of China 1800–1842* (1951), pp.13–14.
4 Greenberg, op. cit., pp. 13–14.
5 Dollars are Spanish dollars worth between four and five shillings.
6 Greenberg, op. cit., pp. 13–14.
7 William Jardine was an exception, sailing in 1802, straight to Canton via Java.
8 Alleged to be so-called because of an early method used by the private merchants of Canton to effect remittances by means of 'respondentia bonds' – loans granted to shippers in Canton to enable them to purchase an export cargo and charter a ship; repayment was to be made within a fixed number of days in India after the landing of the cargo which was security for the loan. Greenberg, op. cit., p. 158.
9 'Hong' comes from the Chinese *hang*, meaning a house of business, a firm.
10 Corrupted from the Chinese title 'Hwai Kwan Pu'. The slightly comic connotation fits with the absurd language known as 'pidgin English', which had become over the years the means of communication of Whampoa and Canton, and which contributed to the patronizing attitude of the British to the Chinese. Compare 'Kitchen Kaffir' in South Africa.

11 It had advantages for some people. George Chinnery, the most famous painter of people and scenes in Macao and Hong Kong was married to and fled from a peculiarly hideous wife in Calcutta. When she threatened him with a visit he repaired quickly to Canton, observing: 'Now I am all right. What a kind providence is this Chinese Government that it forbids the softer sex from coming and bothering us here.'

12 G.J. Yorke, *The Princely House* (unpublished typescript *c*.1937), p. 15.

13 In 1830, the male population was just over 1000, the female nearly 2700.

14 Greenberg, op. cit., pp. 69–70.

15 The dollar in this context is the Spanish dollar, whose Sterling value fluctuated between 4 and 5 shillings.

16 Greenberg, op. cit., p. 106.

17 Alethea Hayter, *Opium and the Romantic Imagination* (1968) p. 34. This fascinating book is the source for much which follows, and is a most illuminating survey of the whole subject.

18 'Opium eater' *pace* De Quincey is a curiously misleading phrase. The author, whose famous *Confessions* first caused addiction to be considered as a special psycho-medical problem, was a laudanum drinker.

19 Sherlock Holmes, though cautioned by Dr Watson, took the drug from time to time. Conan Doyle would hardly have added this feature to his portrait if it had been reprobated at the time, which was much later – 1891 onwards.

20 *Cambridge History of China* vol. 10, part I, p. 178 quoting from 'Opium smoking in Ch'ing China' in F. Wakeham and C. Grant (eds), *Conflict and Control in late Imperial China* (1975).

CHAPTER 3

1 This account of Jardine and his voyages is based on Captain A.R. Williamson, *Eastern Traders* (privately printed by Jardine Matheson & Co., 1975) pp. 51–147.

2 Williamson, op. cit., p. 64.

3 He had a remarkable career, made a great fortune, was renowned for philanthropic works and was created a knight in 1842, the first Indian to receive the honour. He was made a baronet in 1857.

4 Alan Reid in Maggie Keswick (ed.), *The Thistle and the Jade*, p. 22.

5 Jardine Matheson Papers (henceforth JM Papers), *Private Letter Book* (PLB), vol. 1, No. 7, March 1830.

6 JM Papers, PLB, vol. 2, No. 100, January 1833.

7 G.J. Yorke, op. cit., p. 114.

8 Quoted Yorke, op. cit., p. 124.

9 Daniel Magniac, another partner, had transgressed the code of the day by marrying his half-caste mistress in Macao. He was promptly pensioned off and sent home.

10 Williamson, op. cit., p. 143.

11 'The Firm' with a capital 'F' was how Jardine Matheson came to be known colloquially until the Second World War.

CHAPTER 4

1 Quoted Greenberg, op. cit., p. 118.

2 Greenberg, op. cit., p. 120 quoting from Robert Taylor's *Letter Books*, 4 April 1820.

3 Quoted Yorke, op. cit., p. 144 from JM Papers, Yrissari & Co. *Letter Book*, 26 April 1823.

4 Ibid, 29 April 1824.

5 Yorke, ibid.

6 Quoted Greenberg, op. cit., pp 122–3.

7 *Cambridge History of China*, vol. 10, Part II, p. 172.

8 Ibid., p. 31.

9 1803–51. See *Cambridge History of China*, vol. 10, Part I (1976), p. 549. He later acted as interpreter during the First Opium War, then as 'magistrate' of Chusan and later as Chinese Secretary to the British Government of Hong Kong. His nephew-in-law, Harry Parkes, played an important part in the Second Opium War.

10 Yorke, op. cit., pp. 173–4, quoting from a draft letter by William Jardine, October 1832, in the JM archives. See also Maurice Collis, *Foreign Mud* (1946) p. 82, quoting from the same source.

11 Gutzlaff, *Journal of Three Voyages along the Coast of China* (1834), from which this and subsequent quotations are taken. See also Yorke, op. cit., pp. 174–6.

12 'The trade' was of course opium.

13 Or so it would appear from an item in PLB, 13 June 1833, quoted Yorke, op. cit., p. 176. Gutzlaff's private account to the Firm has not survived.

14 Archdeacon Moule, *The Story of the Cheh-Kiang Mission* (1878). The book, though unbelievably boring, ran into four editions, the last published in 1891. Cheh-Kiang is the Chinese province just south of Shanghai.

15 This was about £174, some £50 above Lintin prices. Collis, *Foreign Mud*, p. 88.

16 Yorke, op. cit., p. 179, quoting W. McKay to JM & Co., 6 August 1833.

17 Ibid., quoting McKay to JM & Co., end of August 1833.

18 Ibid., p. 180, quoting McKay to JM & Co., 14 September 1833.

19 Greenberg, op. cit., p. 140, quoting Jardine PLB, 10 March 1831.

20 Clipper, as Alan Reid says (*The Thistle and the Jade*, p.132), was first applied by New England slang to swift privateers of new design built at Baltimore. It became a general term for fast sailing ships of many different rigs.

21 Captain A.R. Williamson, *Eastern Traders* (privately printed 1975), pp. 187–92 on which this account of Clifton and *Red Rover* is based.

22 Williamson, op. cit., p. 192.

23 Yorke, op. cit., pp. 189–90.

24 Ibid., p. 192, quoting PLB, 11 August 1830.

25 Keswick (ed.), op. cit., p. 138.

26 Yorke, op. cit., p. 181 quoting PLB, 26 March 1833.

27 Ibid., p. 184.

28 Greenberg, op. cit., p. 141.

CHAPTER 5

1 Maurice Collis, *Foreign Mud* (1946), p. 107.

2 Ibid., pp. 107–11.

3 Quoted *Foreign Mud*, pp. 109–10.

4 Ibid, p. 110.

5 Ibid, p. 111.

6 JM Papers, PLB, 29 Feb. 1832, Yorke, op. cit., p. 167.

7 Collis, op. cit., pp. 115–19.

8 The person of highest rank in China always sat facing south, which was the direction of happy augury.

9 Collis, op. cit., pp. 59–61, based on C.T. Downing, *The Fan-Qui in China in 1836–7* (1838).

10 Quoted Gerald Graham, *The China Station*, War and Diplomacy 1830–1860 (1978), pp. 48–9.

11 Quoted Ibid., pp. 9–10.

12 JM Papers, PLB, Ch. 3, p. 127, June 1834.

13 PLB, p. 152, 8/34.

14 Quoted *Foreign Mud*, p. 142.

15 Ibid.

16 The ensuing account is based on Collis, op. cit.

CHAPTER 6

1 Keswick (ed.), op. cit., p. 28
2 Quoted Collis, op. cit., p. 184 and also in Graham, op.cit., p. 68, n. 9 who cites *Chang, Hsin-Pao, Commissioner Lin and the Opium War* (1964), pp. 83–4.
3 Quoted Yorke, op. cit., pp. 218–19.
4 Memorandum 24 March 1835, F.O. 17/8. Quoted partly Collis, op. cit., p. 184 and partly in Graham, op.cit., p. 66.
5 Greenberg, op. cit., p. 167, n. 2.
6 J.M. Papers, PLB, p. 165, October 1834. The 'certain party' is clearly Dent. The 'allusion' may be something in Jardine's newspaper, the *Canton Register*, which hinted at Dent's involvement and led to scurrilous exchanges with their own paper, the *Canton Press*. Yorke, op. cit., p. 220.
7 Ernest Bevin's phrase was 'a whelk stall'.
8 *Cambridge History of China*, vol. 10, part I, pp. 178–9.
9 Greenberg, op. cit., p. 202.
10 Ibid., p. 20.
11 Ibid., quoting PLB, WJ, 16.12.1838 and 5.1.1839.
12 Ibid., pp. 194–5.
13 Ibid., p. 195.
14 Yorke, op. cit., pp. 259–60.
15 David Jardine, a nephew.
16 Yorke, op. cit., quoting PLB, 26.1.1839.
17 Alan Reid in Keswick (ed.), op. cit., p. 23. He was not as iron-headed as all that.

CHAPTER 7

1 Quoted *Cambridge History of China* vol. 10 (1978), p. 185.
2 Graham, op. cit., p. 86 quoting F.O. 17/31, 30 March 1839.
3 Quoted Collis, op. cit., p. 224.
4 Yorke, op. cit., p. 235. Luckily he was saved by the opportune arrival of a consignment for Dent & Co. which he purchased at invoice price to keep his word, ibid., p. 239.
5 Ibid., p. 240 and Collis, op. cit., p. 229.
6 Yorke, op. cit., p. 238 quoting *India Letter Books*, 15 May 1839.
7 Yorke op. cit., quoting Jardine to Matheson, 27 September 1839, p. 327.
8 Ibid., p. 328.
9 Quoted Edgar Holt, *The Opium Wars in China* (1964), p. 98.
10 Ibid., pp. 99-100. Gladstone made an unfortunate slip of the tongue in defending the measures taken against the British community by the Cantonese - '... and then of course they poisoned the wells.' The 'of course', despite instant retraction, was held against him for many years. In fact the wells never were poisoned.
11 Disraeli, *Sybil* (1945), Book II, ch. I (Bradenham edition, pp. 54–5). Disraeli was writing as a novelist not a historian. He transfers 'McDruggy's' candidature to the general elections of 1837. In fact Jardine got into Parliament in the election of 1841.
12 Quoted Collis, op. cit., pp. 283–4.
13 Ibid., p. 284.
14 Yorke, op. cit., p. 244 quoting JM Papers ILB, 24 July 1839.
15 Graham, op. cit. quoting Matheson to William Jardine, 1 May 1839, JM Papers PLB (B9).
16 Quoted Collis, op. cit., p. 301.
17 *Letters of Queen Victoria*, vol. l, p. 261.
18 See Graham, op. cit., ch. 4 for an account of this remarkable ship.
19 Graham, op. cit., pp. 196–7.
20 *Cambridge History of China*, p. 205.
21 Yorke, op. cit., p. 461, quoting JM Papers PLB, 21 April 1843.
22 Ibid., p. 351, quoting PLB, 31 July 1843.
23 P.C. Kuo, *A Critical Study of the First Anglo-Chinese War with Documents* (1935), p. 291.
24 Ibid., p. 198.

25 Yorke, op. cit., pp. 352–3, quoting letter in H.T. Easton, *The History of a Banking House* (1903), p. 29.

CHAPTER 8

1 Yorke, op. cit., p. 486 quoting JM Papers, *Coastal Letter Books* (CLB), 22 January 1841.

2 Ibid., p. 487 quoting JM Papers, PLB, 21 August 1841.

3 Ibid., p. 488 quoting JM Papers, PLB, 25 August 1841.

4 Keswick (ed.), op. cit., p. 74 quoting JM Papers, PLB, 23 August 1841.

5 Yorke, op. cit., p. 489 quoting JM Papers, *Local Letter Book* (LLB), 4 December 1841.

6 Ibid., p. 4.

7 W.D. Jones, *Lord Derby and Victorian Conservatism* (1956), p. 86.

8 Ibid.

9 Graham, op. cit., pp. 233–4.

10 Alexander George Fraser 1785–1853, 16th Baron Saltoun was one of the heroes of Waterloo, holding the garden and orchard of Hougoumont Farm against all the onslaughts of the French.

11 Yorke, op. cit., p. 490 quoting from Alexander Fraser, *The Frasers of Philorth* (1879).

12 Ibid., p. 491 quoting JM Papers, PLB, 27 March 1844.

13 Brooks's was a club to which numerous members of the Firm were to belong: Andrew, Joseph and the first and second Sir Robert Jardine. James Matheson also became a member in 1843, his seconder being Edward Ellice. His nephew Alexander was elected in 1848. See *Memorials of Brooks's* (1967).

14 The address is printed in full in *The Thistle and the Jade*, p. 25.

15 Colin Crisswell, *The Taipans* (1981), p. 66.

16 It should not be confused with the title acquired by his nephew Alexander. See Keswick (ed.), op. cit., p. 170.

17 Keswick (ed.), op. cit., p. 26.

18 Quoted Charles E. Harvey, *The Rio Tinto Company* (1981), p. 6.

19 Ibid.

20 Crisswell, op. cit., p. 68, n. 31.

CHAPTER 9

1 See p. 149

2 Edward LeFevour, *Western Enterprise in Ch'ing China 1842–95* (Harvard East Asian Monographs, 1968), p. 13. This is an invaluable study based on the JM Papers.

3 Ibid.

4 Ibid., p. 160, n. 32.

5 Ibid., p. 157, n. 9.

6 The best account is in Graham, op. cit., pp. 256-58.

7 *Cambridge History of China 1800–1911*, p. 223, quoting JMA *Coastal Letter Book*, p. 22, April 1843.

8 Sometimes translated as 'intendant', title of the provincial governor in pre-revolutionary France.

9 Keswick (ed.), op. cit., p. 33.

10 J.V. Davidson-Houston, *Yellow Creek* (1962), p. 48; who quotes the constitution of the British Company: 'any gentleman enrolling cannot unroll himself without the sanction of the Consul.'

11 Douglas Hurd, *The Arrow War* (1967), p. 16.

12 Ibid., p. 17.

13 The figures for the Parliament elected in 1852 and still sitting were Conservatives 290, Peelites 45 and Liberals 319, but the Peelite vote was unpredictable and the Liberals ranged from high Whig aristocrats to Left-wing radicals.

14 Quoted in Douglas Hurd, op. cit., p. 28.

15 Ibid., p. 90.

16 Captain Henry (later Lord) Loch, one of Elgin's staff.

17 Hurd, op. cit., p. 127.

18 Quoted Ibid., p. 127.

CHAPTER 10

1 Vol. 10, Part 1, p. 252.

2 Another partner was Warren Delano, Jr., grandfather of Franklin Delano Roosevelt.

3 LeFevour, op. cit., p. 48, quoting Jardine Archives.

4 Ibid., chapter III passim.

5 Ibid., p. 166, n. 90. Translated into HK $ the figures are roughly 10,190,000 and 17,730,000.

6 Crisswell, op. cit., p. 137.

7 LeFevour, op. cit., p. 27.

8 Ibid. p. 165, n. 80.

9 Ibid., p. 29, n. 88.

10 For the early years of the HKSB see Maurice Collis, *Wayfong* (1965), ch. 1.

11 Crisswell, op. cit., pp. 155–6.

12 The contrast is explained by the fact that goods could not be transhipped at Alexandria or Suez without ruinous expense and had to go round the Cape. This did not apply to passengers and mail.

13 Crisswell, op. cit., p. 134.

14 Collis, op. cit., p. 34.

15 For example: when some of the working partners wanted to sell the Firm's China Coast Fleet in 1876, the question was referred to Robert Jardine, who gave his approval in November, although in the event the deal did not go through.

16 Keswick (ed.) op. cit., p. 32.

17 British Library Add MS 44548, f. 31. I owe this reference to Dr Colin Matthew, editor of the *Gladstone Diaries*.

18 Supplement 1901–11, p. 364.

19 Keswick (ed.), op. cit., p. 62.

20 Ibid., p. 38.

21 Crisswell, op. cit., p. 191.

CHAPTER 11

1 Keswick (ed.), op. cit., p. 154. The account of Jardine in Japan in chapter 6 by Pat Barr is the source of quotations, except when otherwise stated.

2 John Roberts, *The Pelican History of the World* (1980), p. 785.

3 Hugh Cortazzi (ed.), *Mitford's Japan* (1985), p. 31.

4 Ibid., p. 33.

5 Ibid., p. 74.

6 Keswick (ed.), op. cit., p. 156.

7 Ibid.

8 Ibid.

9 Ibid., p. 157.

10 Cortazzi (ed.), op. cit., pp. 25–6.

CHAPTER 12

1 Keswick (ed.), op. cit., pp. 173–4.

2 LeFevour, *Western Enterprise in Late Ch'ing China* (1970), p. 40.

3 Ibid., p. 41.

4 Ibid., p. 43.

5 Ibid., p. 44.

6 Ibid., p. 45.

7 Ibid., p. 46.

8 P.H. Kent, *Railway Enterprise in China* (1907), p. 4.

9 *Jardine Matheson & Co., an Historical Sketch* (n.d.) p. 50.

10 Alan Reid, *The Woosung Road: the Story of the First Railway in China, 1875–1877* (1977), pp. 5-6.

11 LeFevour, op. cit., n. 15, p. 191.

12 Ibid., p.116.

13 Ibid., p. 111.

14 Ibid., p. 114.

CHAPTER 13

1 LeFevour, op. cit., p. 118.
2 Ibid., p. 119.
3 Ibid.
4 Ibid., p. 120.
5 Ibid., p. 121
6 Keswick (ed.), op. cit., pp. 191–2.
7 The complicated details are described in *The Cambridge History of China*, vol. 10, pt. 1, pp. 419–22.
8 Ibid., vol. 10, pt. 1, p. 477.
9 D.G.M. Platt, *Finance, Trade and British Foreign Policy* (1968), p. 265, quoting Alcock, *The Capital of the Tycoon* (1863), II, p. 352.
10 Quoted Platt, ibid.
11 See Chapter XII.
12 Platt, op. cit., p. 271.
13 Quoted Platt, op. cit., p. 272.
14 This is why the whole future of Hong Kong was at stake in 1997. The island itself and Kowloon were British colonies annexed in perpetuity in 1843 and 1860 respectively, but were regarded as unviable without the New Territories, which must then revert to China.
15 Peter Fleming, *The Siege at Peking* (1959), p. 32.
16 LeFevour, op. cit., p. 126.
17 Ibid., p. 128.

CHAPTER 14

1 P.D. Coates, *The China Consuls* (1988), p. 89.
2 Quoted Keswick (ed.), op. cit., p. 35.
3 See the *Economist*, 22 December 1990, p. 126 for an interesting comparison of the cost of various goods and services 1900–90.
4 P.D. Coates, op. cit., p. 96.
5 Ibid., p. 59.
6 Ibid., pp. 160–61.
7 *The Thistle and the Jade*, p. 205.

8 Quoted Fleming, op. cit., p. 229.
9 Ibid., p. 243.
10 See Maurice Collis, *Wayfung, The Hong Kong and Shanghai Banking Corporation* (1965), pp. 118–26 passim for an account of the Bank's joint activities with Jardine Matheson.
11 P.D. Coates, op. cit., p. 122.
12 D.C.M. Platt, *Finance, Trade and British Foreign Policy* (1968), p. 285.
13 Jack Gray, *Rebellions and Revolutions in China from the 1800s to the 1990s* (1990), p. 122.
14 Platt, op. cit., p. 284.

CHAPTER 15

1 Keswick (ed.), op. cit., p. 45.
2 Betty Peh T'i Wei, *Old Shanghai*, p. 219.
3 Keswick (ed.), op. cit., p. 205.
4 Quoted in Nicholas R. Clifford, *Spoilt Children of Empire* (1991), p. 33.
5 Appointed 1894, retired 1901.
6 Quoted Clifford, op. cit., p. 34. Sir Sidney Barton (1876-1946) was ambassador in Abyssinia from 1929 until the Italian conquest in 1936.
7 DNB 1941–50 (1959), p. 65.
8 Quoted Clifford, op. cit., p. 90.
9 Quoted, Ibid. p. 182.
10 Keswick (ed.), op. cit., p. 204.
11 Ibid., p. 205.
12 Ibid., p. 207.
13 Ibid., p. 208.
14 Ibid., p. 210.
15 Quoted Clifford, op. cit., p. 272.
16 Quoted R.A.C. Parker, *Chamberlain and Appeasement* (1993), p. 39.
17 Ibid.
18 Quoted Clifford, op. cit., p. 274.
19 Keswick (ed.), op. cit., p. 212.
20 Ibid., p. 214.
21 Ibid.
22 Story in 'Peterborough', *Daily Telegraph*, 30 November 1993.
23 Keswick (ed.), op. cit., p. 215.

CHAPTER 16

1 Keswick (ed.), op. cit., p. 216.
2 *Allies of a Kind* (1978), 548 n.
3 Quoted Thorne, op. cit., p. 31.
4 Ibid., facing p. xxii.
5 Speech at the Mansion House, 10 November 1942.
6 Oliver Lindsay, *Lasting Honour* (1978). This is the most authoritative account of the fall of Hong Kong and I have relied on it for much that follows.
7 Ibid., p. 13.
8 Ibid., p. 19.
9 Ibid., p. 91.
10 Ibid., p. 92.
11 Ibid., p. 47.
12 Quoted Lindsay, op. cit., p. 155.
13 Both were armed merchant cruisers which engaged German battleships against hopeless odds and were sunk respectively on 5 November 1940 and 23 November 1939. Captain Fegen of *Jervis Bay* was awarded a posthumous VC, but Captain Kennedy of *Rawalpindi* was not, though he certainly deserved it.
14 Jardine Matheson & Company: An Historical Sketch, p. 63.
15 Keswick (ed.), op. cit., p. 217.
16 Ibid., pp. 223–5.

Bibliography

Alcock, R., *The Capital of the Tycoon*, 1863

Clifford, Nicholas R., *Spoilt Children of Empire*, 1991

Coates, P.D., *The China Consuls*, 1988

Collis, Maurice, *Wayfong, The Hong Kong and Shanghai Banking Corporation*, 1965

Collis, Maurice, *Foreign Mud*, 1946

Cortazzi, Hugh (ed.), *Mitford's Japan*, 1985

Crisswell, Colin, *The Taipans*, 1981

Davidson-Houston, J.V., *Yellow Creek*, 1962

Downing, C.T., *The Fan-Qui in China in 1836–7*, 1838

Easton, H.T., *The History of a Banking House*, 1903

Fairbank, John King and Twichett, Denis (eds), *Cambridge History of the World*, 1980

Fleming, Peter, *The Siege at Peking*, 1959

Fraser, Alexander, *The Frasers of Philorth*, 1879

Graham, Gerald, *The China Station, War and Diplomacy 1830–1842*, 1978

Gray, Jack, *Rebellions and Revolutions in China* (1990)

Greenberg, Michael, *British Trade and the Opening of China 1800–1842*, 1951

Gregory, J.S., *Great Britain and the Taipings*, 1969

Gutzlaff, *Journal of Three Voyages along the Coast of China*, 1834

Harvey, Charles E., *The Rio Tinto Company*, 1981

Hayter, Alethea, *Opium and the Romantic Imagination*, 1968

Holt, Edgar, *The Opium Wars in China*, 1964

Hurd, Douglas, *The Arrow War*, 1967

Jardine Matheson Papers, *Private Letter Book* (PLB)

Jones, W.D., *Lord Derby and Victorian Conservatism*, 1956

Kent, P.H., *Railway Enterprise in China*, 1907

Keswick, Maggie (ed.), *The Thistle and the Jade*, 1982

Kuo, P.C., *A Critical Study of the First Anglo-Chinese War with Documents*, 1935

LeFevour, Edward, *Western Enterprise in Ch'ing China 1842–95*, 1968

Letters of Queen Victoria, vol. 1

Memorials of Brooks's, 1967

Moule, Archdeacon, *The Story of the Cheh-Kiang Mission*, Church Missionary Society 1878

Park, R.A.C., *Chamberlain and Appeasement*, 1993

Platt, D.G.M., *Finance, Trade and British Foreign Policy*, 1968

Reid, Alan, *The Woosung Road: the Story of the First Railway in China, 1875–1877*, 1977

Roberts, John, *The Pelican History of the World*, 1980

Williamson, Captain A.R., *Eastern Traders* (privately printed by Jardine Matheson & Co.), 1975

York, G.J., *The Princely House* (unpublished typescript), *c*.1937

Index